Why Turbo Pascal? Why The Beç

Turbo Pascal is the ideal language for the beginner to programming and the Beginner's Guide to Turbo Pascal is your ideal companion on the journey.

Designed by Niklaus Wirth to be easy to learn whilst including the latest programming techniques, Pascal provides the perfect environment for the novice programmer. Borland took this powerful language and added many features to create Turbo Pascal. With version 7 for DOS and version 1.5 for Windows, Turbo Pascal is the best entry to the arcane world of computer programming.

The Beginner's Guide to Turbo Pascal is your perfect introduction to the language. Packed with screenshots so that you can instantly see results and with example programs to clearly illustrate each topic, we make your encounter with Turbo Pascal simple and as straightforward. Relax and let this book do the work. In next to no time you'll be up to speed with Turbo Pascal.

What is Wrox Press?

Wrox Press is a computer book publisher which promotes a brand new concept - clear, jargon-free programming and database titles that fulfill your real demands. We publish for everyone, from the novice through to the experienced programmer. To ensure our books meet your needs, we carry out continuous research on all our titles. Through our dialog with you we can craft the book you really need.

We welcome suggestions and take all of them to heart - your input is paramount in creating the next great Wrox title. Use the reply card inside this book or mail us at:

feedback@wrox.demon.co.uk
or
Compuserve 100063, 2152

Wrox Press Ltd.   **Tel:**   **0101 312 465 3559**
2710 W. Touhy   **Fax:**   **0101 312 465 4063**
Chicago
IL 60645
USA

The Beginner's Guide to Turbo Pascal

Oleg Perminov

Wrox Press Ltd.®

The Beginner's Guide to Turbo Pascal

© 1994 Oleg Perminov

Published by Wrox Press Ltd. 1334 Warwick Road, Birmingham, B27 6PR. UK

Library of Congress Catalog Card Number: 94-78639
ISBN 1-874416-30-3

Trademark Acknowledgements

Credits

Author
Oleg Perminov

Managing Editor
Michael Brunt

Technical Editors
Michael Brunt
Mike O'Docherty

Style Editor
Luke Dempsey

Technical Reviewers
Stephen Parkinson
Mike Fletcher

Proof Reader
Pam Brand

Beta Testers
Samantha Parkinson
Jason Stone

Production Manager
Gina Mance

Book Layout
Ewart Liburd
Eddie Fisher
Kenneth Fung
Greg Powell

**Quizzes, Exercises and
Model Answers**
Mike O'Docherty

Cover Design
Third Wave

Mike O'Docherty works for:
PEVE$_{IT}$ Unit
Department of Computer Science
The University of Manchester
Manchester M13 9PL
UK

For more information on Third Wave, contact Ross Alderson on 44-21 456 1400

About the Author

Oleg Perminov is a professor of computer science at the Moscow Engineering Physics Institute. He has been working with Pascal since 1976 and has written 4 books on the subject. He has also designed a Pascal compiler for the IBM/370. In his spare time, he enjoys reading foreign literature in the original, especially Shakespeare and Burns

CONTENTS

Summary of Contents

CONTENTS

Contents

INTRODUCTION

Why The Beginner's Guide?

There's one reason why anybody reads a programming book, and that's to learn programming quickly and correctly. There are plenty of books out there which aim to cover anything and everything, and succeed in covering nothing. This book is in the hands-on mold of all Wrox books - we show you what you need to know, when you need to know it.

We deal in plain English, and in programming which is exciting and street-wise. Rather than teach you how to log the exchange rates of the dollar since 1900, we'll show you how to solve real problems, and present programs and output in cool and colorful ways. Programming should be useful, and useful quickly. But we also understand the difficulties involved in the programming world, and we'll point out the pitfalls and pratfalls which you might encounter - forewarned is forearmed.

Who's This Book For?

Beginners to programming: those who need to learn for college, or work, or because programming literacy is becoming *the* requirement of this century. We know that there is a limit to your free time, and that semesters don't last forever - we, too, work to deadlines! We won't waste your time - we'll just teach you Turbo Pascal.

Beginners to Turbo Pascal: OK, so you can already achieve things in other progamming languages, but you've always fancied yourself as a Turbo Pascal guru! We won't patronize or cajole - we've learnt programming and we reckon we know what you'll need, and what you don't need.

What You Need To Use This Book

Apart from a real desire to learn Turbo Pascal programming, you'll also need access to a PC, and a copy of Turbo Pascal. Though this book was written for the latest version of Turbo Pascal, version 7.0, the same programming principles apply for any version of Pascal.

We've made an assumption that you are familiar with computers, and that you are aware of how DOS works. If you need to brush up on these areas, now's the time to do so!

As for the source code, we've put it on the Internet. So you can play on the world's airwaves, *and* save yourself some typing! Or, we'll mail you the disk for a small fee - to cover the costs only.

Conventions Used

To enable you to find your way around the language we've used various different styles to highlight different references.

Program Code

```
Program EX_2_1;
Uses Crt;
Var
   Your_Name : String;
Begin
   ClrScr;
   Write('Enter your name: ');
   ReadLn(Your_name);
   WriteLn('Hello ',Your_Name,', Welcome to WroxLand');
End.
```

We shade program code so that you can easily find it.

We also quote extensively from programs to illustrate points as they arise. When code is quoted at other times, we use the following style:

```
TextBackground(Green);
TextColor(White + Blink);
Window(23, 9, 56, 9);
Write (A[1]);
Window(23, 9, 56, 9);
```

When code features in the middle of sentences, we write it in `this_style`.

When for the sake of brevity we have not printed some lines of code we'll use three periods ... to indicate this.

The Turbo Pascal Language

In the text we use this style to highlight words with a specific meaning in Turbo Pascal. These will be reserved words and standard functions and procedures, (but more of that later).

To introduce the 'syntax' of Turbo Pascal commands we use these boxes.

Insert(*Start_String, String_to_add, pos_of_first_char*);

Where *Start_String* and *String_to_add* are both variables of string type and *position_of_first_character* is of integer type. The statement inserts *String_to_add* into *Start_String* at the character whose position is equal to *pos_of_first_char*.

They are all shaded, and the command itself is explained fully in the shaded box. The words you must use are in this style, whilst text that should be replaced with your own choice is in *this style*.

Important Bits, Interesting Bits

Bits that you really must read are in this type of box.

Things that are interesting but not essential are in this type of box.

And, What Else?

- Important words are in **this style**.
- Filenames are in **THIS_STYLE.PAS**.
- Keys that you press are in *this style*.
- Things that appear on output screens are in this style.

How to Use This Book

Load up Turbo Pascal, open up this book, and learn. The book is designed to be like a personal tutor, taking you through each subject thoroughly and testing your comprehension at the end with Quiz Questions. Each chapter ends with some Exercises which will stretch your understanding and help you see the creative possibilities of this language.

The programs in the book are there for you to create useful and exciting programs *of your own*, and we strongly recommend you work through them and amend them to your own requirements. Hey, if you want magenta text on a white background then do it! We won't answer for how your users will react - we'll just show you how it's done. We've included programs as early as we possibly could (we nearly put one in the Introduction!), and you should have no fear of them at all. Go ahead and work with them. You'll soon appreciate how flexible and user-friendly the language is. It really is the ideal language with which to start your programming.

We've given you a bumper chapter on debugging, which takes you through one of our debugging experiences with screenshots for each stage. Debugging experience is a key requirement, and the time you take over it will be time well spent.

We've also included a number of appendices as a handy reference to error messages, command keystrokes and the IDE menu screens. Dip into them when you need them.

Tell Us What You Think

One last thing. We've tried to make the book enjoyable and accurate. The programming community is what we're here to serve, so if you have any queries or suggestions, let us know, so that our future books are even better. Return the reply card at the back of the book, or contact us direct at Wrox. The easiest way is to use email:

feedback@wrox.demon.co.uk
Compuserve: 100062,2152

# CHAPTER 1

Welcome to Turbo Pascal

Congratulations on choosing Turbo Pascal as your entry into the world of programming! Pascal is the perfect language with which to start your journey, and Turbo Pascal from Borland is a powerful, yet easy-to-use implementation of this popular language.

In this first chapter we cover the basic concepts of programming and tell you about the unique features of Turbo Pascal. We'll then move on to your 'toolbox' for creating programs, the Turbo Pascal **Integrated Development Environment (IDE)**. This is a set of software tools which enable you to create Turbo Pascal programs easily and efficiently, and is Borland's 'added value' in the Turbo package. In this first chapter we'll look at the most commonly used and most important functions in the IDE. By the end of the chapter you'll have enough basic information to run your first program.

We're sure you're eager to get started on programming so we will create some very simple Turbo Pascal programs in the course of finding our way around the IDE. This will help us familiarize ourselves with the IDE while working on real projects, and get a glimpse of what makes up a Turbo Pascal program. By the end of the chapter you should be comfortable enough using the IDE to work through the programs in the rest of the book, and have a taste for the kind of things we're going to learn.

To summarize, in this first chapter we'll cover:

▶ What Turbo Pascal is

▶ The Turbo Pascal toolkit

▶ Writing your first Turbo Pascal program

What is Pascal?

Pascal is a high-level computer programming language that allows programmers to write clear, efficient, easily modified and easily maintained programs.

The Pascal programming language was invented in 1970 by Professor Niklaus Wirth of the Technical University of Zurich, Switzerland. It was named after the famous French philosopher and mathematician Blaise Pascal, who invented one of the earliest practical calculators. Professor Wirth gathered together the best ideas about structured programming, and the structured theory of data, to produce a language convenient for teaching students. However, Pascal was soon being used to write many other applications. Nowadays, Pascal is used throughout the world on most types of computer, from the humble PC to super-computers.

The Ideal Language

Because Pascal was initially designed for students, it is the ideal language for beginners to learn. The features are neither complex nor confusing, and the wide variety of different data structures, procedures and functions have simple rules of application. A few hours of basic study will teach you how to write simple programs and from then on you'll just keep adding to your knowledge in leaps and bounds. After no time at all you'll be writing complex programs several pages in length.

One of the most popular implementations of Pascal is Turbo Pascal. The most advanced version of Turbo Pascal now available is version 7.0, and this is the version we'll be covering in this book.

What is Programming?

So we might know something about Pascal and Turbo Pascal, but really we need to establish exactly what our task involves, namely, what are the steps we need to follow in order to program a computer?

Modern society depends a great deal on computers and computer programs. They are part of almost all we do. It's easy to forget that someone has to write the instructions which bridge the gap between the needs of the world and the capabilities of the machine. This is our role as programmers. These instructions take the form of programs and each program conforms to the same basic rules. Whenever you meet a problem all you need to do is apply these rules to create a successful program.

The Seven Steps to Success

The process of creating a working program can be broken down into seven steps.

1   Understand the nature of the problem to be solved.

A program is a set of instructions to **transform input data** into **output data**. To understand how to use a program to solve a problem, you must first decide what the input data is, what the output data is, and what the **process of transformation** is that converts one to the other.

As an example, imagine you want to bake a cake. You'll need eggs, flour, margarine and sugar. This is the input data. The output data will be the actual cake. The process of making the cake is the transformation. Faced with these raw materials it's difficult to see how to get from the input data to the output - this is the nature of the problem!

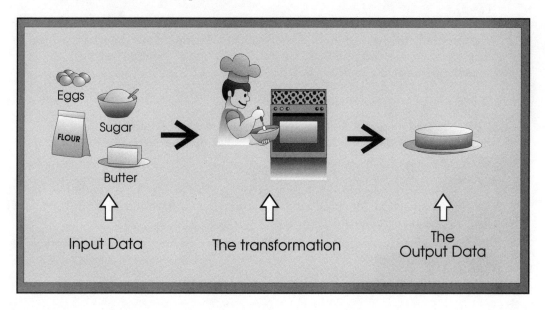

2   Design the algorithm to accomplish the transformation.

An **algorithm** is a sequence of instructions that leads to a result. When solving a problem this is the crucial step. When designing your algorithm you need to work out the steps you need to go through to reach your goal.

The algorithm you would use to bake a cake would be something like:

- Put margarine into a bowl
- Add sugar
- Stir until of a creamy texture
- Beat in eggs
- Fold in flour

and so on.

3   Write the program.

Once you have understood the problem and have designed your algorithm the next step is to produce a set of instructions so that the computer can perform the task. These instructions are written in the programming language Turbo Pascal.

The program for baking a cake is the recipe. Writing down the recipe means that you can ask your mother, kid brother or other assorted relatives to actually perform the task.

4   Prepare the input data.

We've defined programming as the transformation of input data into the required output data. We have to decide what data to feed into the program, and how.

This is where we decide what type of margarine to use and whether or not to use self-raising flour. In preparing the input data we would also make sure we had all the necessary cooking utensils to hand.

5   Compile the program.

You find a new recipe for cake making but unfortunately it's written in French. For you to understand even the ingredient list, let alone the processes involved, you'll have to wait for your neighbor, Madame Patisserie, to come home from the cake shop and translate it for you.

Computers need 'translations' too. Not only do they *not* understand English, they don't understand Pascal either! The only instructions a computer can follow are those written in **machine code**. Machine code consists of a series of 1s and 0s, and the computer is actually just a series of switches activated by these changing numbers. **Compiling** a program involves translating a program from Pascal into machine code.

6   Run the program.

Once the program has been compiled, it's in a form the computer can understand. We can now run the program and the output data we wanted will appear. This is the actual 'doing' part of programming.

In our cake scenario, the actual blending of the ingredients and the baking of the cake in an oven (not to mention our cutting and eating the thing!) correspond to the **executing** of the program.

> You'll often come across the phrase 'executing a program'. This doesn't involve the electric chair, it's just a way of saying 'run the program'!

7   Debug the program.

If only Mme. Patisserie were here! Maybe the self-raising flour was too old to raise! Maybe (gasp!) it was the eggs! You open the oven and look what's there - a soggy mess of floating excuses!

Everyone makes mistakes and programmers are no exception. The final step in creating a great program is to sort out any errors. (Did you use the wrong flour?). In computing, errors in programs are called **bugs**, and the process of finding and correcting bugs is called **debugging**.

It's said that Grace Hopper, one of the programmers who wrote the COBOL compiler, discovered that a program wasn't printing because a moth had been trapped in the printer. As a result, errors in programs became known as bugs.

A lot of the errors you get at first will be trivial, such as typing mistakes. However, as your programs get longer and more complex, you'll come to appreciate the value of the powerful debugging tools that come with Turbo Pascal in Turbo Debugger. In Chapter 7 we give you a full breakdown of these tools.

A Typical Program - DIR.EXE

Whenever you interact with a computer, you are executing some form of program. MS-DOS itself is a collection of programs. Take the familiar DIR command as an example.

```
METALDUS      <DIR>        29/04/94     9:09
ACCESS        <DIR>        29/04/94     9:11
WINPROJ       <DIR>        29/04/94     9:12
WP51          <DIR>        29/04/94     9:13
SETUP         <DIR>        29/04/94     9:14
MS-BTTNS      <DIR>        29/04/94     9:14
POWERPNT      <DIR>        29/04/94     9:14
EXCEL         <DIR>        29/04/94     9:15
WINWORD       <DIR>        29/04/94     9:17
CLIPART       <DIR>        29/04/94     9:18
INTERNET      <DIR>        06/05/94     9:21
TC            <DIR>        17/05/94    13:23
WINZIP5B      <DIR>        23/05/94    16:14
HJPRO         <DIR>        02/06/94     7:23
TP            <DIR>        19/06/94    10:38
ST            <DIR>        19/06/94    18:52
         66 file(s)         711,727 bytes
                       146,784,256 bytes free
```

When Microsoft wrote MS-DOS, they went through the same seven steps that we just looked at.

1 *Understand the nature of the problem to be solved.*

The problem Microsoft identified was how to produce a list of the files in any directory on the computer's monitor. The input data for the problem is names of the files in the directory stored on the disk in the computer. The output data is the list of files on the screen.

2 *Design the algorithm to accomplish the transformation.*

Microsoft then decided how the program would sort through the information on the disk, select the names of the files, and then display them. This defined the algorithm.

3 *Write the program.*

Microsoft then wrote the program, **DIR.EXE**.

4 *Prepare the input data.*

There are two sources of input data for the **DIR.EXE** program, input from the user and input taken from your computer.

▶ The input you provide is the directory that is to be sorted. You can leave this information out as MS-DOS will then assume you are talking about the current drive and directory.

▶ The second input is all the information contained on the disk that DIR must sift through to find the file names you want.

5   Compile the program.

Once the programmers at Microsoft had finished writing the program they would have compiled it into an executable file. An executable file is a file that holds the program so that it can be run or executed. In Turbo Pascal the compiler translates your programs into instructions the computer can understand and stores these instructions in an the executable file.

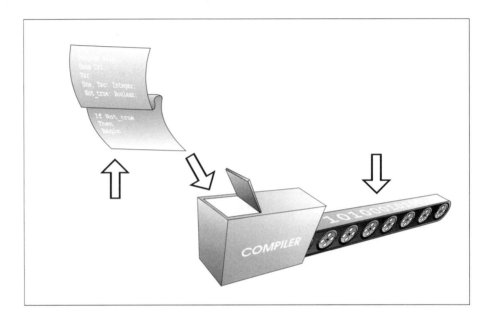

6   Run the program.

Running the program is now easy. By typing **DIR** at the C:> prompt MS-DOS loads and runs the program **DIR.EXE**.

7   Debug the program.

After all these years, DIR seems to work fine. Who knows whether it worked first time at Microsoft. All we can say is that even the very best programmers spend a good part of their time debugging.

Examining the IDE - Turbo Pascal's Toolkit

Having seen how to go about writing a program we will now go through the special tools that Turbo Pascal provides. This is the Integrated Development Environment or the **IDE**. In the IDE you have all the software tools you need to create Turbo Pascal programs.

Starting the IDE

If you accepted the default settings for Turbo Pascal when you loaded it, type Turbo at the C:> prompt to start Turbo Pascal. If you didn't accept these settings then we'll assume you know what you're doing and can start up Turbo Pascal on your own. You should see the screen below.

This is the menu line

This is the name of the program you are working on

This is the number of the window

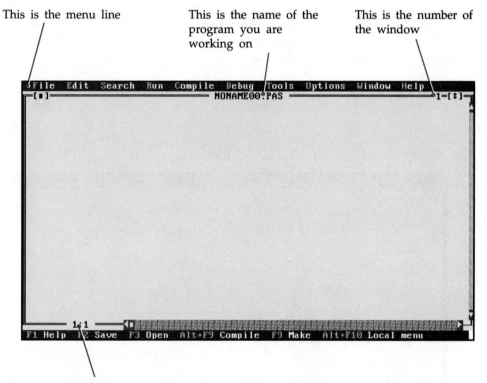

These figures tell you where the cursor is. The first figure says how many characters from the left and the second figure how many lines down

The Main Turbo Pascal Menu

The main Turbo Pascal menu has ten options: File, Edit, Search, Run, Compile, Debug, Tools, Options, Window and Help. If you are restricted to using the keyboard each option can be selected in any one of three ways:

1 By pressing the F10 . This activates the menu line by highlighting the word File. You then use the ← and → keys to highlight the option you need. Once you have highlighted the relevant option, press the *Enter* key and Turbo Pascal will perform the relevant task.

2 The second way to select a menu option also begins by pressing the *F10* key. But instead of using the arrow keys, press the letter in red in the option name. This executes the selected option. For example, if you wish to select the Compile option, press C.

3 The third way to select a menu option is by holding down the *Alt* key together with the letter in red of the main menu option. For example, if you wish to select the Compile option, press *Alt+C*.

Turbo Pascal also fully supports the use of a mouse. This gives you some more options to select on the main screen as below.

Click on here to close a window

Click on the word to activate the menu

Click on here to re-size the window

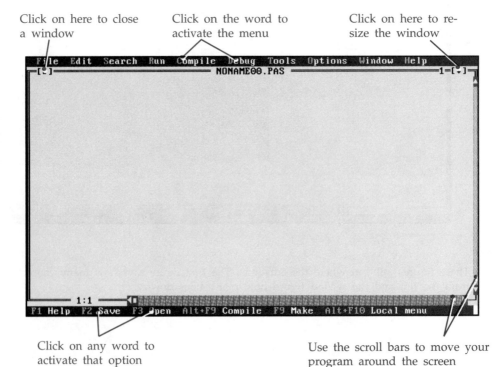

Click on any word to activate that option

Use the scroll bars to move your program around the screen

The File Menu

The File menu lets you create new files, load previously created files, save new files, exit Turbo Pascal, and so on.

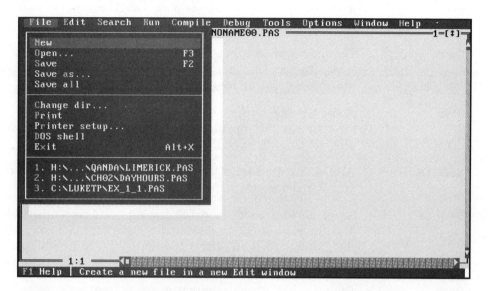

When you open the File menu, the New option is highlighted. You can select an option by using the ↑ and ↓ keys, highlighting the appropriate option, and then pressing the *Enter* key.

When looking at the File submenu, you can see that *F3* is on the same line as the word Open, *F2* is next to Save, and *Alt+X* is next to Exit. These characters are the hot keys which execute the option without going through the menu structure. For example, if you want to save a file you can simply press *F2*.

Option	What It Does
New	This opens a new file to edit and gives it the name **NONAME00.PAS**. After this, you can load the file to be edited or write new source text.
Open	This opens an existing file. The prompt appears to help you select the file. Use the *Tab*, ←, ↑, → and ↓ keys to search through the list of files..
Save	Saves the file in the current window to your hard disk with the name at the top of the window. It is a good idea, from time to time, to save the file being edited.
Save as...	Also saves the file in the current window to disk, but offers you the chance to change the name.
Save all	Saves all files being modified during your current session. The files are saved to disk under their current name. One of the features of the Borland IDE is its ability to edit multiple files at the same time.
Print	Prints a copy of the program in the current window.
Printer setup	This option allows you to change the settings on your printer.
DOS shell	This option allows you to temporarily quits the Integrated Development Environment to execute DOS commands. To return to the IDE, you must type Exit. You will then return to the screen you were on before you went into DOS.
Exit	This option takes you completely out of the Integrated Development Environment.

Having given you an overview of each command, we'll now go into detail on some of the more important options.

Loading a Program File

To show you how to load a program we are going to choose one of the demo programs that comes with Turbo Pascal. With the file menu open, to load a program:

1 Type O.

2 Type the filename (with all the directories), or browse through the files in the dialog box.

Type the name of the file here (with all the directories)

With a mouse, you can click here to open a submenu of your previous choices

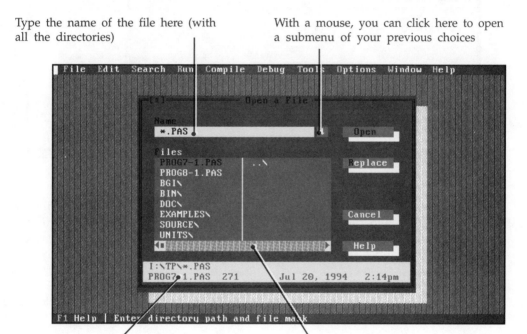

This shows your current directory

With a mouse you can use the scroll bars to look through the file names

Select the demo program **DIRDEMO.PAS** from the list and press *Enter.* You should see a screen similar to the one below.

```
  File  Edit  Search  Run  Compile  Debug  Tools  Options  Window  Help
 ┌─[■]═══════════════════ TP\EXAMPLES\DIRDEMO.PAS ════════════════1═[‡]═┐
 │{*******************************************************}         ▲
 │{                                                       }         ▓
 │{ Turbo Directory Demo                                  }         ▓
 │{ Copyright (c) 1985,90 by Borland International }              ▓
 │{                                                       }         ▓
 │{*******************************************************}
 │
 │program DirDemo;
 │{ Demonstration program that shows how to use:
 │
 │     o Directory routines from DOS unit
 │     o Procedural types (used by QuickSort)
 │
 │  Usage:
 │
 │    dirdemo [options] [directory mask]
 │
 │  Options:
 │
 │    -W        Wide display
 │    -N        Sort by file name                                 ▼
 ├─── 1:1 ═══◄─┼─────────────────────────────────────────────────►┘
  F1 Help  F2 Save  F3 Open  Alt+F9 Compile  F9 Make  Alt+F10 Local menu
```

To see the results of the program we need to compile the source code into an executable file, and then run it. We have two options: we can compile the program first then run the compiled program as a separate process; or choose the Run command directly, which will compile the program automatically beforehand.

As explorers of the system, we'll go via the Compile menu, to better understand the process.

The Compile Menu

Compiling is the process by which we translate the instructions written in Turbo Pascal into executable code that the computer can understand. These machine-ready instructions are contained in an executable file. This file is given the same name as the program, but the extension is changed to **.EXE**. When we've compiled the above program, Turbo Pascal will produce a file called **DIRDEMO.EXE.**

To compile the program select Compile and the following menu should appear on screen.

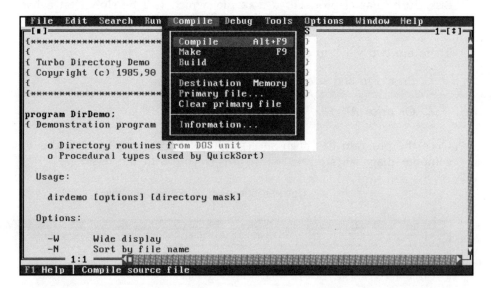

The only options we need for now are the Compile and the Destination options.

Option	What It Does
Compile	Causes the current source code file to be compiled. The destination of the code is decided by the option below.
Destination	This option allows you to select the destination of the compiled code. You have two choices. Either the code can go into the computer's memory or to your hard disk. You select the different options by pressing Enter at this option. The setting toggles between the two options.

As a rule, during writing and debugging, your program compiles to memory. This is why the default value of the destination is Memory. The code is stored in the memory of the computer and runs immediately when you select Run.

If the destination is Disk you need to quit the IDE to run the program so it's best to only use this option when the program is bug-free. If the destination is Disk, Turbo Pascal produces a **.EXE** file, which will be stored on a hard disk. As a **.EXE** file the program can be run independantly from Turbo Pascal.

There are two ways to compile your program:

1 Press *F10* and select Compile

2 Or press *Alt+F9*.

Once the program has been successfully compiled, you'll get Turbo Pascal's compiler diagnostics screen which greets you with the message:

Compile successful : Press any key

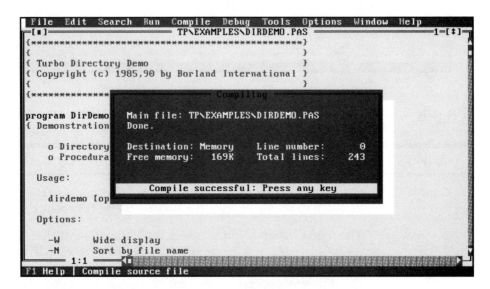

The words Press any key will be blinking. This means the process of compilation has been successful. Once you have pressed any key, Turbo Pascal is ready to run the compiled program, and the Run option enables you to do this.

The Run Menu

To run the current program you select Run from the Run menu.

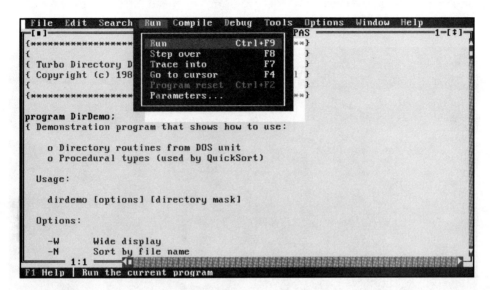

There are other options on the menu which are used to debug your programs. We explain these in more detail in Chapter 7. The only option we will consider now is the Run option.

Option	What It Does
Run	This option lets you run the current program stored in the editor. If a program wasn't previously compiled, the Run option will cause it to compile before execution

From the keyboard there are two ways to run the program:

▶ Press *F10* and select Run

▶ Or press *Ctrl+F9*

Seeing the Result

Having run the program the screen flickers, but stays the same as before. To see the message produced by the program you need to swap to the DOS screen using *Alt+F5*:

```
SPIKE     LUK          0  26-Jul-94  21:01
PROG7-3   PAS        317  21-Jul-94  14:14
PROG7-4   PAS        812  21-Jul-94  14:22
DIGGER               768  27-Jul-94  14:00
SPURIOUS            2304  26-Jul-94  22:36
MY_SYSX   PAS       6188  26-Jul-94  22:30
MY_SYSX   BAK       6186  26-Jul-94  22:30
NETALDUS        <DIR>     29-Apr-94   9:09
ACCESS          <DIR>     29-Apr-94   9:11
WINPROJ         <DIR>     29-Apr-94   9:12
WP51            <DIR>     29-Apr-94   9:13
SETUP           <DIR>     29-Apr-94   9:14
MS-BTTNS        <DIR>     29-Apr-94   9:14
POWERPNT        <DIR>     29-Apr-94   9:14
EXCEL           <DIR>     29-Apr-94   9:15
WINWORD         <DIR>     29-Apr-94   9:17
CLIPART         <DIR>     29-Apr-94   9:18
INTERNET        <DIR>      6-May-94   9:21
TC              <DIR>     17-May-94  13:23
WINZIP5B        <DIR>     23-May-94  16:14
HJPRO           <DIR>      2-Jun-94   7:23
TP              <DIR>     19-Jun-94  10:38
ST              <DIR>     19-Jun-94  18:52
73 files, 727265 bytes, 150093824 bytes free
```

As you can see the **DIRDEMO.PAS** produces similar results to the DOS command DIR.

Exiting the IDE

The final command to show you in this first section is that which lets you exit the system. You can do this in one of two ways:

▶ Press *F10*, select File and then select Exit.

▶ Or press *Alt+X*.

Writing Your First Pascal Program

Now it's time to write your first program. To prepare for this you need to start with a clear screen:

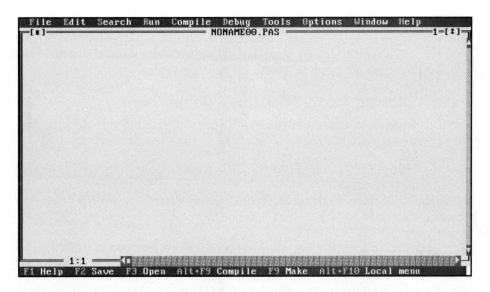

If your screen looks different to this, it could be that the IDE has kept the same configuration from the last exit. To get back to the standard layout:

▶ Press *F10*, select Window and then select Close all

▶ Or press *F10*, select File and then select New.

Using a Program Template

Your first program will write the following message on the screen:

Hello John, welcome to WroxLand!

To start with, you need to type in the three words shown below.

```
Program
Begin
End.
```

This outline is a useful template for the general structure of a Turbo Pascal program and should be the basis for any program you write. Later, between the lines Program and Begin you'll insert what are known as **declarations**, and between the lines which say Begin and End you'll insert what are known as **statements**.

There must be a Begin for every End in a Turbo Pascal program. Therefore, every time you write Begin you should immediately write the word End. This will help you avoid creating errors in your programs.

Try It Out - Adding Code That Does Something

Firstly, we need to name the program. This is the name for the program *itself*. To call the program **MyProg1** you need to change the first line to

```
Program MyProg1;
```

Note the semi-colon at the end - this is Turbo Pascal's way of indicating that a statement is finished. It's a very important thing to remember.

The next step is to add some statements that do something. In this case we want to produce our screen message, so our statement needs to be as follows:

```
WriteLn( 'Hello John. Welcome to WroxLand !');
```

This line must be inserted between the Begin and End statements. To do this, position the cursor just after the word Begin and then press *Enter*. A new blank line will appear. Then type the line exactly as it's printed above. Your screen should now look something like the one below.

```
  File  Edit  Search  Run  Compile  Debug  Tools  Options  Window  Help
 =[■]=                      NONAME00.PAS                            1=[‡]=
 Program MyProg1;
 Begin
 WriteLn ('Hello John, Welcome to WroxLand');
 End.




 
 
 
 
 
 
 
 
 
 
 
    4:5
 F1 Help  F2 Save  F3 Open  Alt+F9 Compile  F9 Make  Alt+F10 Local menu
```

Saving Your New Program

Having written your first program the next thing you should do is save the file. To save it:

1 Press *F2*. Turbo Pascal prompts you for the name of the file with the message Save file as.

2 Enter the name of the file, and the file will be written to disk with that specified name. For example, if you specify the name as **MYPROG1.PAS**, your program will be saved on the disk under this name. Also, the name **NONAME00.PAS** will be replaced *on screen* with the name **MYPROG1.PAS**.

> You must use names which end with **.PAS** as Turbo Pascal will only process **.PAS** files.

Compiling and Running MYPROG1

In our first example, the program was compiled before being run. However, providing there are no errors, the program can be run immediately. Simply use *Ctrl+F9*. This compiles *and* executes the program. If you press *Alt+F5* you'll see the program's message on the screen.

```
Luke C:\>i:

Luke I:\>tp

Luke I:\>i:\tp\bin\turbo
Turbo Pascal  Version 7.0  Copyright (c) 1983,92 Borland International
Hello John. Welcome to Wroxland!
```

If you see any other message on-screen, check that you have copied the program exactly as it's typed in the book.

Errors in Source Code

Let's see what happens if we intentionally put an error in the program. For example, instead of the word Begin, move the cursor down and write the word Bgin. Now, if you run the compiler again, this message is output:

Error 36: BEGIN expected

The cursor is positioned under the letter B of the word Bgin. You must now correct the error and compile the program again. This is a good example of why the Borland editor is called an Interactive Development Environment!

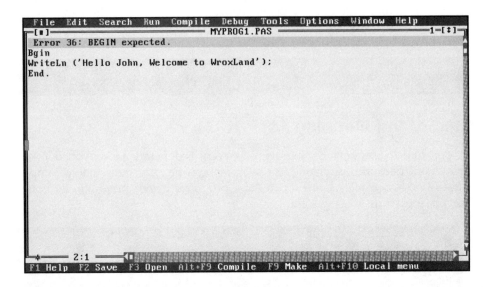

Compiling to Memory

The default value of the Destination option is Memory. This means that the executable code will be stored in the computer's internal memory or RAM. When you exit Turbo Pascal this information will be lost, because no file has been produced.

To save your program more permanently, we need to compile the program to Disk. To change the value for destination you need to:

▶ Press F10, select Compile and then select Destination

This toggles the value of Destination to Disk.

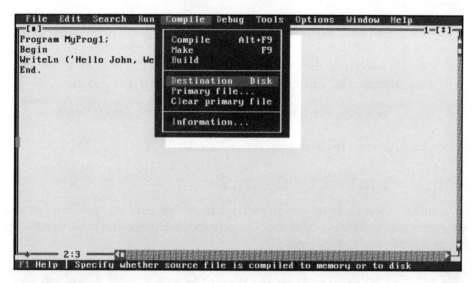

You can now compile your program again (Press *Alt+F9*). The file **MYPROG1.EXE** will now be stored on your hard disk. This program can now be run from DOS. To do this you need to exit Turbo Pascal again.

Exiting the IDE

To recap, you can do this in one of two ways:

▶ Press *F10*, select File and then select Exit.

▶ Or press *Alt+X*.

Saving That File

The last thing that you did was to correct the deliberate mistake, so Turbo Pascal knows the program has been changed. To keep your work up-to-date, Turbo Pascal checks whether you saved your work before you exit. As you didn't save it, you'll see the following message on screen:

MYPROG1.PAS has been modified. Save?

You now have three options. Using the *Tab* key, you can choose between these three options:

1 Select Yes and the program will be saved with the name **MYPROG1.PAS.**

2 If you select No, the program on the screen will NOT be saved and the file **MYPROG1.PAS** will contain the old version of the program.

3 If, in fact, you *don't* want to quit Turbo Pascal, select Cancel.

In our case, choose Yes and exit Turbo Pascal.

Running MyProg1 in DOS

Back in DOS we want to run **MYPROG1.EXE**. To execute the program now, enter the command MYPROG1.EXE at the C:> prompt. You'll see the same results as before appear on your screen:

```
Luke C:\>i:

Luke I:\>tp

Luke I:\>i:\tp\bin\turbo
Turbo Pascal  Version 7.0  Copyright (c) 1983,92 Borland International
Hello John. Welcome to Wroxland!
```

As with any DOS command, you can leave off the **.EXE** part.

Starting Again

Start up Turbo Pascal and you'll see the starting screen again. To load your first program (**MYPROG1.PAS**) again, there are two options:

1 Press *F10*, select File and then select Open.

2 Press *F3*.

In both cases you will see the Filename Dialog box:

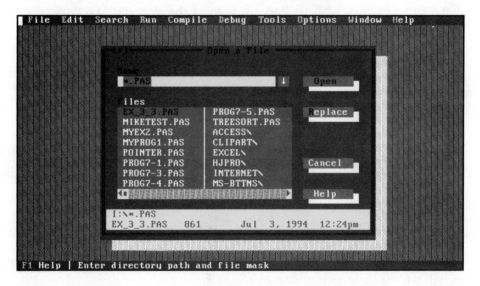

Again, there are two choices:

1 Write the name **MYPROG1.PAS** at the line where it says Name and press *Enter*.

2 Press the *Tab* key. This skips you to the part of the prompt where it says Files. Use the ←, ↑, → and ↓ keys to find **MYPROG1.PAS**, and press *Enter*. The name of the file will appear at the line of the prompt under Name. Press *Enter* again.

Assigning a Start-Up File

If you know the program you want to start up with, a simpler method is to enter the command

TURBO MYPROG1.PAS

at the C:> prompt. Turbo Pascal will start up with the file already loaded.

The Default Start-Up File

If the program you wish to start up with is the one you last worked on, Turbo Pascal makes it even easier. When you load a program Turbo Pascal will make that program the default start-up file as long as you do the following:

▶ Press *F10*, select Options and then select Save TURBO.TP

If you exit Turbo Pascal and go back into it, **MYPROG1.PAS** will automatically be displayed on the screen.

> Whenever you want to save what you are working on before your next session, use the Save TURBO.TP option.

The Window Menu

The Turbo Pascal IDE can work on a number of different source files at the same time, by assigning each file its own window. The Window menu gives access to various functions for managing a multi-window environment. The pull-down menu is shown opposite.

Window Option	What It Does
Tile	This arranges all the open windows like tiles.
Cascade	This arranges all the open windows in a cascade with the windows overlapping. The window at the front is the active window.
Close all	Closes all windows on the screen.
Size/Move	Changes the size or the location of the window currently being used. The *Shift* +↑ and *Shift* +↓ keys move the lower border of the window and the *Shift* +← and *Shift* +→ arrow keys move the window's right border. To move the whole window use the ↑, ↓, ← or → keys. To fix the size or location press the *Enter* key.
Zoom	Zooms into and pulls out of the active window.
Next	Activates the next window.
Previous	Activates the previous window.
Close	Closes the current active window.

The Turbo Pascal Text Editor

In this last section of the chapter we will look at the Turbo Pascal Text Editor. This is like a wordprocessor and it lets you add, delete or modify the source code of a program. These changes can be made using the editing commands and can be made to characters, words, lines or specified sections of the source code called 'blocks'. As you become more proficient with Turbo Pascal, the value of these powerful features will become apparent. For the moment, we'll take a brief tour of the menus, and then look at some ways to make use of the features they provide.

The functions available in the Turbo Pascal editor can be broken down into four categories: **Cursor Movement Commands**, **Insert & Delete Commands**, **Block Commands** and **Miscellaneous Editor Commands**.

Cursor Movement Commands

The cursor indicates your position when you are editing a program. It is represented by a flashing underline character. The following keystrokes move the cursor around the screen.

Keystroke(s)	Moves the Cursor ...
Ctrl+S **or** ←	One character to the left.
Ctrl+D **or** →	One character to the right.
Ctrl+A **or** *Ctrl+* ←	One word to the left.
Ctrl+F **or** *Ctrl+* →	One word to the right.
Ctrl+E **or** ↑	Up one line.
Ctrl+X **or** ↓	Down one line.
Ctrl+R **or** *PgUp*	One screen, or 20 lines, up.
Ctrl+C **or** *PgDn*	One screen down.

Continued

Keystroke(s)	Moves the Cursor ...
Ctrl+W	Moves the source code text up one line, whilst maintaining the position of the cursor on the display screen. This function allows you to scroll line by line through the source code whilst staying in the same vertical cursor position.
Ctrl+Z	As above, but moves the source code text down one line.

Insert and Delete Commands

The following commands are used to insert and delete characters, words and lines in the program.

Command	Keystroke(s)	What It Does
Insert mode on/off	*Ctrl+V* **or** *Ins*	Lets you choose between insert and overwrite modes. The insert mode moves all text after the insertion point to the right whilst new text is inserted. The overwrite mode replaces old text with new text whilst it's being entered.
Insert line	*Ctrl+N*	Inserts a line at the current cursor location. All text on the current line is moved to the next line. A blank line appears at the cursor position.
Delete line	*Ctrl+Y*	Deletes the current line. All characters are deleted, including the carriage return and line feed characters
Delete to end of line	*Ctrl+Q Y*	Deletes all characters to the end of the current line, including the current character.

Continued

33

Command	Keystroke(s)	What It Does
Delete character left	*Ctrl+H* **or** *Backspace*	Deletes the character to the left of the current cursor position
Delete character	*Ctrl+G* **or** *Del*	Deletes the character directly above the cursor.
Delete word right	*Ctrl+T*	Deletes the current word. The entire word is deleted when the cursor is positioned on the first character of the word. When the cursor is positioned on a character other than the first, this command deletes all characters to the end of the word, including the current character.

Block Commands

The following commands are used to mark a section of text and then to manipulate it as a single item. Turbo Pascal only allows you to mark one block at a time, but you can copy or move that text around in your program. You can also read and write text from files stored on your disk.

Block Command	Keystroke(s)	What It Does
Mark start of block	*Ctrl+K B.*	Marks the start of a block beginning from the current cursor position. This command must precede *Ctrl+K K* .
Mark end of block	*Ctrl+K K*	Marks the end of the block. This command must follow *Ctrl+K B.*
Mark single word	*Ctrl+K T*	Marks a single word. If the cursor is positioned on a word, that word is marked. If the cursor is positioned on a space between two words, the word to the left of the cursor position is marked.

Continued

34

Block Command	Keystroke(s)	What It Does
Copy block	Ctrl+K C	Copies the marked block to the current position of the cursor.
Move block	Ctrl+K V	Moves the marked block to the current position of the cursor. The editor re-arranges the text to fill the gap left behind.
Delete block	Ctrl+K Y	Deletes the marked block.
Read block from disk	Ctrl+K R	Reads source code from the disk into the editor at the current cursor position. Turbo Pascal prompts you for the name of the file with the message Read block from. Enter the name of the file and the text will appear at the specified location
Write block to disk	Ctrl+K W	Writes the marked block onto a disk. Turbo Pascal prompts you for the name of the file with the message Write block to. Enter the name of the file and the block will be written to disk with the specified name
Hide/display block	Ctrl+K H	Hides or displays the current marked block.
Print block	Ctrl+K P	Prints the current marked block.
Indent block	Ctrl+K I	Moves the current marked block one position to the right.
Unindent block	Ctrl+K U	Moves the current marked block one position to the left.

Miscellaneous Editor Commands

The following commands are general purpose commands which don't fit into any of the previous categories. All miscellaneous Editor Commands are shown in the following table:

Editor Command	Keystroke(s)	What It Does
Menu bar	*F10*	Activates the Menu bar.
Save and edit	*Ctrl+K S* **or** *F2*	Saves the file in the active window to disk and returns to the Turbo Pascal Editor.
New file	*F3*	Opens a file and displays it in the active window.
Close active window	*Alt+F3*	Closes the current active window.
Find	*Ctrl+Q F*	Finds the text written at the prompt Text to find. If the text is found then it is highlighted, otherwise you will get the message Search string not found.
Find & replace	*Ctrl+Q A*	Finds the text written at the prompt Text to find and replaces it with the text written at the prompt New text. Turbo Pascal will ask you again to make sure Replace this occurrence? and will replace the text if you answer Yes.

Editing a Program With the Turbo Pascal Text Editor

Let's have a look at some of the useful features which help you to write programs more efficiently. Firstly, load your first program, **MYPROG1.PAS**, which you should be able to do for yourself by now!

Suppose you want to print the message Hello John, welcome to WroxLand! to the screen more than once. Rather than re-typing the same program text, a better way is to **copy** the statement WriteLn 'Hello John, welcome to WroxLand'; as many times as you want inside your program. Here's how you do it:

1   Position the cursor under the letter W of the word WriteLn.

2   Mark the beginning of the block using *Ctrl+K B*.

3   Press the *End* key. The cursor will skip to the position after the semicolon.

4   Mark the end of the block using *Ctrl+K K*. The marked block will be highlighted.

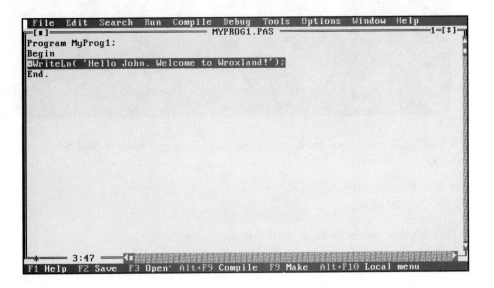

5   Press *Enter*. A blank line will appear.

6   Copy the block using *Ctrl+K C*. The contents of the marked block will appear at the place where the blank line was.

7   Press the keys *Ctrl+K K*. The block will cease to be highlighted.

There are now two WriteLn statements in the program. Run the program, and you will see the message twice.

```
Luke C:\>i:

Luke I:\>tp

Luke I:\>i:\tp\bin\turbo
Turbo Pascal  Version 7.0  Copyright (c) 1983,92 Borland International
Hello John. Welcome to Wroxland!
Hello John. Welcome to Wroxland!
```

A block can mark out more than one line. To mark both WriteLn statements as a block:

1   Position the cursor under the letter W of the first occurrence of the word WriteLn.

2   Mark the beginning of the block using *Ctrl+K B*.

3   Press the *Down* arrow key.

4   Press the *End* key. The cursor will skip to the position after the semicolon.

5   Mark the end of the block using *Ctrl+K K*. The marked zigzag shaped block is highlighted.

In this way, you can mark any number of lines as a block.

To delete these two lines press the keys *Ctrl+K* U twice. The text of the program will return to its original state.

Finding and Replacing Code

The following features help to find, or to find and replace, parts of your programs.

If you wanted to find the word **John** in the program it's possible for you to look through the whole text. Turbo Pascal has another way of doing it. Press the keys *Ctrl+Q F* and the prompt

Text to find

appears. Write the word **John** in either upper or lower-case and press the *Enter* key. Turbo Pascal then searches the document and highlights the word **John.** You can then press any arrow key and the word will stop being highlighted.

In case the word you're looking for isn't in the text, the message

Search string not found

will appear on screen. At this point, all you can do is press the *Enter* key.

Turbo Pascal begins looking for the text from the position of the cursor. This means that if you want to search through the whole program, then the cursor must be at the very top on the left.

Occasionally, you may want not only to find the text but also to replace it with different text. To do this, you need to use the command Find & Replace. To replace the word **John** with the word **Mary** press the keys *Ctrl+Q A*. The prompt

Text to find

will again appear. Write the word **John** in either upper or lower-case and press the *Tab* key. This time the prompt

New text

will appear. Write the word **Mary** in either upper or lower-case.

Press the *Enter* key. After this, the new prompt

Replace this occurrence

will appear, and the word **John** will be highlighted. You now have three
options. By using the *Tab* key you can select Yes, No or Cancel. If you select
Yes and press the *Enter* key, then **John** will be replaced with **Mary**. Otherwise,
the text remains as it was.

Deleting a Block

The last action we will look at is deleting the block. We'll use this to return
MYPROG1.PAS to it's original state. To do this, you must delete one of the
WriteLn statements.

1 Mark the block containing the WriteLn statement.

2 Press the keys *Ctrl+K Y* and a blank line will appear.

3 Press the keys *Ctrl+Y* and the blank line will be deleted.

Note that by using the keys *Ctrl+Y*, it's possible to delete, line by line, any number of lines. This is OK if you only want to delete one, two or three lines. Otherwise, use the method described above.

Summary

Your first voyage through the Turbo Pascal Integrated Development Environment is over. You now have enough knowledge to write, compile and run simple programs in Turbo Pascal. You can also carry out different editing operations on the program.

You have seen that Turbo Pascal allows you to carry out actions in different ways. Choose the way that best suits you. However, don't forget to save the program you are editing. From time to time, press *F2*. This saves the current version of the program. Even if something unexpected happens in the middle of your editing session, at least the most recent version of the program will be saved. Otherwise, all will be lost and you will have to start entering all your changes again.

In the next chapter, we will start to build our own programs from the ground up. We will look at what each of the components of **MYPROG1.PAS** really does, and how we can add more useful features to it.

Quiz Questions

1   Why can't we write programs in English?

2   What are the advantages of Turbo Pascal as a programming language?

3   What do the following terms mean: algorithm, program, compile, run, debugging?

4   A program transforms what into what?

5   Identify three different ways of saving a program and three different ways of running a program in the IDE. Which methods do you prefer?

6   How do you mark the beginning and end of a block of text in the IDE editor?

Exercises

1   Write an algorithm (in English!) that describes the process of making a cheese and pickle sandwich. What do you think the input data is? What do you transform them into? If you have the ingredients, try out your algorithm!

2   Type in the program **MYPROG1.PAS** and save it as **MY_PROG2.PAS**. Edit **MYPROG2.PAS** by replacing the current WriteLn( ) statement with

```
WriteLn('This is an odd line of output.');
```

between Begin and End.

▶   Use the block facilities of the editor to make ten copies of this line.

▶   Use the search and replace facility to find each occurence of the word 'odd'.

▶   Replace **every other** occurence with the word 'even'.

▶   Compile your program in memory and run it. Check that it produces the following result:

```
This is an odd line of output.
This is an even line of output.
This is an odd line of output.
This is an even line of output.
This is an odd line of output.
This is an even line of output.
This is an odd line of output.
This is an even line of output.
This is an odd line of output.
This is an even line of output.
```

When your program is working, save it.

3   Make **MYPROG2.PAS** your default start-up file.

▶   Compile **MYPROG2.PAS** to disk.

▶   Exit the Turbo Pascal IDE and run **MYPROG2.PAS.**

▶   Re-start Turbo Pascal and close **MYPROG2.PAS.**

▶   Reset your compile method to Compile to Memory.

The Nuts and Bolts of a Turbo Pascal Program

In the English language, words must be spelt correctly and sentences must obey certain rules of grammar for us to understand what is being said. (*Wrods tpels correctly must be* proves the point.) Turbo Pascal is an artificial language where correct spelling and the obeying of rules are similarly essential. However, even with correct spelling and correct grammar, an English sentence can still cause confusion. Take the example 'time flies'. Does this mean 'time passes rapidly', or is it a command to measure the speed of insects?

Computers need clear and precise instructions to perform the tasks we set them so the rules governing the 'grammar' of a programming language have to be very strict. Learning these rules is the key to learning a programming language and in this chapter we will teach you the basic rules for Turbo Pascal.

The topics we'll cover include:

- Program headers, statements, and the structure of programs
- Reserved words, variable identifiers, comments and constants
- Strings and numbers

In the last section we will also cover some aspects of how to program with style.

The Building Blocks of a Turbo Pascal Program

The first chapter took you for a tour round Turbo Pascal's 'toolbox', the IDE. In this chapter we'll introduce the basic elements, the nuts and bolts of a Turbo Pascal program, and explain a bit more about the basic structure or template of a program. To do this we'll use a modified version of program **MYPROG1**.

MYPROG1 has an obvious disadvantage if you want to greet anyone whose name isn't John. Program **EX_2_1** is a modified version of program **MYPROG1** which greets the user personally.

```
Program EX_2_1;
Uses Crt;
Var
    Your_Name : String;
Begin
    ClrScr;
    Write('Enter your name: ');
    ReadLn(Your_name);
    WriteLn('Hello ',Your_Name,', Welcome to WroxLand');
End.
```

The following screenshot shows a typical result of running the program.

```
Enter your name: Mary
Hello Mary, Welcome to WroxLand
```

The Basic Template of a Turbo Pascal Program

The next figure shows the template and the elements of this program.

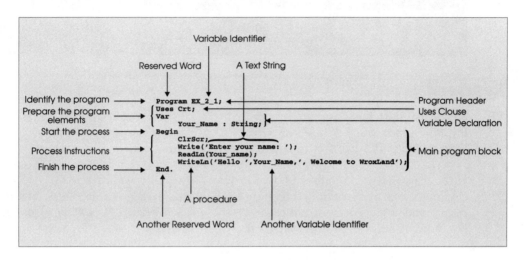

The Program Header

Let's take a closer look at these various elements. The first line of your program is the **program header**. You must use the program header to show that what follows is a program, and to give your program a name. Though this may seem unnecessary, remember that computers will only do *exactly* what you tell them to. It also stops you returning to your computer to find that you have compiled your end of term paper on Quantum Mechanics, instead of your program to draw fractals (the second of these programs will be possible after you have read this book - the first requires a course in sophomore physics!)

The structure of the program header is:

> Program *Variable_Identifier;*
>
> The word Program is compulsory, and the word *Variable_Identifier* is replaced by your name for the program (**EX_2_1** in the above case).

> Note the semi-colon which marks the end of the program header. Though it may look trivial, the semi-colon is vital. If you don't include it, Turbo Pascal won't be able to compile or run your program and will send you the (dreaded) error message:
>
> **Error 85: ';' expected**

Reserved Words

You must start the program header with the word Program, and this is also the *only* place you can use the word Program. Because of this unique characteristic, Program is called a **reserved word**.

Turbo Pascal has a number of words which are reserved for special circumstances. For example, other reserved words in **EX_2_1** are Uses, Var, Begin and End. We'll introduce and explain each one as we come across it. For now, it suffices to say that these words exist!

> All the reserved words in Turbo Pascal are listed in Appendix A.

Variable Identifiers

The other part of the program header, **EX_2_1**, is the **variable identifier**. This consists of one word which is used to identify the program.

Your_name, which appears later on in the program, is also a variable identifier. As they are a fundamental concept in programming, we'll spend some time on variable identifiers now, and return to the structure of the program later.

Go back to **EX_2_1** and run the program again. This time when you are asked for your name, type Quasimodo. The results displayed on screen are different from the previous time you ran the program (see the following figure), but we haven't changed the program in any way. The secret to how Turbo Pascal does this is in variable identifiers.

```
Enter your name: Quasimodo
Hello Quasimodo, Welcome to WroxLand
```

How It Works - The Variable Identifier

Imagine that you are inside a warehouse surrounded by a huge stack of empty boxes. A phone call from *Var* asks you to label a box with the word *Your_Name*.

You then receive a delivery from *Readln()* with the instruction to store the letters Q, U, A, S, I, M, O, D and O in the box labeled *Your_Name.*

Having put the letters in the box, *Writeln()* phones and asks what's in the box labeled *Your_Name.* You tell him, he makes a copy, and on he goes.

This scenario describes the memory system inside your computer, when program **EX_2_1** is running with you in the starring role as the processing unit.

A computer's 'memory' is like the warehouse. Each individual memory cell in the computer is like a single box in the warehouse. Your computer stores and handles data by identifying a particular memory cell with a variable identifier. Your computer then uses this identifier to refer to this memory cell. Other commands in the program can then instruct the computer to store data in the cell with this identifier, or to examine the contents of the specified cell.

Once the cell has been labeled we can vary the contents of the cell. In the above example, we could have stored the name 'John' in the box labeled **Your_Name** instead of 'Quasimodo'. So we use variable identifiers to identify cells whose contents can vary. Good choice of name!

How to Write Variable Identifiers

For Turbo Pascal to recognize a variable identifier three rules **must** be followed:

1 It must start with a letter or an underscore character (_).

2 The first letter must be followed by a sequence of letters (A-Z), digits (0-9), or underscore characters.

3 Your identifier must be distinguishable from other identifiers within its first 63 characters. Turbo Pascal only recognises these first 63, though there is no maximum length as such.

If an identifier follows these rules, we say it's a **legal** identifier (just think of Turbo Pascal as the programming cops and you'll get the idea!).

Identifier Chic - The Fourth 'Rule'

There is also a fourth 'rule' for writing identifiers. However, if you break this rule it isn't a violation and doesn't lead to illegal identifiers - it just leads to very confusing programs. This rule is 'when you create an identifier, use a word that means something to you'.

When we see the program identifier **EX_2_1**, it's easy for us to remember that this is the **EX**ample program from Chapter **2** and it's the **1**st program in the chapter. When you look at the program itself it's easy to see that your name is stored in the variable **Your_Name**. Check out the following legal identifiers to see what we mean:

Identifier	Comment
Number_of_Pages	Helpful
Counter	Fine and dandy
Area	Meaningful
N	What on earth does this mean?
X1	Your guess is as good as mine
_X	Time to give up

UPPER or lower?

Turbo Pascal is not case-sensitive. This doesn't mean Turbo Pascal is unfeeling towards luggage (though in fact it is). It means it doesn't distinguish between the upper-case or lower-case of a letter. To Turbo Pascal PROGRAM is the same as program. You can therefore use either when you create an identifier.

DON'T Try It Out - Duplication

Look at the following two identifiers:

VeryVeryVeryVeryVeryVeryVeryVeryVeryVeryVeryVery_Long_Identifier_1

and

VeryVeryVeryVeryVeryVeryVeryVeryVeryVeryVeryVery_Long_Identifier_2

If you used both of these identifiers in the same program you'd get the error message:

Error 4: Duplicate identifier

Only the first 63 characters in an identifier are significant, but the two examples above only differ at the 66th position. You won't need such long signifiers - but the lesson stands.

DON'T Try It Out - Illegal Characters

It's important that you follow the conventions for writing identifiers otherwise Turbo Pascal will refuse to run your programs. The following is a list of illegal identifiers and the reasons why they are not valid:

Illegal Identifiers	Problem
First Number	You can't have a space. Turbo Pascal uses spaces to separate elements in a program. The example on the left would be treated as two distinct identifiers.
1st_Number	Identifiers must start with a letter or an underscore (_).
A+B	You must only use letters, numbers and underscores. The + sign is illegal.
A&B	The character & is illegal.

The Basic Template of a Turbo Pascal Program - Continued

Now that you're familiar with three of the elements of a Turbo Pascal program - program headers, reserved words and variable identifiers - we can continue to examine the program template. After the program header comes the uses clause.

The Uses Clause

You include in the uses clause all the **units** that Turbo Pascal can have access to in a program. Units are special programs written and supplied by Borland. They provide an interface between your programs and external devices (such as printers and monitors) and are controlled by your computer's operating system. Because of the standard nature of DOS and Windows, it's logical for Borland to write these program parts. However, it's also useful to know how to write your own, so in Chapter 6 we'll find out more about units and actually write one.

The structure of the uses clause is

Uses *Unit_Variable_Identifier;*

where Uses is a reserved word and *Unit_Variable_Identifier* is the name of the unit. If you are using more than one unit you can include a list of their names separated by commas, before the semi-colon.

In our programs we need to include the line:

```
Uses CRT
```

so that we can control the monitor.

CRT is shorthand for Cathode Ray Tube, the electronic device in a monitor.

Variable Declaration

Once you have identified the program and told Turbo Pascal which units your program will be using, then it's time to make some **declarations**. Here you list all the variable identifiers you are going to use in this program. Turbo Pascal then uses this information to allocate cells in your computer's memory for each variable. You also tell Turbo Pascal here what **type** the variable identifier is. The type of a variable defines the range of values a variable can take and what operations can be performed on that variable.

Typing

In the front of your computer there will be a disk drive. This has a slot of a certain size and shape to only accept computer disks. Because of this standardization of input, two things are ensured. Firstly, there are certain standard functions your disk drive will perform, such as letting the disk rotate. Secondly, it stops objects other than disks being placed in the drive (such as a pastrami sandwich on rye).

Types in Turbo Pascal place similar restrictions on a variable identifier. The type defines which functions can be performed on the variable (you can rotate a disk in a disk drive) and which values a variable can take (pastrami on rye is not an acceptable alternative to a disk).

Types in Turbo Pascal define whether a variable is a number (integer or real type), a string of letters (string type) or takes the value 'true' or 'false' (boolean type). Setting the type of a variable stops you trying to add together 'blue' and '14' or answering the question 'is 1 true?'

The structure of the variable declaration is:

Var
    Variable_Identifier   : *Type_Identifier;*

Where Var is a reserved word to indicate the start of the variable declaration, *Variable_Identifier* is the name of the variable and *Type_Identifier* is the name of the type.

In **EX_2_1** the variable declaration looks like this:

```
Var
   Your_Name : string;
```

This sets aside memory for the variable identifier **Your_Name** which is of type string.

Strings

In Turbo Pascal a string is a sequence of zero or more characters and a variable of string type is used to store such a sequence. Strings and variables of string type are Turbo Pascal's way of manipulating text in a program. In **EX_2_1**, the variable **Your_Name** is of string type and is used to store the string of characters that make up your name or Quasimodo's. There's a whole lot more to handling text in Turbo Pascal so we have dedicated Chapter 4 to a complete introduction to strings.

The Main Program Block

Back in the program we must now create our **main program block**. This is the sequence of statements in the program which actually processes the data. The main program block starts with the reserved word Begin. It finishes with the reserved word End.

How to End a Program

Any fool can fly a plane - it takes an expert to land. End indicates the finish of the main program block, but to tell Turbo Pascal that your program is complete you must use a period (.).

Statements

A statement is an instruction to Turbo Pascal which tells it to process certain data or perform certain actions. Statements are separated from each other by semi-colons.

In **EX_2_1**, the main program block consists of this sequence of statements:

```
Begin
   ClrScr;
   Write('Enter your name: ');
   ReadLn(Your_name);
   WriteLn('Hello ',Your_Name,', Welcome to WroxLand');
End.
```

Let's look at each line to see what's going on.

Procedures

ClrScr, Write(), ReadLn() and WriteLn() are all **procedures**. These are special programs that Borland provide with Turbo Pascal to make your work easier. When Turbo Pascal reads these words, it 'runs' these separate programs and then returns to your program.

For instance, when Turbo Pascal finds the instruction ClrScr in a program, it clears the output screen, while Write() and WriteLn() send what is contained between the parentheses to the output screen. In further chapters you'll actually write some of your own procedures, so we'll save a more formal definition of procedures until later. For now though, because the input and output of data is so important, we'll take a closer look at Write(), WriteLn() and ReadLn().

Turbo Pascal comes equipped with a large number of pre-defined procedures which you can use in any program, such as Write, WriteLn() and ReadLn(). These are stored in the **System** unit. Because these procedures are so important, Turbo Pascal doesn't even ask you to include the line **Uses System** in your program.

The exception is the procedure Clrscr. This is specific to manipulating the monitor through DOS and is stored in the **CRT** unit. Hence the inclusion of the line **Uses CRT** in all our programs

Input and Output Procedures

ReadLn()

The user inputs data into a program using the ReadLn() procedure. This takes the data typed in by the user and, when the *Enter* key is pressed, stores it in the variable whose identifier appears inside the parentheses.

So, in **EX_2_1**, the statement

```
ReadLn(Your_Name);
```

takes the name you typed (either yours or Quasimodo's), and after you've pressed the *Enter* key, stores that name in the variable **Your_Name**.

Character Strings

The procedures Write() and WriteLn() do the opposite to ReadLn(), in that they output the data inside the parentheses. However, we must understand more about character strings before we examine these procedures in detail.

A character string is a sequence of zero or more characters written on one line and enclosed between 2 apostrophes. Turbo Pascal treats a character string as literal text, so that when a character string is output, you see exactly the same characters in the same sequence.

Literal Text	On Screen Appearance
'a'	The letter a
'B'	The letter B
' '	A space
'Turbo Pascal'	Two words - Turbo Pascal
'BORLAND'	The word BORLAND

Because character strings are literal, the text is case-sensitive. So upper-case and lower-case letters are treated differently. The character string 'This is a string' is not the same as the string 'THIS IS A STRING'.

If you want to display an apostrophe, you should type two apostrophes. For example, 'Don''t' appears on the screen as the word Don't.

As a final note on character strings, Turbo Pascal allows an empty or 'null' string which contains zero characters.

Write() and WriteLn()

You use these two procedures to output data. The program

```
WriteLn('Hello ',Your_Name,', Welcome to WroxLand');
```

produces the output

Hello Quasimodo, Welcome to WroxLand

(assuming that the string Quasimodo is stored in the variable **Your_name**). WriteLn() forms output from a combination of the character strings and the contents of a variable (in this case the variable **Your_Name**). Remember to separate the elements of the output using commas.

Write() vs WriteLn()

However, we still haven't answered that nagging question, namely, what's the difference between Write() and WriteLn()? Time to take the plunge! Let's take a look at Program **EX_2_2**.

```
Program EX_2_2;
Uses Crt;
Var
    Your_Name : String;
Begin
   ClrScr;
   Write('Enter your name: ');
   ReadLn(Your_name);
   Write('Hello ');
   Write(Your_Name);
   Write(', Welcome to WroxLand');
   WriteLn;
End.
```

The output from this program is shown oppposite.

```
Enter your name: Luke
Hello Luke, Welcome to WroxLand
```

It's the same as the earlier shot (the output from the program without the modification). This is because using WriteLn() prints the text and then moves the cursor to the beginning of the next line. Write(), on the other hand, leaves the cursor at the end of the printed text, but on the **same** line. As a result, the three Write() procedures in **EX_2_2** all output data on the same line.

Comments

We have now covered each element of this program and introduced you to the basic template. Now take a look at another version of the same program.

```
Program EX_2_3;
{This first line identified the program as EX_2_3}

{*********************
*Author : Oleg N. Perminov
*Date: 28th of January 1994
*Input data: Users name
*Output data: Greeting the user
*Function: Ask for the users name and then greet them
*Date of last changes: 6/12/94
*Status: Done
*********************}

{Set up system to output data to the screen}
```

```
Uses Crt;
{Declare Your_Name as a variable of string type}
Var
    Your_Name : String;
{Start the main program block}
Begin
{ Clear the screen }
    ClrScr;
{ Output the character string as a prompt }
    Write('Enter your name: ');
{ Input the user name and store this name in the variable Your_Name}
    ReadLn(Your_name);
{ Output the greeting with the Users name}
    WriteLn('Hello ',Your_Name,', Welcome to WroxLand');
{Finish the main program block and then the program}
End.
```

The output of the program is shown below.

```
Enter your name: Luke
Hello Luke, Welcome to WroxLand
```

Even with all the extra lines, the output remains the same. This is because the extra lines are included to make it easier to follow what is happening in the program. They are merely **comments** on the program and don't change the way the program behaves.

Comments - Definition

> To write a comment enclose your message between curly brackets {} or between the symbols (* and *). All comments in a program are ignored by Turbo Pascal. They are there for you to be able to make sense of a program when you return to look at it.

Comments About Comments

Some say the best comment of all is the clear and well-structured text of the program itself. This is very true. However, comments don't make a program any worse; they can only improve it and make the program text clearer. This won't only help other people who try to read the program, but will also help you as the author of the program. That's why it's strongly recommended to include comments in your programs.

Here are a number of different kinds of comments.

1 *Comments at the head of the program.* Include some general information about the function of the program, input and output data, name of the programmer, version of the program, and so on. Enclose them in a box of asterisks so that you can tell at glance what the program is for.

2 *Comments which describe which variables are used in the program.* Understanding the data used is the key to understanding the whole program. This is why you need to add comments about all data, explaining why it is used in your program.

3 *Comments which delineate different parts of programs.* As your programs grow in size, they may become split into independent parts. In this case it is a good idea to add comments in each part of the program to show where one part ends and another begins.

4 *Comments which clarify the most complicated sections of your program.* If you've used some exotic algorithm, for example, then give it a brief description.

EX_2_3 is a useful tool with which you can re-cap what we have discussed so far in the chapter, but generally there's no need to explain every line of a program. The best way to decide where to insert comments is to read through your program and type in any answers to the questions the future readers of your programs might come up with.

Extending Turbo Pascal - Constants and Numbers

Program **EX_2_4** adds a bit more spice to the earlier program. In this new example the program reads in your name and age. It then calculates how old you will be in the year 2000, and if it's also after your birthday it will give you the year in which you were born. It then displays the now well-worn greeting on screen alongside this new information.

```
Program EX_2_4;
{This program asks for the user's name and age,
then greets them and displays the user's age in the year 2000
 and the year the user was born }
Uses Crt;
{Declare a constant}
Const
    Current_year = 1994;
{Declare 4 variables, 1 of type string and 3 of type integer}
Var
    Your_Name : String;
    Your_Age, Age_in_2000, Born_Year : Integer;
Begin
    ClrScr;
{Prompt the user for their name and their age and store
them in the appropriate variables}
  Write('Enter your name: ');
  ReadLn(Your_name);
  Write('Enter your age: ');
  ReadLn(Your_Age);
{------------------------------------------}
{Calculate the users age in the year 2000 and store in the value}
    Age_in_2000 :=  2000 - Current_year + Your_Age;
{------------------------------}
{Calculate the year the user was born and store in the value}
    Born_year := Current_year - Your_Age;
{------------------------------}
{Greet the user}
    WriteLn('Hello ',Your_Name,', Welcome to WroxLand');
{Tell the user their age in the year 2000 and the year they were born}
    Write('In the year 2000 you will be ', Age_in_2000:4,' years old');
    WriteLn(' and if it is after your birthday you were born in',Born_year:5);
End.
```

Declaring Constants

If we work through the program, the first 2 instruction lines (ignoring the comments) are the program header and the uses clause. The next line is the first new style of instruction: declaring **constants**. To state the obvious, the value stored in a constant identifier remains constant. This allows you to refer to the same piece of information in your program a number of different times.

In **EX_2_4** for instance, we refer to the current year twice in the program. We could have typed the number '1994', but this is simply the number between 1993 and 1995. By using the identifier **Current_Year** we give the value 1994 a meaning. If we need to refer to the current year in our program we can use the constant identifier each time, which makes the program easier to follow. It also means that if we want to use the program in 1995 we only have to change one line at the top.

The structure for declaring a constant is

Const
    Constant_Identifier = *Constant_Value;*

where Const is a reserved word, *Constant_Identifier* is a legal identifier and *Constant_Value* is the value you wish to remain constant in your program.

Listing Variable Identifiers

The next part of the program is the variable declaration (which we've already met). We can now extend the scope of the declaration to include more than one variable of the same type, and also to introduce a new type.

When you declare variables, each declaration statement needs to be separated by a semi-colon. When you declare more than one variable of the same type, a complete statement should consist of a list of variable identifiers separated by commas. A colon separates the final identifier from the type.

So declaring a list of variables you write:

```
Var
    T1_Variable_1,   T1_Variable_2,...   T1_Variable_n   :Type_1;
    T2_Variable_1,   T2_Variable_2,...   T2_Variable_n   :Type_2;
    ...
    Tn_Variable_1,   Tn_Variable_2,...   Tn_Variable_n   :Type_n;
```

Where Var is the reserved word followed by lists of Variable Identifiers.

Types Revisited - Integers

In **EX_2_4** we used two variables of integer type. In Turbo Pascal there are two basic kinds of number: **integer** and **real**. For those of a less mathematical mind, integers are whole numbers (no finicky fractions or dreary decimal points thank heavens!). Real numbers are those which include a decimal point, and a fractional part.

As with all types, declaring variables as integer type restricts the kind of information you can store *in* that variable. It also restricts the operations you can perform *on* that variable. However, Turbo Pascal has 5 types which deal with integers (in the mathematical sense of whole numbers), one of which is the one called integer (in the Turbo Pascal sense of a type). Because this can get confusing, we have devoted the whole of Chapter 3 to numbers.

Assignment Statements

This moves us to the final element in the nuts and bolts of Turbo Pascal - **assignment statements**.

The structure of an assignment statement is very simple

```
Variable_identifier  :=   expression;
```

The special symbol := is called an assignment operator and the **expression** can be any value or any calculation giving a single value.

In **EX_2_4** assignment statements are used to assign the results of calculations in the two variables. In the first instance

```
Age_in _2000 := 2000 - Current_Year + Your_Age;
```

When Turbo Pascal reads this it takes the number '2000', subtracts the value stored in the variable **Current_Year**, and then adds the value stored in **Your_Age**. The result of this calculation is assigned to the variable **Age_in_2000**.

It's important to differentiate between the assignment operator := and the equals sign =. The equal sign is a static remark that states that two expressions are equal. When you declare a constant you set the identifier equal to the value. This is then fixed for the program. Assignment is a dynamic process. Suppose the result of the above calculation was 30. The value stored in **Age_in_2000** would be equal to 30. If later in the program you wrote the statement

```
Age_in_2000 := 2;
```

you would have changed the value stored in the variable **Age_in_2000** to **2** (and the person would not have been born yet!). Using the assignment operator := you replace any previously stored value with the new value.

The expression on the right of an assignment statement can be any mathematical expression. This will consist of a sequence of variables separated by mathematical operators such as +, -, *. For example, if the current year is 1994, the line

```
Age_in_2000 := 2000 - Current_Year;
```

would store the value 6 in **Age_in_2000**. Later you can write

```
Age_in_2000 := Age_in_2000 + 1;
```

to make the value stored in **Age_in_2000** equal to 7. It may seem odd to have the same variable on both sides of the assignment, but assignment works in two stages. **First** it evaluates the expression and **then** it stores the result in the variable (on the left).

> Standard functions can also be used in an expression (but more about that later!).

Unlike the declaration statements for variables of more than one type, the left side of an assignment statement can only have one variable. If you wanted to assign zero to several variables you need to write:

X := 0;

Y := 0;

Z := 0;

Don't Try It Out!

Turbo Pascal will not allow you to write

X := Y := Z := 0;

or

X, Y, Z := 0;

Outputting Numbers

You have already seen the procedures Write() and WriteLn() in operation on strings. Look at the statements using these functions in Program **EX_2_4** and note the slight difference.

```
Write('In the year 2000 you will be ', Age_in_2000:4,' years old');
WriteLn(' and if it is after your birthday you were born in', Born_year:5,);
```

These two statements give the output shown in the following shot:

```
Enter your name: Luke
Enter your age: 25
Hello Luke, Welcome to WroxLand
In the year 2000 you will be   31 years old and if it is after your birthday you
   were born in 1969
```

As you can see, the identifiers are followed by a colon and a digit (in the first case 4, in the second case 5). When you look at the output, however, these digits don't appear.

These digits are Turbo Pascal codes for **formatting** the output of a number, defining how the number should appear on screen. These 'invisible' digits show the number of character positions the output number occupies on screen. If the field width is bigger than the item then it makes the field just big enough to print the item. If the item is narrower than the specified field width then it makes up the field width with spaces to the left of the item.

Programming in Style

Finally for some style! Let's briefly consider how to make our programs easier to follow by making them better-looking. The following figure shows the output from the programs **STYLE1.PAS** and **STYLE2.PAS**.

```
Enter first side:
15
Enter second side:
12
Enter angle:
40
Third side=  9.6552576598E+00
```

Now take a look at the layout of the two programs

```
Program Style_2;Uses Crt;Var Side_1, Side_2, Side_3, Angle :
Real;Begin ClrScr;WriteLn('Enter first side: ');ReadLn(Side_1);
WriteLn('Enter second side: ');ReadLn(Side_2);WriteLn(
'Enter angle: ');ReadLn(Angle);Side_3 := Sqrt(Sqr(Side_1)+
Sqr(Side_2)-2*Side_1*Side_2*Cos(Angle*Pi/180));WriteLn('Third side= '
,Side_3);End.
```

Rather confusing? Check-out program **STYLE_1** and see how much easier a well-written program is to read.

```
Program Style_1;
Uses Crt;
Var
  Side_1, Side_2, Side_3, Angle : Real;
Begin
  ClrScr;
  WriteLn('Enter first side: ');
  ReadLn(Side_1);
  WriteLn('Enter second side: ');
  ReadLn(Side_2);
```

```
   WriteLn('Enter angle: ');
   ReadLn(Angle);
   Side_3 := Sqrt(Sqr(Side_1)+Sqr(Side_2)-2*Side_1*Side_2*Cos(Angle*Pi/180));
   WriteLn('Third side= ',Side_3);
End.
```

To write a well-structured program in Turbo Pascal follow these simple rules:

1 Never write more than one statement per line.

2 All the statements in a compound statement should start from the same position. A sequence of statements between the reserved words Begin and End is called a **compound** statement. The main program block is an example of a compound statement.

3 Indent all the statements in the current compound statement by three to five spaces.

4 Separate independent parts of the program with blank lines or dashes.

Summary

In this chapter, we have introduced you to the building blocks of a Turbo Pascal program.

This has included identifying parts of a program so that we understand the basic template for a program - the program header, the uses clause, constant declarations, variable declarations and the main program block. We have also covered the basic elements of a program - reserved words, variable identifiers and constants. We have seen how we combine these pieces to write a complete program.

We have also spoken about types and we have briefly mentioned numbers and strings. Because of their importance each of these subjects has a complete chapter.

Finally we talked about writing clear, well commented and well-structured programs. You will find it very useful to follow these guidelines when writing your programs, as you will find it much easier to follow your programs.

Quiz Questions

1 What do the following terms mean?
Reserved word, program header, variable identifier, constant, unit, type, statement, procedure, comment, assignment.

2 Which of the following variable identifiers are legal in Turbo Pascal?

123
ABC
QwErTy
widget37
This_identifier_is_too_long_to_bother_typing_it_again_and_again.
This_identifier_is_too_long_to_bother_typing_it_again_and_again
beryl_
x,y

3 Which of the following variable identifiers are useful?

t1
username
r
r (in a program for calculating a circle's area from its radius)
Day_of_week
distance_of_the_earth_from_the_sun
Alices_height

4 How do you write comments in Turbo Pascal programs? How would you use them?

5 What is the effect of the following assignment (where number is an Integer)?

```
number := number * 10;
```

6 What is wrong with the following program?

```
program silly;
var
     a_string: String;
uses
     crt;
begin
     a_string := 'A value';
end.
```

Exercises

1   Write a program which will print an address label for your home or business. Here's a fancy one we prepared earlier:

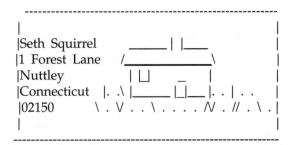

2   Write a program which reads a user's name and then uses it to personalise a limerick. A suitable template for the limerick is:

"Hey! These computers are great!"
Said XXXXX, a coder of late.
"They can calculate stuff
"And, if that's not enough,
"They can even arrange you a date!"

XXXXX is the user's name!

3   Write a program which will request a number of days from the user and convert it into the equivalent number of hours. For example, a run of your program might produce the following:

Please enter the number of days: 45
45 days is the same as 1080 hours.

CHAPTER
3

Processing Numbers

The only thing that computers can actually process is numbers, and the very first models were simply expected to be number crunchers. Since those early days, many more uses have been developed (including some fairly hot games). However, it's still useful to know how to get your computer to handle numbers (even if only to make a quick buck from doing your kid brother's math homework!).

In this chapter, we'll introduce you to the different types in Turbo Pascal which handle numbers. Turbo Pascal treats whole numbers differently from numbers with a fractional or decimal part, so we'll look at each of them separately.

In the chapter we will:

▶ Define the different number types

▶ Show you how to declare the different variables

▶ Introduce you to math and standard Turbo Pascal functions for working with numbers in programs

▶ Show you how to use the For and If statements to make your programs more interesting

Numbers and Types

Defining the **type** of a variable restricts the range of values the variable can store, and also defines the operations that can be performed on that variable. In Turbo Pascal, there are 10 different number types, but we can simplify our study by looking at two groups - **integers** (whole numbers) and **real** numbers (numbers with a fractional or decimal part). Whilst the specific range of values is different for each type, the set of operations that can be performed on integers is the same for each of the 5 integer types, and the set of operations that can be performed on real numbers is the same for each of the 5 real types.

Because we've already had some dealings with integers we'll look at them first.

Integers

What's an Integer?

Integer is the mathematical term for a whole number. In Turbo Pascal, to process whole numbers, you must declare variables as one of five integer types. Each of the integer types can store values which follow these rules:

- The value doesn't include a decimal point
- The value consists of the digits 0 through 9
- The value can contain the signs + or - to denote that it is more (+) or less (-) than zero

So 1, +1, -1, 100 or -100 are integers. 1.5, on the other hand, is **not**!

Declaring an Integer

You declare integer variables in the same way that you declare any other variables, by including the statements below:

```
Var
    Integer_Variable_Identifier :   Integer_Type_Identifier;
```

Where Var is the reserved word, *Integer_Variable_Identifier* is the name of the integer variable and *Integer_Type_Identifier* is the name of the type. This must be one of the types listed in the following table.

Five Kinds of Integers

The five integer types are listed in the following table:

Type Identifier	Range of Values	Number of Bytes
Longint	-2,147,483,648 through 2,147,483,648	4
Integer	-32,767 through 32,767	2
Word	0 through 65,535 .	2
Shortint	-128 through 128	1
Byte	0 through 256	1

The difference between each type is the range of values that can be stored. This affects the amount of memory that Turbo Pascal allocates to the variable when it's declared. You only need to worry about this when a program tells you it doesn't have enough memory to run - which won't happen for a few years yet so don't worry.

Standard Pascal only allows you to declare variables of **Integer** type, so as a rule we will declare variables only in this type.

When we are referring collectively to the above types we will write integer in normal text. If we wish to refer to the type identifier integer, the word will appear as it does here - integer

Bits and Bytes

Hold on, you may be saying, what's all this about **memory** and **bytes**? For those of you who are scratching your heads on this one, let's take time out to look at how computers store information.

Computers are limited by the amount of memory they have. We've already described the internals of a computer as a warehouse full of empty boxes. Imagine each of these empty boxes represents an area of memory in the computer. Memory in a computer is measured in bytes. A byte is just enough memory to store one character. When you declare a variable, Turbo Pascal sets aside a certain number of bytes of memory for each variable. As you can see from the previous table, the greater the range of the type, the greater the number of bytes Turbo Pascal uses to store the variable.

Integers in Action

The example program **EX_2_4** from Chapter 2 shows integers in action.

```
Program Ex_2_4;
{This program asks for the user's name and age,
then greets them and displays the user's age in the year 2000
 and the year the user was born }
Uses Crt;
{Declare a constant}
Const
   Current_year = 1994;
{Declare 4 variables, 1 of type string and 3 of type integer}
Var
   Your_Name : String;
   Your_Age, Age_in_2000, Born_Year  : Integer;
Begin
   ClrScr;
{Prompt the user for their name and their age and store
them in the appropriate variables}
  Write('Enter your name: ');
  ReadLn(Your_name);
  Write('Enter your age: ');
  ReadLn(Your_Age);
{-------------------------------------------------------------------
-}
{Calculate the users age in the year 2000 and store in the value}
   Age_in_2000 := 2000 - Current_year + Your_Age;
{-------------------------------------------------------------------
-}
{Calculate the year the user was born and store in the value}
   Born_year := Current_year - Your_Age;
{-------------------------------------------------------------------
-}
{Greet the user}
   WriteLn('Hello ',Your_Name,', Welcome to WroxLand');
{Tell the user their age in the year 2000 and the year they were born}
   Write('In the year 2000 you will be ', Age_in_2000:4,' years old');
   WriteLn(' and you were born in', Born_year:5,);
End.
```

At the start of the program we declare three variables of integer type and use one integer variable to store **Your_age** in years, and the other two integer variables to store the results of two calculations. The final part of the program outputs the values stored in the variables as part of the messages shown.

Because we have used variables of integer type, if the user were to enter a number other than a whole number Turbo Pascal would output the error message:

Error: Invalid numeric format

So we can't process anyone who is over 32,767 years old.

Real Numbers

What's a Real Number?

Now, we move to real numbers. These include all numbers with something after the decimal point (even if that something is a zero). You use real type variables to store values which follow these rules:

- The value includes a decimal point and there must also be a digit either side.

- The value uses the digits 0 through 9.

- The value can contain the signs + or - to denote that it is more (+) or less (-) than zero.

So the following are valid real numbers:

Real Number	Value Represented
100.0	one hundred
-100.0	minus one hundred
1.5	one and a half
1000000.0	one million
1.0e6	one million
1.0E6	one million
1.5e-6	0.000001

Exponential Format

The last 3 numbers may need a little explanation.

Real numbers can also be written in **exponential** format. This takes the format: *x.y*e*n*.

This means: '*x.y* multiplied by 10 raised to the power of *n*'.

So, for example:

1.5e2 = 1.5 x 10^2 = 1.5 x 100 = 150.

Also:

10^{-n} = $1/10^n$ so

. 1.5e-2 = 1.5 x 10^{-2} = 1.5 x $(1/10^2)$ = 1.5 x (1/100) = 1.5 x 0.01 = 0.015

Forceful Types

Also, you can actually store a whole number in variables of real type. Because of this, Turbo Pascal will automatically convert an integer number into a real number if necessary. This doesn't work the other way round.

Unreal Numbers

To avoid any unnecessary error messages, here are a few examples of invalid real numbers.

Not a Real Number	Reason
1,000	Commas are illegal
1 000	Spaces are illegal
.5	There must be a digit before the decimal point
5.	There must be a digit after the decimal point
1.0e2.5	The value following the 'e' must be an integer

Declaring a Real Variable - Definition

Declaring a variable of real type is as simple as declaring any other type:

```
Var
    Real_Variable_Identifier :   Real_Type_Identifier;
```

Where Var is the reserved word, *Real_Variable_Identifier* is the name of the real variable and *Real_Type_Identifier* is the name of the type. This must be one of the 5 types in the table below.

Five Kinds of Reals

The 5 different kinds of real type are listed in the table below:

Type	Range of Values (Each value can be plus or minus)	Number of Significant Digits	Number of Bytes
Real	2.9e-39 through 1.7e38	11 - 12	6
Single	1.5e-45 through 3.4e38	7 - 8	4
Double	5.0e-324 through 1.7e308	15 - 16	8
Extended	3.4e-4932 through 1.1e4932	19 - 20	10
Comp	-9.2e18 through 9.2e18	19 - 20	8

Standard Pascal only allows you to declare variables of real type, and even in Turbo Pascal your use of the other 4 types is restricted. For you to use the extra precision or flexibility available from these other four types, Turbo Pascal requires a 80x87 math co-processor, or emulation routines.

An 80x87 math co-processor is a special chip that can be installed in your PC and that which executes arithmetic very quickly. However, you don't actually need this hardware, as you can link in Turbo Pascal's emulator routines. These routines are software programs that pretend to be a piece of hardware, namely an 80x87 chip. When the program is compiled, the compiler generates special pieces of code for the 80x87 or the emulator.

To tell Turbo Pascal that it has access to an 80x87 or the emulator, you need to include a **compiler directive** in your program. A compiler directive is an instruction to the compiler which appears as a comment in your program. When the compiler reads the directive it will 'switch' on (or off) the appropriate feature. To turn on the 80x87 or the emulator, you need to include {$N+} in your program. To turn this feature off you include the comment {$N-}.

However, for the most part this is wholly unnecessary, and you'll find the real type covers all your needs.

The *Accuracy of Real Numbers*

When using integer numbers, you never need to worry about the accuracy of calculations. The exact whole number is stored in the computer and the result of the calculation is also an exact number.

By contrast, because a computer has limited memory, real numbers are stored as approximations. The different sorts of real types provide you with different compromises between accuracy and memory usage. This is the meaning of the significant digits for each number. This is the number of digits either side of the decimal point that are used to store a number.

For example, a real variable uses 6 bytes of memory, but only stores the first 12 digits of a number (at most). Digit number 13 and beyond are lost to the wind. Of course, this number of digits will be sufficient for most of our programs. After all, it does give the value of Pi as 3.1415926536. Plenty!

Example: Money in the Bank

So, having seen some of the properties of real numbers, we'll take a look at a program that uses them. The following example uses real variables to calculate your new savings after one year.

```
Program ex_3_2;
Uses CRT;
{A program to calculate your new savings after 1 year }
Var
    Deposit,           {initial deposit of money}
    Savings,           {To store value of savings after one year}
    Interest           {annual interest rate as a percentage}
                       : Real;
Begin
   ClrScr;
 {Read in values for initial deposit and then interest rate as a percentage}
   Write('Enter your initial deposit: ');
   ReadLn(Deposit);
   Write('Enter the bank''s annual interest rate as a percentage: ');
   ReadLn(Interest);
 {-------------------------------------------------------------------------}
 {Calculate the value of the savings after one year}
   Savings := Deposit + Deposit * Interest / 100;
 {-------------------------------------------------------------------------}
 {Output this new value to the screen}
   Write('After one year you will have ');
   Write(Savings:5:2);
   WriteLn(' in the bank');
End.
```

Firstly, we declare the three variables we'll need. They are all of real type, so we can declare them as one list. The variable identifiers are separated by commas, then after the last variable identifier comes a colon, then the type identifier (real in this case), then a semi-colon to end the statement. So long as you include all of this punctuation in the correct order, you can separate out the text with comments and spaces to make the program more readable. Previously, with integers, if you tried to enter a real number you got an error. This time, if you entered an integer (by not including a decimal point for example), Turbo Pascal will convert the values to real.

When we write the value of **saving** to the screen, we use some formatting codes to show dollars and cents in our savings. As you know, the first number is the width in characters of the output. We use the second colon and number to show the cents. This second number tells Turbo Pascal that we want to see a decimal point, and also states the number of digits to display after the decimal point.

This is one of the possible outputs from this program.

```
Enter your initial deposit: 56
Enter the banks annual interest rate as a percentage: 6
After one year you will have 59.36 in the bank
```

Math in Programs

We're talking about numbers, so at some point we have to talk about math. Below, we review the math operations and how they are used in Turbo Pascal.

Whilst we don't like using jargon, operands is the best word we know to replace the phrase 'variables being operated on', so we have used it in these tables.

This table shows operations on a single operand:

Symbol	Operation	Example where number = 1
+	Has no effect	+ **number** = 1
-	Makes the value less than zero	- **number** = -1

If + and - have only one operand, they indicate whether the value of the variable is greater (+) or less (-) than zero. Turbo Pascal assumes your numbers are positive, so you won't often find much use for the (+) operator on its own.

This table shows the operations on two operands:

Symbol	Operation	Example where $num1 = 5$ and $num2 = 3$
+	Addition	$num1 + num2 = 5 + 3 = 8$
-	Subtraction	$num1 - num2 = 5 - 3 = 2$
*	Multiplication	$num1 * num2 = 5 * 3 = 15$

Addition, subtraction and multiplication are standard operations in Turbo Pascal and translate directly from ordinary math. Division in Turbo Pascal is slightly different.

> Before we discuss division, a word about types. For all the above operations, if the operands are both of integer type, then the result will be of integer type. If either of the operands is of real type, the result will be of real type

Division

Symbol	Operation	Type of Operands	Type of Result
/	Division	integer	real
		real	real
div	Division with truncation	integer	integer
mod	The modulus or remainder	integer	integer

The / (division) operator is the standard division operation in Turbo Pascal. For example, if $num1 = 5$ and $num2 = 2$, $num1 / num2 = 2.5$

This operator always gives a result of real type, even when both operands are of integer type. For example, if $num1 = 4$ (integer type) and $num2 = 2$ (integer type) and $num3 = num1 / num2$, then $num3 = 2.0$ (real type).

To do division on integer types, you need to use the operators Div and Mod. The result of Div is the whole number part of the division, and the result of Mod is the **remainder** or **modulus**.

Examples of Div and Mod

3 divides into 14, 4 whole times, with 2 as the remainder. So:

14 div 3 = 4

14 mod 3 = 2

3 divides into 15, 5 whole times, with no remainder. So:

15 div 3 = 5

15 mod 3 = 0

Priority of Operations

We also need to know in which order to do operations. Look at the following calculation:

2 + 3 * 4

Is the answer 5*4 = 20 or 2 + 12 = 14? In Turbo Pascal, all calculations with *, /, Div and Mod are of equal importance and are done first. These are followed by + and - calculations. So the answer to 2 + 3 * 4 is 14.

Calculations of the same importance are done by starting on the left and working through to the right. So

-5 +7 = 2 (not -12)

5 is made negative first and then added to 7. (**Not** 'add 5 and 12 and then make the number negative').

18 div 2 * 3 = 27 (not 3)

18 div 2 is 9, which is then multiplied by 3. (**Not** 'multiply 2 by 3 and then do 18 div 6').

However, you can alter the order by using parentheses. For example:

18 div (2 * 3) = 3, (not 27)

When you use parentheses, you tell Turbo Pascal to do the calculations in parentheses first, and only then will it go on to do the other calculations. Not only is this a neat trick if you are in doubt about the order, but it also helps to make your programs more readable. We recommend that you use parentheses and tell Turbo Pascal the order you want.

List of Functions

The four basic operations are all very well, but what if you want to do any more high-powered math? Turbo Pascal provides a set of common math functions that you can use in your programs. These **functions** are actually other programs that have previously been written and can now be used in your programs. We'll show you how to write your own functions in Chapter 6, but as the math functions are so common, Turbo Pascal provides them for you.

The table below gives a list of some of the most common math functions.

Name	Function	Type of x	Result Type	Example
Abs(x)	Absolute value	Any	Same as x	Abs(1) = Abs(-1) = 1
Cos(x)	Cosine	Real	Real	Cos(Pi) = -1
Frac(x)	Fractional part	Any	Real	Frac(3.456) = 0.456
Int(x)	Integer part	Real	Real	Int(123.321) = 123.0
Pi	Value of Pi		Real	3.1415926536
Round(x)	Rounded value	Real	Integer	Round(123.321) = 124
Sin(x)	Sine	Real	Real	Sin(Pi) = 0
Sqr(x)	Square	Any	Same as x	Sqr(2) = 4
Sqrt(x)	Square root	Any	Real	Sqrt(4) = 2.0
Trunc(x)	Truncated value	Real	Integer	Trunc(123.321) = 123

In the table we have given a short example of each function, but we reckon the best way to understand these functions is to see them in action. In the next program, we use a couple of them to give you an idea of how they work.

Example: Meters to Yards, Feet and Inches

If you'd wanted to learn math, you'd have picked up a math text book and not one on Turbo Pascal. What you want to learn is how to program. In the following example, we've combined all of the types and some of the operations and functions you've just learnt to show them in action. The purpose of the program is to take a length in meters, and show the equivalent length in yards, feet and inches.

```
Program Ex_3_3;
{A program to convert a length in meters into yards, feet and inches}
Uses CRT;
Const    {First declare all the constants}
   Inches_per_yard = 36;
   Inches_per_foot = 12;          {Notice these are both integers}
   Inches_per_meter = 39.372;   {Whilst this value is a real}
Var      {Next declare all the variables we need}
   Total_meters, Total_inches, Fractional_part, Number_inches : real;
   Whole_part, Number_yards, Number_feet : integer;
Begin
   ClrScr;
   {Accept the value we are to convert}
   Write('Enter the length in meters to convert and press Enter: ');
   ReadLn(Total_meters);
   {--------------------------------------------------------------}
   {Convert the length into inches using the standard conversion}
   Total_inches := Total_meters * Inches_per_meter;
   {Store the whole part of the length as an integer variable}
   Whole_part := Trunc(Total_inches);
   {Work out how many times 36 divides into this whole number of inches}
   Number_yards := Whole_part div inches_per_yard;
   {Work out how many times 12 divides into the remainder
   of the previous division}
   Number_feet := (Whole_part mod inches_per_yard) div inches_per_foot;
   {Add the remainder from the previous calculation to
   the fractional part of the original calculation}
   Number_inches := (whole_part mod inches_per_foot) + Frac(Total_inches);
   {--------------------------------------------------------------}
   {Output the answers to the screen and
   use the output format to space the text}
   Write(Total_meters:7:3,' meters is equal to');
   Write(Number_yards:4,' yards');
   {There can be a maximum of 3 feet so 2 characters is sufficient
   to leave a space and one digit}
   Write(Number_feet:2,' feet and');
   {There can be a maximum of 12 inches so with 3 digits after the decimal
   point plus one character for the point itself, 7 characters gives one
   space and a maximum of 2 digits}
   Write(Number_inches:7:3,' inches');
End.
```

Starting from the top of the program, so that we can use div and mod operations, we are careful to define the constants and variables with the correct type. Then, converting the length from meters to inches gives a value of real type. To use div and mod we need to find the whole part of this value and store this as an integer type. To do this we use the standard Turbo Pascal function Trunc().

Using div we then find out how many times 36 (the number of inches in a yard) divides into this whole number of inches. This gives us the number of yards. Finally, we work out the number of inches. This is the remainder after dividing the whole number of inches by 12 (the number of inches per foot), plus the fractional part which is there from when we converted the number of meters to inches. We use the standard Turbo Pascal function Frac() to work out this last part.

Below is typical output from this program.

```
Enter the length in metres to convert and press Enter: 27
 27.000 metres is equal to  29 yards 1 feet and  7.044 inches
```

Making Math More Interesting

Impossible, we hear you cry! If we were left with just numbers and math functions, we'd have to agree. So that we can take our programming further, we're going to introduce a couple of Turbo Pascal's control structures - the For loop and the If statement. We'll cover these statements in far more detail in Chapter 5, when we deal more fully with control structures. For now, we'll have to content ourselves with a brief introduction and an example program.

The reason for introducing these structures here is to enable us to write the final example in the chapter. This is a program to draw a sine wave on your screen. Having introduced the If and For statements, we'll need to introduce one more topic, and then we'll be ready.

The For Statement

The program we looked at earlier to calculate our savings was all very well, but really we could do with a program that worked for any number of years. To do this we need to use the new Turbo Pascal structure the For ... To loop.

A For statement allows you to perform a group of statements a specified number of times. A general For statement looks like this:

```
For loop_index := starting_value to ending_value do
Begin
   Statement_1;
   Statement_2;
   ...
   Statement_N;
End;
```

Where For, to, do, Begin and End are reserved words, *loop_index* is an integer variable and *starting_value* and *ending_value* are two integers.

The loop works by performing **all** the statements for each value in the sequence *starting_value*, *starting_value+1*, *starting_value+2*, through to *ending_value*. The term loop is associated with this kind of Turbo Pascal structure, because the control in the program keeps looping back to the top each time. Each time the loop is performed *loop_index* is assigned the next value in the sequence.

Example: Money in the Bank 2

In this revised example, we've added just a few lines to the program, but these few lines make it far more flexible.

```
Program Ex_3_4;
Uses CRT;
{A program to calculate your new savings after however many years }
Var
    Deposit,                    {initial deposit of money}
    Savings,                    {To store value of savings after one year}
    Interest                    {annual interest rate as a percentage}
                    : Real;
    Num_years,                  {number of years to leave money in bank}
    Counter                     {Counter for the For statements}
                    : Integer;
Begin
    ClrScr;
    {Read in values for initial deposit and interest rate as a percentage}
    Write('Enter your initial deposit: ');
    ReadLn(Deposit);
    Write('Enter the bank''s annual interest rate as a percentage: ');
    ReadLn(Interest);
    Write('Enter the number of years to save: ');
    ReadLn(Num_years);
    {-----------------------------------------------------------------------}
    {Set the value of savings to equal deposit}
    Savings := Deposit;
    {-----------------------------------------------------------------------}
    {Calculate the new value of the savings.}
For Counter := 1 to Num_years do
        Begin
        Savings := Savings + Savings * Interest / 100;
        End;
    {-----------------------------------------------------------------------}
    {Output this new value to the screen}
    Write('After ', Num_years:2,' years you will have ');
    Write(Savings:9:2);
    WriteLn(' in the bank');
End.
```

Using the For ... to loop, for each value of **counter** from 1 to **Num_years** we work out a new value for **savings**. We then store this new value in the **savings** variable ready for the next pass through the loop.

When we've stepped through the values all the way to the value of **num_years**, control in the program doesn't loop back to the top again, but moves on to the last lines to output the result.

If we had a deposit of 1000 and left the money there for 5 years with an interest rate of 6%, we get the result shown below:

```
Enter your initial deposit: 1000
Enter the bank's annual interest rate as a percentage: 6
Enter the number of years you will save for: 5
After  5 years you will have $  1338.23 in the bank
```

The If Statement

The second control structure we are going to introduce is the If statement. This is a vital part of programming, as it allows you to ask a question in your program and to do different things depending on the answer.

The general form of an If statement is set out below:

```
If Condition
    Then
        Begin
        Statement_1;
        Statement_2;
          ...
        Statement_N;
        End
    Else
        Begin
        Else_Statement_1;
        Else_Statement_2;
          ...
        Else_Statement_N;
        End;

If, Then, Else, Begin and End are reserved words
```

When Turbo Pascal reads an If statement, it tests the *condition*, and depending on the result, chooses one of two actions:

▶ If the *condition* is satisfied (the result is 'yes'), then the *Statements* written after the reserved word Then are performed.

▶ Or if the *condition* is not satisfied (the result is 'no'), then the *Else_Statements* written after the reserved word Else are performed.

Remember how precise Turbo Pascal is about spelling. In the If statement, you shouldn't write a semi-colon between the reserved words End and Else.

Example: Do They Divide?

In the following example, we use the If statement to choose between two statements to print. The condition we are testing is whether one integer is divisible by another. Because number A is divisible by number B if and *only if* the remainder of the division is equal to zero, we can use the mod operation to test this condition.

```
Program Ex_3_5;
{Program to test whether one integer is divisible by another}
Var
    Number_to_test, Number_to_divide : Integer;
Begin
    Write('Enter the number to be tested and press Enter: ');
    ReadLn(Number_to_test);
    Write('Enter the number to divide by and press Enter: ');
    ReadLn(Number_to_divide);
{Check whether the condition answers yes or no}
    If (Number_to_test mod Number_to_divide) = 0
        Then
{if the number is divisible output the following statements}
        Begin
        WriteLn(Number_to_test,' is divisible by ',Number_to_divide);
        End
    Else
{If the number is NOT divisible output this statement}
        Begin
        WriteLn(Number_to_test,' is not divisible by ',Number_to_divide);
        End
End.
```

Below is a screenshot which shows the result after running the program with several different values. The If statement selects the correct statement depending on the values entered.

```
Enter the number to be tested and press Enter: 4
Enter the number to divide by and press Enter: 2
4 is divisible by 2
Enter the number to be tested and press Enter: 6
Enter the number to divide by and press Enter: 3
6 is divisible by 3
Enter the number to be tested and press Enter: 7
Enter the number to divide by and press Enter: 3
7 is not divisible by 3
Enter the number to be tested and press Enter: 7
Enter the number to divide by and press Enter: 5
7 is not divisible by 5
Enter the number to be tested and press Enter: 1024
Enter the number to divide by and press Enter: 16
1024 is divisible by 16
Enter the number to be tested and press Enter: 99
Enter the number to divide by and press Enter: 5
99 is not divisible by 5
```

Drawing on a Computer Screen

The final program in the chapter draws a sine curve on the screen. Before we move to this section we need to tell you something about the screen.

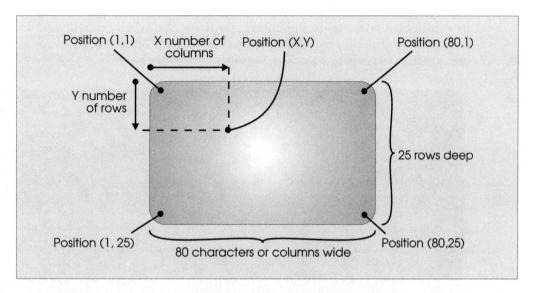

The X-axis starts from the left border of the screen and ends at the right border, and the Y-axis starts from the top of the screen and ends at the bottom. So when you describe a position on the screen the first value or X coordinate gives the number of columns, and the second value or Y coordinate gives the number of rows. There are 80 columns on the screen and 25 rows, and the coordinates must be whole numbers between these values.

Finally, before we start the main program, we'll just recap on the Write() procedure. The Write() procedure works across from the left to the right of the screen along one line, writing the characters as it goes. It does not move to the next line until it reaches the right-hand edge.

Drawing Graphs of Trig Functions

In this last section, we'll pull together what we have learnt in this chapter to write a program that draws a graph of the sine function from 0 to 2*pi. Because we are using Write() to output the values, our graph will come out on its side, but it's still fairly impressive! To draw the graph we will use an 'I' to represent the central axis, write an asterisk to mark the point equal to sin(x), and spaces everywhere else. The output is shown below:

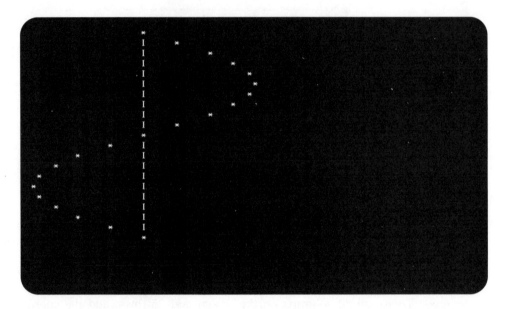

Dividing Up the Number of Rows

We're going to use the first 21 rows to draw the graph. This means we need to divide the output range 0 ... 2*Pi into twenty parts, giving the 21 points:

0, (2*Pi/20), (2*Pi/20)*2, (2*Pi/20)*3, through (2*Pi/20)*20

So the first asterisk marks Sin(0), the next asterisk marks sin(2*Pi/20), the next asterisk marks sin((2*Pi/20)*2) and so on as we move down the screen, until we get to the 21st asterisk which marks sin((2*pi/20)*20).

In the actual program, we'll replace the value 20 with the constant identifier **no_lines** to make the program easier to read. You should be able to see that as we move down a row, the value taken by sin() increases in steps of **2*pi/no_lines**.

The For Loop

So if we use a For loop we can step down through each row by letting the variable **line** take the value from 0 through to the value of **No_lines**. At each pass through the loop we need some statements to fill in the spaces and symbols for the line. This can be expressed in Turbo Pascal as follows:

```
Step := 2*Pi / No_Lines;
For Line := 0 to No_Lines do
Begin
< Fill in the current line >
End;
```

<Fill in the current line> is called **pseudo-code**, and is our way of noting what we're going do in this part of the program without writing the full code.

Refining the Pseudo-code

Let's begin to refine the pseudo-code. On each line the program has to find the position of the asterisk and then print it out. This can be expressed as follows:

```
Step := 2*Pi / No_Lines;
For Line := 0 to No_Lines do
Begin
    Pos_of_star := Sin(Step * Line);
    <Write an asterisk in this position>
End;
```

Here **Pos_of_star** must be an integer variable as each coordinate of a position on the display screen can only be expressed as a whole number.

However, the sin() function always results in a real value. According to the rules of Turbo Pascal it's impossible to assign a real value to an integer variable. So we have to convert the real value to an integer one. Turbo Pascal has two functions that will do this: trunc() which gives the whole part of the real number and round() which results in the real value rounded up to the nearest integer. We'll choose round() for this program.

The fragment of source code now looks like this:

```
Step := 2*Pi / No_Lines;
For Line := 0 to No_Lines do
Begin
   Pos_of_star := Round(Sin(Step * Line));
   <Write the asterisk in this position>
End;
```

Extending the Range

This still isn't finished, as you will see if you take a closer look at this section. $Sin(x)$ outputs real values between -1 and +1. Applying round() to this formula means that the variable **Pos_of_star** can only have three values: zero, plus one, and minus one. As we are expecting 21 points, this is no use - especially as there is no position on the screen represented by minus one.

To avoid negative numbers cropping up, and to extend the number of possible values for **Pos_of_star**, we'll use the following expression:

```
Half_no_columns + Round(Sin(Step * Line))* Half_no_columns
```

Half_no_columns is a constant that denotes half the number of columns on the screen that we will use to draw the graph. As round(sin(x)) only has values +1, 0 & -1, the minimum value of this expression is zero, and the maximum value is 2***Half_no_columns**. There are 80 columns in the display so **half_no_columns** must be less than 40.

Drawing the Central Axis

The central axis will be in the middle column so when we have reached the **half_no_columns** column we will draw an 'I' to mark it. From this we can see that we need to refine the pseudo-code to test whether the value of **Pos_of_star** is greater or less than the value of **half_no_columns**. We can then decide how to write the line.

Also, on three occasions the value of sin() will be zero and the following expression

```
Half_no_columns + Round(Sin(Step * Line))* Half_no_columns
```

will be equal to **Half_no_columns**, so the asterisk needs to appear on the central axis. To see if this is the case, we test whether **Pos_of_star** is equal to **Half_no_columns**.

So we include two If statements and the pseudo-code becomes:

```
<If Pos_of_star is less than or equal to Half_no_columns>
   Then
{ For Negative or zero values of Sin(x) }
        <write spaces>
        <then write asterisk>
        <then write spaces>
        <If Pos_of_star is not equal to Half_no_columns>
        <then write X-axis>
Else
{ Positive value of Sin(x) }
        <write spaces>
        <then write X-axis>
        <then write spaces>
        <then write asterisk>
```

Comparing Variables

Turbo Pascal uses the following symbols to compare variables:

Symbol	Comparison
=	Equal to
<>	Not equal to
>	Greater than
>=	Greater than or equal to
<	Less than
<=	Less than or equal to

Refining the Pseudo-code

So, the first If statement becomes

```
If Pos_of_star <= Half_no_columns
```

and the second statement becomes

```
If Pos_of_star <> Half_no_columns
```

We can refine the rest of the pseudo-code even further using the Write() and WriteLn() procedures. All this results in the final program below.

```pascal
Program  Ex_3_6;
{A program to draw a sine graph on screen}
Uses CRT;
Const
   Half_no_columns = 20; {Half the number of columns we will use}
   No_Lines = 20;        {Number of lines on the screen we will use}
Var
   Line,                 {Number of the line being processed}
   Pos_of_star,          {number of column to mark with an asterisk}
   Column_Counter        {Variable used to count through the columns}
               :Integer;
   Step                  {To store the value of the step between x values}
               : Real;
Begin
   ClrScr;
   Step := 2*Pi / No_Lines;
   For Line := 0 to No_Lines do
   Begin
      { First calculate the position of the asterisk for this line}
      Pos_of_star := Half_no_columns + Round((Sin(Step * Line))*
Half_no_columns);
      If Pos_of_star <= Half_no_columns
         Then {the asterisk must be printed out to the left of the X-axis }
         Begin
         {Print spaces before the asterisk }
         For Column_Counter := 0 to Pos_of_star - 1 do
            Begin
            Write(' ');
            End;
         { then print out the asterisk }
         Write('*');
         { Print spaces between the asterisk and the X-axis }
         For Column_Counter := Pos_of_star + 1 to Half_no_columns - 1 do
            Begin
            Write(' ');
            End;
            { If the asterisk and X-axis are not in the
              same place then the symbol 'I' is drawn}
      If Pos_of_star <> Half_no_columns
         Then
            Begin
            Write('I');
            End;
         { Move down to the next line }
      Writeln
      End
```

```
        Else {the asterisk must be printed out to the right of the X-axis }
          Begin
          { Print spaces before the X-axis }
          For Column_Counter := 0 to Half_no_columns - 1 do
             Begin
             Write(' ');
             End;
          { Print out symbol 'I'}
          Write('I');
          { Print spaces before the asterisk }
          For Column_Counter := Half_no_columns + 1 to Pos_of_star - 1 do
             Begin
             Write(' ');
             End;
          { Print out the asterisk }
          Write('*');
          { Move down to the next line }
          Writeln
          End
     End
End.
```

Summary

In this chapter we've seen how numbers are used in Turbo Pascal programs. Numbers are handled in different types, and these types both restrict the range of values that variables can store, and define the operations that can be performed on that variable. Numbers in Turbo Pascal can be divided into two different kinds: **integers** and **real** numbers. **Integers** are whole numbers and **real** numbers have a decimal or fractional part. These terms are also used for the two main types of numbers (which can make life a bit confusing to start with).

We've also covered math in programs, including the standard operations addition, subtraction and multiplication. We've also looked at division, and have seen the different kinds depending on whether variables are real or integer type.

In the final program we looked at using the built in math functions to draw a sine curve on screen. To achieve this we also looked at two control structures, the For loop and the If statement, and we also touched on how to draw images on screen.

Quiz Questions

1 What are the basic differences between the integer types and the real types in Turbo Pascal?

2 What are the results of the following calculations in Turbo Pascal?

```
1 + 2 * 3
(4 + 7) * 4 + 2 / 3
5 div 9
1e6 * 10
-1e5 * 10
7 div 3 * 3 + 7 mod 3
((7 div 3) * 3) + (7 mod 3)
```

3 Given the declarations

```
var
    an_integer: Integer;
    a_real: Real;
```

which of the following assignments are legal?

```
an_integer    := 37  mod  12;
a_real        := 37  mod  12;
an_integer    := 37  /  12;
an_integer    := 3.0  *  563;
a_real        := (3  mod  7)  *  1e6  -  7.3009;
an_integer    := trunc(22  /  7);
a_real        := round(32.47);
```

4 What would the following If statement write to the screen?

```
if (3 * -7.3) < -2.5 then
    begin
    writeln('Less than.');
    end
else
    begin
    writeln('Greater than.');
    end;
```

5 Given the declaration

```
var
    index: Integer;
```

what would the following For loop write to the screen?

```
for index := 1 to 12 do
   begin
   writeln(index, ' times 12 is ', index * 12);
   end;
```

6 Write a WriteLn() statement that will print on your screen

The formatted number is 3.14.

using the real value of Pi = 3.141592653.

Exercises

1 In the 'chickens and rabbits' puzzle, you are asked to imagine a pen containing chickens and rabbits. Given the total number of heads and the total number of legs, your task is to work out how many chickens and how many rabbits are in the pen.

Write a program to solve the chickens and rabbits puzzle for totals entered by the user. For example, if the user indicates that there are 104 legs and 32 heads, your program should conclude that there are 20 rabbits and 12 chickens in the pen.

Hint: number of rabbits = (leg count - twice the head count)/2

2 Write a program to help work out the total price of an article being bought from a shop. Assume a fixed sales tax of 7.5%. A run of your program should produce the following:

Please type in the net price (dollars.cents): 68.95
Tax (7.5%): $5.17
Total price: $74.12

3   Write a program that works out how many quarters, nickels and dimes to give to a customer as change. For instance, if the change is 65 cents, you should give the customer two quarters, one dime and one nickel.

Assume that the change amount, which should be read from the user, is never more than 99 cents.

CHAPTER
4

Manipulating Text

We said in the last chapter that the first computers were designed purely to 'crunch' numbers. Since those early days, however, we've moved on to a point where whole businesses have risen and fallen based on the ability of computers to process words. This chapter looks at Turbo Pascal's techniques and methods for manipulating text.

In programming parlance, a **string** is a sequence of characters. In Turbo Pascal, string is also the name of the type for handling sequences of characters. This chapter describes the different features of strings, and then looks at the functions and procedures for manipulating variables of string type.

As well as the string type, Turbo Pascal has another type for dealing with single characters called the char type. In the second half of the chapter, we study the functions associated with variables of this type. We finish with a look at how to display text on screen in different colors.

In this chapter we'll look at:

   ▶ What exactly makes a string a string

   ▶ Functions for manipulating strings

   ▶ Selecting individual characters within a string and comparing strings

   ▶ The char type and handling characters

   ▶ Displaying information on screen

Strings

What's a String?

As with integer and real types, defining a variable as string type defines the values the variable can store, and the functions that can operate on the variable. Declaring a variable as string type restricts the values to sequences of characters, and restricts the operations to the functions and procedures outlined in this chapter.

Declaring Strings

To declare a variable as string type, you use the following variable declaration statement:

Var
String_variable_identifier : String[*Int_num*];

where the number in square brackets *Int_num* is an integer number which defines the maximum number of characters in the string. This number is optional. If you don't specify a value here, Turbo Pascal gives your variable the default maximum size of 255 characters. If you do specify a number, it must be between 1 and 255.

The actual length of the string stored in the variable may change while your program is running. The number in the square brackets is used to define the maximum length you want your variable to be. If you try to store a string longer than the maximum size you have defined, Turbo Pascal will just ignore the extra characters.

Assigning Strings

When you come to assign a string of characters to a variable of string type, you must enclose the characters between quotes. When Turbo Pascal sees quotes around characters, it treats those characters as text.

The following lines of code in your program would declare the variables **Simple_String** with a maximum length of 16 characters, and **Short_String** with a maximum length of 27 characters. We then assign two strings.

```
Var
    Simple_String : String[16];
    Short_string : String[27];
Begin
    Simple_String := 'This is a string';
    Short_string := 'The characters don''t all fit';
    Writeln('Simple_String stores the string', Simple_string);
    Writeln('Short_string stores the string', Short_string);
End.
```

The output from this fragment of code would be as follows:

Simple_String stores the string This is a string
Short_string stores the string The characters don't all fi

As you can see, because **Short_string** can only take 27 characters, Turbo Pascal ignores the last character in the sequence.

To attain a single quote (as in *don't*), you use a double quote in the string.

String Functions

We've defined the values which string type variables can hold. To complete the description, we'll also need to define the operations and functions that you can perform on variables of this type. Turbo Pascal has eight functions for manipulating strings.

Joining Strings 1 - The Concat Function

You use Concat() to join two or more strings together. This has the following format:

Concat(*string_1*, *string_2*, ... , *string_N*)

Where *string_1*, ..., *string_N* are string variables

Take the program below as an example:

```
Program Ex_4_1;
Uses CRT;
Var
{First define 6 string variables, 5 without defining a maximum length
        and one variable defined of maximum length of one character}
   String_1, String_2, String_3, String_4, String_5, Result : String;
   Space                                                   : String[1];
Begin
   ClrScr;
   Space := ` ';
   String_2 := `Latin';
   String_1 := `Concatenate';
   String_3 := `for';
   String_4:= `join';
   String_5 := `is';
   Result :=
Concat(String_1,Space,String_5,Space,String_2,Space,String_3,Space,String_4);
   WriteLn(Result);
End.
```

In the first series of statements we assign strings of characters to the variables and we then use Concat() to join the strings together and WriteLn() to send the result to the screen. If you run the program, you'll see the output as shown below.

Joining Strings 2 - Using +

In the previous examples, we used the function Concat() to join strings. In Turbo Pascal, you have a second option. The + operator performs the same action as the function Concat(). So the program below gives the same result as the one above.

```
Program Ex_4_2;
Uses CRT;
Var
{First define 5 string variables, 4 without defining a maximum length
        and one defined with a maximum length of one character}
   String_1, String_2, String_4, Result : String;
   Space                                 : String[1];
Begin
   ClrScr;
{Assign strings of characters to the variables}
   Space := ' ';
   String_2 := 'Latin';
   String_1 := 'Concatenate';
   String_4:= 'join';
{Use '+' to join the strings together and writeln() to send the result to the
screen}
   Result := String_1 + Space + 'is' + Space + String_2 + ' for ' +
String_4;
   WriteLn(Result);
End.
```

Copying Strings

You use the Copy function to do what it says - 'copy' a section of a string from one variable to another. The function has the following structure:

Copy(*Test_String, Number_of_first_character, Number_of_chars*)

where *Test_string* is the string to be operated on and *Number_of_first_character* and *Number_of_chars* are both positive integers. The function copies *Number_of_chars* from *Test_string* counting from *Number_of_first_character*. If *Number_of_first_character* is greater than the length of the string, nothing is copied, and if *Number_of_chars* counts beyond the end of the string, only the remainder of the string is copied.

Example of the Copy Function

Take the variable **Rope** which stores the string 'My name is John'. Counting from the left, Turbo Pascal gives each character in the string a number. The first character 'M' is number 1, through to the last character, the letter n in the word 'John', which is number 15. To use Copy, you specify the number of the character you wish to start at and also the number of characters you wish to copy. So

```
Oh := Copy(Rope, 1, 2);
```

copies the section of the string 'My' to the variable **Oh**.

```
Call_me := Copy(Rope, 4, 4);
```

copies the string 'name' to **Call_me**.

```
Wayne := Copy(Rope, (8+4), 4);
```

assigns the string 'John' to the variable **Wayne**.

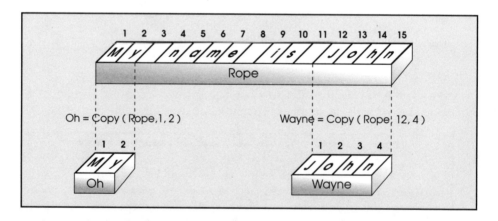

In each of these functions and procedures, the integer numbers marking the starting character or the number of characters can be replaced with calculations that give a positive integer result.

Deleting

To remove part of a string, you use the Delete function. This has the following format:

> Delete(*Test_String*, *Number_of_first_character*, *Number_of_chars*);
>
> where *Test_string* is the string to be operated on and *Number_of_first_character* and *Number_of_chars* are both positive integers. The function deletes *Number_of_chars* from *Test_string* counting from the position indicated by *Number_of_first_character*. If *Number_of_first_character* is larger than the length of *Test_String,* no characters are deleted and if *Number_of_chars* counts beyond the end of *Test_string,* all the characters to the end of the string are deleted.

An Example of Delete

To use the function, you specify the number of the character from which Turbo Pascal should start to count, and the number of characters you want to delete. So to trim the string 'This string is except this bit right', Turbo Pascal should delete sixteen characters counting from the 15th character (the space between 'is' and 'except'). The statement:

```
Trimmed := Delete('This string is except this bit right', 15, 16);
```

would store the value 'This string is right' in the variable **Trimmed**.

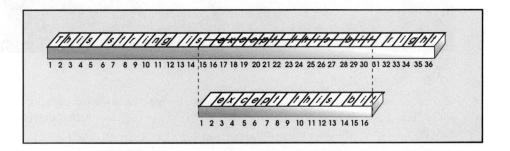

> In each of the functions, you can substitute a string of characters for a variable.

How Long is My String?

You use the Length function to determine the number of characters **currently** stored in a string. The format is as follows:

> Length(*Test_String*)
> which gives the result as an integer.

> As the string of characters stored in a variable can be changed during a program, the length of the variable will change. **Length** tells you the number of characters in the string at the time you run the function. The value in the declaration in square brackets is the maximum number of characters that can be stored in a variable - this can't be changed during the program.

Examples of the Length Function

So Length('123456789') = 9, and if **Test_string** holds the value 'A sentence of 27 characters' then the following statement

```
Len := Length(Test_string);
```

assigns the value 27 to the variable **Len**.

> The statement
>
> ```
> Len := Length('');
> ```
>
> assigns the value 0 to the variable Len.

Adding to Your String

You've seen how to delete part of a string, so for the sake of balance we'll show you how to add to a string. To do this you use the Insert function. The function is used in the following way:

> Insert(*Start_String*, *String_to_add*, *pos_of_first_char*);
>
> Where *Start_String* and *String_to_add* are both variables of string type and *position_of_first_character* is of integer type. The statement inserts *String_to_add* into *Start_String* at the character whose position is equal to *pos_of_first_char*.

Examples of Insert

If the variable **rope** has the value 'My name is John' then

```
Insert(rope, 'first ', 4)
```

will change the value in **rope** to 'My first name is John'.

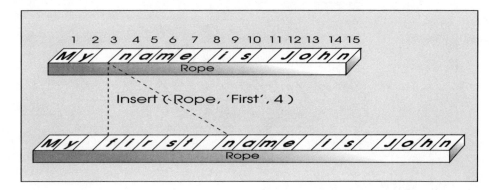

Where's the Word?

The Pos() function tells you the position where one string starts within a second string. This is its structure:

Pos(***Str_looked_in***, ***Searched_for_Str***);

This looks through the string ***Str_looked_in*** for the string ***Searched_for_Str***. If it is found, Pos() returns the postion number of the first character of ***Searched_for_Str***. If ***Searched_for_Str*** is not found in ***Str_looked_in***, Pos() returns the value 0.

An Example of Pos()

As an example of Pos(), look at the statements below.

```
Searched_for_Str:= 'is';
Str_looked_in := 'My name is John';
Start_Pos := Pos(Searched_for_Str, Str_looked_in);
```

Start_Pos returns the value 9.

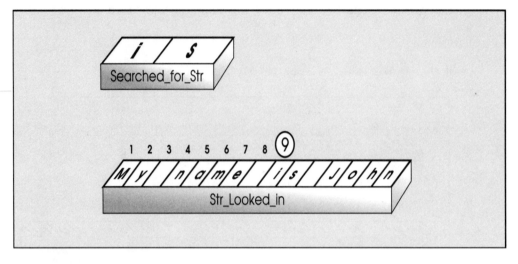

'My Full Name is John Smith'

After being bombarded with so many new functions, your head may be reeling. To give you a chance to catch your breath and to let it all sink in, we'll take a look at some programs that use these functions.

Suppose you want to take the string

'My name is John'

and convert it to the string

'My surname is Smith'.

Analyzing this problem we can see that we need to take the following steps:

1   Find the word 'name'

2   Then insert the string 'sur'

3   Find and delete the word 'John'

4   Insert the word 'Smith'

As you can see, we'll need to use the string functions we've just met. The program is listed below.

```
Program Ex_4_3;
Uses CRT;
Var
   Working_String, Sur_string, Smith_string : String;
   Current_position                         : Integer;
Begin
   ClrScr;
   Working_String := 'My name is John';
   Sur_string   := 'sur';
   Smith_string := 'Smith';
   WriteLn('Starting with the string ', '''', Working_String, '''');
   WriteLn;
   Current_position := Pos('name', Working_String);
   Insert(Sur_string, Working_String, Current_position);
   WriteLn('Changing it to ',  '''', Working_String, '''');
   WriteLn;
   Current_position := Pos('John', Working_String);
   Delete(Working_String, Current_position, 4);
   WriteLn('Then to ', '''', Working_String, '''');
   WriteLn;
   Insert(Smith_string, Working_String, Current_position);
   WriteLn('We end up with ', '''', Working_String, '''');
   WriteLn;
End.
```

Taking a 'walk' through the program, firstly we declare the necessary variables - three as string variables to hold the text we'll manipulate, and one integer variable for the position of the character. We then assign the correct strings to these variables. Throughout the program, we store the current value of the string in the variable **Working_String** and we display this string as we are altering it.

To show what we are doing, we display the string we are starting with. The displayed string appears between double quotes. To display single quotes, you write two quotes together; so to display double quotes, you need to write four.

The first task was to locate the number of the starting character of 'name' in the working string using Pos(). We stored this number in the variable **Current_position** and then used this variable in subsequent functions. Once you know the position where the word 'sur' should go, you can make the insertion using the function Insert.

The next step was to find the start of the word 'John' and then to delete the next four letters starting from this position. To store the value of this new position, we reused the variable **Current_position**. The final step was to insert the word 'Smith' starting where the word 'John' started.

The output of this program is shown below.

```
Starting with the string 'My name is John'

Changing it to 'My surname is John'

Then to 'My surname is '

We end up with 'My surname is Smith'
```

Converting Strings to Numbers and Back Again

Having seen how to manipulate straight text we need to consider the occasions when you need to convert text to numbers and vice versa.

The Function Str()

If you have a value of integer or real type, the function Str() will convert this number into text to be stored as a string. Str() has the following format:

Str(*number_to_convert*:*width*:*Decimal_places*, *String_variable*)

where *number_to_convert* is the number to be changed and *String_variable* is an identifier which has been declared as string type. *Width* and *Decimal_places* are optional integers separated by colons. *Width* describes the minimum length in characters of the number. *Decimal_places* describes the number of digits after the decimal place that are to be shown.

In its simplest form, the following statement

```
Str(1234, String_1);
```

will assign the string '1234' to the string variable **String_1**.

If you use *width* to denote the length in characters of the number, then if **Num_to_Change** has the value 1234,

```
Str(Num_to_Change:10, Str_1);
```

assigns the 10 character string value

'   1234'

to the variable **Str_1**. (You can't see the spaces, but there are 10 characters in this string).

With real numbers, the default conversion for Str() is to store the value in exponential format. If the real variable **Real_to_change** has the value 12.34 then the statement

```
Str(Real_to_change:10, Str_1);
```

assigns the 10 character string

' 1.234E+01'

to the string variable **Str_1**.

Finally, you can include another digit to establish the length of the fractional part of the number. The statement

```
Str(Real_to_change:10:2, Str_1);
```

assigns the string

'   12.34'

to the variable **Str_1**. Again, the length of the string is 10 characters, two positions are used to represent the fractional part, and the exponential format is dropped.

> **The first digit is actually the minimum field width. If you make this value 1, Turbo Pascal will always fit the field exactly to your number**

> This is the same method for formatting numbers as is used in Write() and Writeln().

The Function Val()

This function does the opposite of Str() and has the following format:

> Val(*string_to_convert*, *Number_Variable*, *Error_code*);
>
> Where *string_to_convert* is a string, *Number_Variable* is an identifier of integer or real type, and *Error_code* is an integer variable. If *String_to_convert* actually contains non-numeric characters, *Error_code* will contain the position of the offending character in the string, and *Number_variable* will be assigned the value zero. On the other hand, if there is no error, *Error_code* will be assigned zero. The only exception to this is leading spaces. Turbo Pascal will strip these away and return the number and *error_code* will be zero

Using the variables from the above example, if **Str_1** has the value '1234' the statement

```
Val(Str_1,Result,Check);
```

stores the value

1234

if **result** is declared as an integer type, or

1234.0

if it's declared as a real type. The conversion is successful, so **Check** has the value zero.

If **str_1** had the value '1234A' instead, **Result** would have the value zero. **Check** would equal 5 as the offending non-numerical character, the letter 'A', occupies the fifth position in the string.

Working Out the Date

Now that we can convert strings to numbers, we can write a program that accepts a date input as MM-DD-YY and outputs three integer values representing the month, the day and the year.

The Date Is

The algorithm for this program is as follows:

1 Extract the 1st and 2nd characters in the string and convert them to their integer value. This is the number of the month.

2 Repeat the above for the 4th and 5th characters in the string which give the number of the day

3 Repeat part 1 again for the 7th and 8th characters which gives the number of the year

4 Print the results.

The first three steps resemble each other, involving just one transformation operation.

Suppose the entered string is as follows:

Str_1 = '12-31-99'.

To extract the characters and convert them, you will need an additional string variable, **Temp**, and the function Copy():

```
Temp := Copy(Str_1, 1, 2);
```

The variable **Temp** now contains the value '12'. This value must be converted into an integer value and assigned to the variable **Month**. The procedure Val() can be used here.

```
Val(Temp, Month, Error_code);
```

The variable **Month** now has the integer value '12' so you have performed the conversion. However, there is one disadvantage with this method - you had to use the additional string **Temp** to save the intermediate result. You can avoid the extra string by specifying the function Copy(), complete with the expression as the first argument in Val(). This means you only need one statement to achieve the same result:

```
Val(Copy(Str_1, 1, 2), Month, Error_code);
```

So the final program becomes as follows:

```
Program Ex_4_4;
Uses CRT;
Var
   Str_1                    : String;
   Day, Month, Year, Error_code  : Integer;
Begin
   ClrScr;
   WriteLn('Enter a date in the following format: MM-DD-YY : ');
   ReadLn(Str_1);
{ extract and convert month }
   Val(Copy(Str_1, 1, 2), Month, Error_code);
{ extract and convert day }
   Val(Copy(Str_1, 4, 2), Day,   Error_code);
{ extract and convert year }
   Val(Copy(Str_1, 7, 2), Year,  Error_code);
{ print out results }
   WriteLn('Current date is : ');
   WriteLn('          Month = ', Month);
   WriteLn('          Day   = ', Day);
   WriteLn('          Year  = ', Year + 1900);
End.
```

Si Etad Eht - Doing the Reverse

This time, the task is to write a program that inputs three integer values (the month, the day, and the year) and then outputs the date in the form MM-DD-YY. To do this you should take the following steps:

1 Convert the first integer value to a string and save in the variable **Temp_1**.

2 Repeat point 1 for the second variable and store the string in variable **Temp_2**.

3 Repeat point 1 again for the third variable stored in **Temp_3**.

4 Concatenate the strings **Temp_1**, **Temp_2** and **Temp_3** with hyphens in-between.

The procedure Str() will convert the integer value to its string representation. So for the integer **Month** we need the statement:

```
Str(Month, Temp_1);
```

The string **Temp_1** then saves the integer value in **Month** as a string.

We need two more statements for **Day** and **Year** and then a final statement using Concat() to join the strings together:

```
Str_1 := Concat(Temp_1, '-', Temp_2, '-', Temp_3);
```

The string **Str_1** now contains the required value, for instance '02-14-64'.

The simple program to perform this action is shown below.

```
Program Ex_4_5;
Uses Crt;
Var
   Str_1, Temp_1, Temp_2, Temp_3  : String;
   Day, Month, Year               : Integer;
Begin
   ClrScr;
   WriteLn('Enter a date as three numbers separated by returns: ');
   Write('        Month = ');
   ReadLn(Month);
   Write('        Day   = ');
   ReadLn(Day);
   Write('        Year  = ');
   ReadLn(Year);
{ convert month }
   Str(Month, Temp_1);
{ convert day }
   Str(Day,   Temp_2);
{ convert year }
   Str(Year,  Temp_3);
{ form result string }
   Str_1 := Concat(Temp_1, '-', Temp_2, '-', Temp_3);
{ print out result }
   WriteLn('Result string is : ', '''', Str_1, '''');
End.
```

Selecting a Character in a String

As you know, a string is a sequence of characters. Up to now, we've always dealt with strings as whole objects, but you can also extract single characters from a string. Turbo Pascal locates each character by numbering each character position starting from the left. So if you had the string variable **Upper** declared as follows:

```
Upper : String[26];
```

and then assigned this value:

```
Upper := 'ABCDEFGHIJKLMNOPQRSTUVWXYZ',
```

Turbo Pascal would give each letter a number from 1 through 26. To extract or represent a particular letter in the string, you write **Upper[number]**, where **number** is the number of the letter. So **Upper[1]** has the value 'A', **Upper[2]** the value 'B', **Upper[14]** the value 'N' and so on. The number in the brackets is called the **index** of the character.

By combining the variable identifier for the string and the index for the character, you create an identifier for the character. This character identifier can then be used as part of an expression, can be assigned to a variable identifier, can basically act *as* a variable identifier and go where a variable identifier goes. However, caution is required - if you assign a value to the identifier, you'll change the character in the string!

Comparing Strings

Is 'Dog' greater than 'Cat'? Whilst this may sound like a stupid question, in programming there *is* an answer, because each letter has a corresponding number in the **ASCII character set**.

The ASCII Character Set

Pronounced 'Asky', ASCII stands for the American Standard Code for Information Interchange. Your computer (like any other) can only process numbers. So that it can tell which key was pressed, each character on your keyboard has a corresponding number. The ASCII Character Set is the agreed standard which details which number corresponds to which character. As the full set is just a boring table of characters and numbers (it appears in Appendix F), we'll give you a taster with this snippet of the table below:

Keyboard Character	ASCII Code Number	Keyboard Character	ASCII Code Number	Keyboard Character	ASCII Code Number
A	65	Z	90	$	36
a	97	z	122	Space	32
B	66	1	49	Enter	13
b	98	9	57	Esc	27

The ASCII code is the number the computer uses internally to represent the keyboard character, so every character on the keyboard is represented in the ASCII character set. This includes the digits '1' through '9' and all the symbols such as '$', '%', or '@'.

Comparing Characters

The fact that the ASCII character set is ordered means it is possible to compare characters. When you compare characters you should remember the following rules:

1 The space character is less than all letters and digits.

2 Digits are less than letters and '0' < '1' < '2' < ... < '9'

3 Upper-case letters are less than lower-case letters and 'A' < 'B' < ... < 'Z' < 'a' < 'b' < ... < 'z'.

Comparing Strings

We use the method of extracting individual characters in a string to make comparisons between strings.

Equal Strings

Two string variables S1 and S2, which each have N characters, are equal if (and only if) all characters in all positions in the string are the same. So

S1 = S2 *if and only if* S1[1] = S2[1], S1[2] = S2[2], ... , S1[N] = S2[N].

Unequal Strings

On the other hand, if the characters in both strings are equal in the first few positions, but the character in position number X in string S1 is not equal to the character in the same position in string S2, then S1 is not equal to S2.

In other words, if

S1[1] = S2[1], S1[2] = S2[2], ... , S1[X-1] = S2[X-1], but S1[X] <> S2[X]
then S1 <> S2.

Strings Are Sensitive

Strings are case-sensitive, so if S1 = 'abcdef' and S2 = 'abcdef', then S1 = S2.

However, if S3 = 'Abcdef' then S1 <> S3 and, since 'a' > 'A', S1 > S3.

Strings of Different Length

Strings of different length are obviously unequal. However, to decide which is greater you still need to compare the individual characters. As soon as you reach characters that differ, you can decide which string is the greater.

Of course, if you run out of characters to compare, then the shorter string must be less than the longer string. So, if you had the strings S1 = 'abcd' and S2 = 'abc', you can see that S1 > S2 as 'd' > ''.

Now that you know how to compare two strings, we can write programs that make decisions based on this fact. We just need one more component - the If statement.

The If Statement

We've already introduced the If statement in Chapter 3, but in case you are reading this book out of sequence, we will go over the essentials here again.

Structure of the If Statement

The If statement takes the following form:

```
If Condition
   Then
      Begin
      True_Statement(s);
      End
   Else
      Begin
      False_Statement(s);
      End;
```

Where **Condition** can be any expression that Turbo Pascal can interpret as 'true' or 'false'. If **Condition** is true, then only the **True_Statement**(s) will be executed. If **Condition** is false, then only the **False_Statement**(s) will be executed.

> The punctuation of the **If** statement is very important. You must not put a semi-colon between the reserved words **End** and **Else**.

The If statement is invaluable for comparing variables or values.

For example, to compare the strings **S1** and **S2**, you would write the following statements:

```
If (S1 = S2)
   Then
      Begin
      WriteLn('S1 is equal to S2');
      End
   Else
      Begin
      WriteLn('S1 is not equal to S2');
      End;
```

We can work through this programming code statement by statement. The first statement checks to see whether it is true or false that string **S1** is equal to string **S2**. If the condition **S1 = S2** is true, the program will execute the statement which outputs 'S1 is equal to S2'. If **S1** is not equal to **S2**, the condition is false and as a result the other statement is executed which outputs 'S1 is not equal to S2'.

However, this statement can only answer the question 'equal' or 'not equal'? What happens if you want to know which string is greater? The solution is to use the following statement:

```
If (S1 < S2)
   Then
      Begin
      WriteLn('S1 is less than S2');
      End
   Else
      Begin
      WriteLn('S1 is greater than S2');
      End;
```

By **nesting** one If statement inside the other, you can do two tests. Firstly, you test whether the two strings are equal, and if the answer is 'no', you then test which one is greater. This gives the simple program **EX_4_6** for you to try out:

```
Program Ex_4_6;
Uses Crt;
Var
   S1, S2 : String;
Begin
   ClrScr;
   Write('Enter string S1: ');
   ReadLn(S1);
   Write('Enter string S2: ');
   ReadLn(S2);
   WriteLn;
   If (S1 = S2)
      Then
         Begin
         WriteLn('S1 is equal to S2');
         End
      Else
         If (S1 < S2)
            Then
               Begin
               WriteLn('S1 is less than S2');
               End
            Else
               Begin
               WriteLn('S1 is greater than S2');
               End;
End.
```

We will make more use of the If statement later in this chapter.

Char Type

Turbo Pascal includes another type for dealing with characters. This is the char type. Char variables differ from string variables in that they can only take a single value, but this single value can be any member of the ASCII character set. This means a variable of char type can contain letters, digits, symbols and even symbols with no printed form, as long as they are all ASCII characters.

Declaring Chars

To declare a variable of type char, you need to write the following:

Var
        Variable_Identifier(s) : Char;

where Var and Char are reserved words and *Variable_Identifier* is a legal identifier. If you include a list of identifiers they should be separated by commas.

Classic Chars

To assign values to variables of char type, you need to enclose the ASCII character between quotes. Having declared the variables you can then assign different characters such as:

   Char1 := 'A';

   Char2 := 'a;

   Char3 := '5';

   Char4 := ' ' (the space character);

   Char65 := ''''

The output from Char65 would be double quotes, because to assign the value of a quote you must write it twice.

You'll notice that the character '5' and *not* the number 5 is stored in the variable Char3. This leads the expression Char1 + Char3 to equal the string 'A5'.

Control Characters

In the ASCII table there are also some non-printable or **control** characters. These control characters include:

▶ ASCII code number 7 called Bell which emits a 'beep' from the internal speaker.

▶ ASCII code 10, Line Feed, which moves the cursor down one line

▶ ASCII code 13, Carriage Return, which moves the cursor to the left edge of the screen.

These codes and the others in the ASCII character set can all be stored in variables of char type.

Driving Chars

As with strings, Turbo Pascal includes three functions for getting the best out of high performance chars.

The Function Chr()

The char type and the ASCII character set correspond exactly. You'll see this if you look at the two functions Chr() and Ord(). Firstly, Chr():

> The function Chr(*Integer*) returns the character which is represented by the number *Integer* in the ASCII table. The value of *Integer* must be between 0 and 255.

For example, in the ASCII table

▶ The letter 'A' is represented by the number 65, so Chr(65) returns the letter 'A'.

▶ The letter 'a' is represented by the number 97 so Chr(97) returns the letter 'a'.

▶ The digit '5' is represented by 53 and so Chr(53) returns the digit '5'.

This means that the statements below have the same effect as the first three examples above:

    Char1 := Chr(65)

    Char2 := Chr(97)

    Char3 := Chr(53)

Try It Out!

Program **EX_4_7** let's you try out the function. You can compare the results with the ASCII table in Appendix F

```
Program Ex_4_7;
Var
   I : Integer;
Begin
   Write( 'Enter any integer from 0 to 255 : ');
   ReadLn(I);
   Write('Integer ''',I:1,''' represents the character ''');
   WriteLn(Chr(I),''' in the ASCII table.');
End.
```

An example of some output is shown in the screenshot below:

```
Enter any integer from 0 to 255 : 65
Integer '65' represents the character 'A' in the ASCII table.
Enter any integer from 0 to 255 : 97
Integer '97' represents the character 'a' in the ASCII table.
Enter any integer from 0 to 255 : 53
Integer '53' represents the character '5' in the ASCII table.
Enter any integer from 0 to 255 : 32
Integer '32' represents the character ' ' in the ASCII table.
Enter any integer from 0 to 255 : 10
Integer '10' represents the character '
                                       ' in the ASCII table.
```

In the output you can see the effect of using integers which represent control characters in the ASCII code. If you try running the program and enter the number 7, you should also **hear** the difference!

127

The Function Ord()

The function Ord() does the reverse of Chr().

> Ord(**Char_Variable**) returns the number that represents the value of **Char_Variable** in the ASCII table where **Char_Variable** is of char type.

For example,

Ord('A') = 65

Ord('a') = 97

Ord('5') = 53

Try It Out!

The program below shows what Ord() can do.

```
Program Ex_4_8;
Var
   Ch : Char;
Begin
   Write( 'Enter any letter or digit: ');
   ReadLn(Ch);
   Write('Character ''',Ch,''' is represented by  ',Ord(Ch):1);
   WriteLn(' in the ASCII table.');
End.
```

An example of some output is shown in the screenshot below.

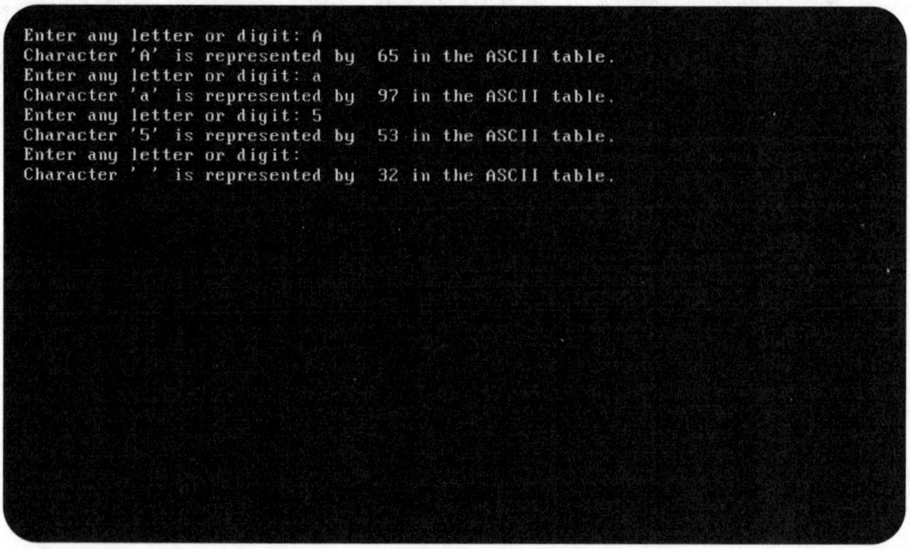

```
Enter any letter or digit: A
Character 'A' is represented by  65 in the ASCII table.
Enter any letter or digit: a
Character 'a' is represented by  97 in the ASCII table.
Enter any letter or digit: 5
Character '5' is represented by  53 in the ASCII table.
Enter any letter or digit:
Character ' ' is represented by  32 in the ASCII table.
```

> As you can see, the two functions are strongly associated as:
>
> `Chr(Ord(Ch)) = Ch`
>
> and
>
> `Ord(Chr(I)) = I` for values of `I` between 0 and 255.

Readkey

The procedure Readkey also uses the char type. If we had declared the variable **Ch** as char type earlier in a program, including the statement:

```
Ch := Readkey;
```

in the program will cause it to pause until a key is pressed. When a key is pressed, the character isn't shown on the screen, but *is* stored in the variable **Ch**.

You can also write the procedure without assigning the character. Including this statement

```
Readkey;
```

in your program will also suspend execution of the program until a key is pressed, and again the character won't appear on screen. In this instance, however, the value of the character is lost.

Try it Out!

The simple program **EX_4_9** demonstrates using Readkey.

```
Program Ex_4_9;
Uses Crt;
Var
   Ch : Char;
Begin
   ClrScr;
   WriteLn('Press a key to continue : ');
   Ch := Readkey;
   WriteLn('You pressed the ', Ch, ' key');
End.
```

Programs That Manipulate Characters and Strings.

You've now seen all the functions and procedures available for handling strings and characters. So that you can see them in action, we're going to build a program that pulls all the techniques together. The program will eventually test whether a line of text is a palindrome or not, but we will build up to this by examining each section of the program. However, before we plunge into the world of string manipulation, we need to cover the For loop. This is a control structure that will add real power to your program.

The For ... To ... Do Loop

A For ... To... Do loop is a way of repeating statements in Turbo Pascal. We introduced this method in Chapter 3 and we will do a complete study of it in Chapter 5, but it makes our programs far more interesting, so we'll use it here. The structure of the For loop is as follows:

```
For loop_index := starting_value to ending_value do
Begin
    Statement_1;
    Statement_2;
    ...
    Statement_N
End;
```

Where For, to, do, Begin and End are reserved words, loop_index is an integer variable and starting_value and ending_value are two integers.

The loop works by repeatedly performing the list of statements for each value in the sequence starting_value through to ending_value. The term loop is associated with this kind of Turbo Pascal structure, because the control in the program keeps looping back to the top each time. Each time the loop is performed, loop_index is assigned the next value in the sequence.

We'll now resume our study of the program and bring the For loop in when we need it.

Stripping a String of Punctuation

First we want to solve the following problem. With a string made up of lower-case letters and punctuation marks, we want to strip out all the punctuation marks.

Our program needs the following steps:

1   Extract the current character.

2   Determine whether the current character is a lower-case letter.

3   If the current character is a lower-case letter then copy the character to another string; otherwise don't do anything.

4   Repeat the previous three steps for all the characters in the string.

Selecting Each Character

If you don't know how many characters there are in the string, you can use the function Length(), which returns the actual length of a string. As the position of each character is numbered, the sequence of characters in the string **s** is:

S[1], S[2], S[3], ... , S[Length(S)]

Using the index we can examine each individual character by writing **S[I]**. The statement

```
For I := 1 to Length(S) do
```

will then process each character in the string.

Selecting Only Lower-Case Letters

Our original string consisted of lower-case letters and punctuation marks. We want our resulting string to consist of lower-case letters only, so the next step is to determine whether the current character is a lower-case letter. The lower-case letters are ordered:

'a' < 'b' < 'c' < ... < 'z'

so if the current character **S[I]** is greater than or equal to 'a', and at the same time less than or equal to 'z', then it is a lower-case letter. In Turbo Pascal you can write this condition as follows:

```
('a' <= S[I]) and (S[I] <= 'z');
```

131

So you can use an If statement:

```
If ('a' <= S[I]) and (S[I] <= 'z')
   Then
      ...
   Else
      ...
```

to test whether or not the current character **S[I]** is a lower-case letter.

Once we've established the status of the character, we need to decide what to do with it. We'll want to save all the lower-case characters in a new string and ignore all the punctuation marks. So after the word Then you need to write a statement which adds the lower-case characters to the new string (which we have declared as **Res_str**). If the current character **S[I]** is not a lower-case letter, you needn't do anything. This means there is no need for the word Else or any statements to follow it.

Adding Characters to a String

To add characters to the string we need the statement

```
Res_str := Res_str + S[I];
```

using the plus operator to join the strings together.

To make sure **Res_str** only consists of the lower-case letters from our original string, we make the initial value of the variable the null or 'empty' string with the following assignment statement

```
Res_str := '';
```

This technique of setting the initial value of a variable is called **initializing**.

Stripping a String of Punctuation - The Code

The complete solution of this task is then as follows:

```
For I := 1 to Length(S) do
   Begin
   If ('a'<=S[I]) and (S[I]<='z')
      Then
         Begin
         Res_str := Res_str + S[I];
         End;
   End;
```

going lower-case

Most sentences of text will contain upper and lower-case letters. In this section, we want to look at replacing all the upper-case letters with lower-case ones.

The solution to this problem is as follows:

1 Extract the current character.

2 Determine whether the current character is an upper-case letter.

3 If the current character is an upper-case letter then replace this character with the corresponding lower-case character; if not, do nothing.

4 Repeat the previous three steps for all characters in the string.

The task is very similar to the previous one, the only difference being that you are *replacing* the character, not copying it.

You already know how to extract a character and determine whether it's a lower-case letter. So it should be no problem to see that the following statements will select the upper-case letters:

```
For I := 1 to Length(S) do
   Begin
   If ('A'<=S[I]) and (S[I]<='Z')
      Then
         ... ;
```

Replacing Characters

We are trying to replace the characters, so we need to use the ASCII character set. The full table is in Appendix F. If you look at this table, you'll see that the letter 'A' has the ASCII number 65 and the letter 'a' has the ASCII number 97; 'B' has the ASCII number 66 and 'b' has the ASCII number 98. It doesn't take long to see that the difference between the ASCII numbers for the upper and lower-case versions of a letter is 32.

So, for an upper-case letter **s[I]** with an ASCII number of **Ord(S[I])**, the corresponding lower-case letter will have the ASCII number **Ord(S[I]) + 32**. To translate this value into the letter, you need to use the function Chr(). The expression **Chr(Ord(S[I]) + 32)** will write the lower-case letter that corresponds to the upper-case letter **s[I]**.

going lower-case - The Code

From this analysis we can see that to solve the task we need the following statements:

```
For I := 1 to Length(S) do
  Begin
  If ('A'<=S[I]) and (S[I]<='Z')
    Then
      Begin
      S[I] := Chr(Ord(S[I]) + 32);
      End;
  End;
```

Notice that each time the assignment statement only affects the character at position **I** in the string **S**. All the other characters are unaffected.

Reverse Characters

The next of our tasks is to reverse a string.

Choosing the Method

Suppose you have a string S with the value 'abcdefg'. Reversing it would give the string 'gfedcba'. One way of solving the problem would be to swap pairs of characters. The string S consists of the characters S[1], S[2], S[3], S[4], S[5], S[6], S[7]. The first exchange we need to do is the first and seventh characters.

Try these two statements:

```
S[1] := S[7];
S[7] := S[1];
```

The first statement means that the value of the first character in the string is replaced by the value of the seventh character. This means the string will have the value

'gbcdefg'.

The second statement replaces the seventh character with the value of the first character, and so replaces 'g' with 'g' to give the result:

'gbcdefg'

Not quite what we wanted!

The problem is that the first statement destroys the value of the first character. To avoid this, we need to start by saving the value of the first character in an additional variable **Ch** of Char type. So step 1 is to use the statements:

```
Ch := S[1];
S[1] := S[7];
S[7] := Ch;
```

The first statement saves the value currently in **S[1]** (that is, 'a') in the variable **Ch**. The second statement places the value from **S[7]** (the letter 'g') into **S[1]**. The last statement replaces the value stored in **S[7]** with the value of the variable **Ch** (the letter 'a'). The result is

'gbcdefa'.

and we have successfully swapped the first and last characters.

Using the same method you can now exchange the values of **S[2]** and **S[6]** so the next step is as follows:

```
Ch := S[2];
S[2] := S[6];
S[6] := Ch;
```

This gives the string:

'gfcdeba'.

Finally, you exchange **S[3]** and **S[5]** with

```
Ch := S[3];
S[3] := S[5];
S[5] := Ch;
```

to get the string:

'gfedcba'.

This is the correct result, but rather than write out all the assignments, we want to use a For loop so that we can work with a string of any length. To write the For loop we need to work out what values the loop parameter needs to take, and how we need to change the values of the index to make sure every variable is swapped.

Looking at the steps, we swapped:

1 S[1] and S[7], that is S[1] and S[length(S)] or S[length(S) + 1 - 1]

2 S[2] and S[6], that is S[2] and S[length(S) -1] or S[length(S) + 1 - 2]

3 S[3] and S[5], that is S[3] and S[length(S) -2] or S[length(S) + 1 - 3]

so we need the body of the loop to look like this:

```
Ch := S[Len + 1 - I];
S[Len + 1 - I] := S[I];
S[I] := Ch
```

Now we need to calculate the upper limit of the loop parameter. Swapping seven characters took three swaps.

- Swapping six characters 'abcdef' also takes three swaps: fbcdea, fecdba, fedcba;

- Swapping five characters 'abcde' takes two swaps: ebcda, edcba;

- Swapping four characters 'abcd' also takes two swaps: dbca, dcba.

Using integer division

> 7 div 2 = 3;
>
> 6 div 2 = 3;
>
> 5 div 2 = 2; and
>
> 4 div 2 = 2.

So we can draw the conclusion that the upper limit of the loop should be the value **(Length(S) div 2)**.

Creating another variable to make the code easier to read, we can write the following statements to reverse any string **s**:

```
Len := Length(S);
For I := 1 to Len div 2 do
   Begin
      Ch := S[Len + 1 - I];
      S[Len + 1 - I] := S[I];
      S[I] := Ch
   End;
```

Is This a Palindrome emordnilaP a siht sl

The final example deals with palindromes - strings that are the same whether you read them from left to right or right to left. Here are some examples:

Otto

Madam, I'm Adam

A man, a plan, a canal - Panama

(You have to ignore the punctuation marks, spaces and the case of the letters).

Our task was to write a program that determines whether or not a string is a palindrome. The task can be divided into these simple steps:

1   Enter the string.

2   Replace all upper-case letters with lower-case letters.

3   Delete all punctuation marks and spaces.

4   Save the transformed string.

5   Reverse the string.

6   Save the reversed string.

7   Compare the transformed string and the reversed string. If they are equal then the entered string is a palindrome.

Drawing on the analysis we have done, you will be able to follow the complete program below.

```
Program Ex_4_10;
Uses Crt;
Var
    S, Res_str, Temp, Init_str : String;
    I, Len                                   : Integer;
    Ch                                       : Char;
Begin
    ClrScr;
    WriteLn('Enter any string of letters: ');
    ReadLn(S);
    {Save the original string}
    Init_str := S;
    { replace upper-case letters}
    For I := 1 to Length(S) do
        Begin
        If ('A'<=S[I]) and (S[I]<='Z')
            Then
                Begin
                S[I] := Chr(Ord(S[I]) + 32);
                End;
        End;
    { delete punctuation marks }
    Res_str := '';
    For I := 1 to Length(S) do
        Begin
        If ('a'<=S[I]) and (S[I]<='z')
            Then
                Begin
                Res_str := Res_str + S[I];
                End;
        End;
    { save temporary string }
    Temp := Res_str;
    { reverse string }
    Len := Length(Res_str);
    For I := 1 to Len div 2 do
        Begin
        Ch := Res_str[Len + 1 - I];
        Res_str[Len + 1 - I] := Res_str[I];
        Res_str[I] := Ch;
        End;
    { compare strings}
    If Res_str = Temp
        Then
            Begin
            WriteLn('''', Init_str, '''',' -is a palindrome!');
            End
```

```
      Else
         Begin
         WriteLn('''', Init_str, '''',' -is not a palindrome');
         End;
End.
```

This program illustrates a very important concept in programming. The task is divided up into various stages which are all quite simple. You then just have to follow the steps to solve the problem. The output data of one step is the input data for the next step, and so on. This method was invented by Niklaus Wirth and is called 'stepwise refinement'. Remember that if any stage is too complex, it can be divided into simpler steps. You can carry on dividing steps into simpler steps until you get a task with an obvious solution. If you combine all the bits of code that solve each step into one program, you'll solve the problem. Using this method will help you with all complex programming tasks.

Displaying Information

As you know, your screen can display text. It can display up to 80 characters per line, and up to 25 lines per page. This means that up to two thousand characters (80 * 25 = 2000) can be displayed on the screen at any one time.

So far, you have only used the procedures Write() and WriteLn() to display results on the screen. The procedure Write() writes data onto the screen starting at the far-left position of the first line. The next time you use the Write() procedure it will continue writing at the end of the previous output. The procedure WriteLn(), on the other hand, automatically moves the cursor to the beginning of the next line, so the output of subsequent WriteLn() statements always starts at the left side of the screen. This is very limiting, so Turbo Pascal gives you other methods for controlling the position of the cursor.

The Procedure Gotoxy

The procedure Gotoxy(x,y) allows you to place the cursor at the coordinates (X,Y) on the screen.

To re-cap, the coordinate system for the text screen is illustrated below.

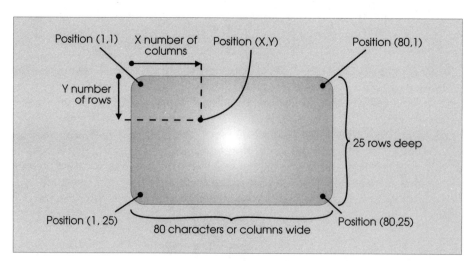

The top left corner of the screen has the coordinates (1,1), where the first number is the X coordinate and the second number is the Y coordinate. The X coordinate can be from 1 through 80, and denotes the number of characters or columns from the left edge of the screen. The Y coordinate can be from 1 through 25 and denotes the number of rows from the top of the screen. The other corners of the screen have the coordinates (80,1), (1,25), and (80,25) respectively. This means that the top right corner of the screen contains the 80th character of the first line. The bottom left corner contains the first character of the 25th line and the bottom right corner contains the 80th character of the 25th line.

So if you write

```
Gotoxy(20,1);
Write('message');
```

the cursor will move to the 20th column and the 1st row which is where the letter 'm' will be written. You could then move the cursor to another position and write another message.

Program **EX_4_11** writes messages in the corners and the middle of the screen as you can see on the next page.

```
Program Ex_4_11;
Uses Crt;
Var
    Len : Integer;
Begin
   ClrScr;
   Gotoxy(1,1);
   Write(' <- Cursor position (1,1)');
   Len := Length('Cursor position (80,1)-> ');
   Gotoxy(80-Len,1);
   Write('Cursor position (80,1)->');
   Gotoxy(1,25);
   Write(' <- Cursor position (1,25)');
   Gotoxy(80-Len,25);
   Write('Cursor position (80,25)->');
   Gotoxy(40,12);
   Write('<- The middle of the screen');
End.
```

So now you can move the cursor in any direction. However, you must specify coordinates that are on the screen, otherwise Gotoxy() won't work.

The Functions WhereX and WhereY

The reverse of Gotoxy() is the two functions WhereX and WhereY. These return the coordinates of the cursor.

▶ WhereX returns the X coordinate of the cursor's current position.

▶ WhereY returns the Y coordinate of the cursor's current position.

So the following statements can be used to store the X and Y coordinates of the cursor's position:

```
X_coord := WhereX;
Y_coord := WhereY;
```

Coloring Magic

Turbo Pascal also provides procedures and functions which allow you to select the background and foreground color.

The Procedures TextBackground and TextColor

The procedure TextBackground() allows you to select the background color for each character.

> TextBackground(*color*);
>
> where *color* can be any of the following: **Black, Blue, Green, Cyan, Red, Magenta, Brown** or **LightGray.**

For example, you can write:

```
TextBackground(Red);
```

and the background color for each character will be red.

The procedure TextColor() on the other hand selects the actual color of the character.

> TextColor(*color*);
>
> where *color* is any of the following: **Black, Blue, Green, Cyan, Red, Magenta, Brown, LightGray, DarkGray, LightBlue, LightGreen, LightCyan, LightRed, LightMagenta, Yellow** or **White.**

By writing

```
TextColor(Blue);
```

the color of the characters will then be blue.

You can also make your text flash on and off by including a plus sign and the word 'blink'. The following statement would bring up flashing blue letters (as opposed to a flashing blue light):

```
TextColor(Blue + Blink);
```

Program **EX_4_12** shows how these features work:

```
Program Ex_4_12;
Uses Crt;
Begin
   TextBackground(Red);
   TextColor(Blue);
   ClrScr;
   WriteLn('Red background and blue characters');
   TextColor(Green);
   WriteLn('Red background and green characters');
   TextBackground(Black);
   TextColor(White + Blink);
   WriteLn('Black background with flashing white characters');
End.
```

We've used a couple of interesting techniques in this program. Unfortunately, the only way to show you them is to ask you to run the program. If you do (and we highly recommend you do) you'll see the following results.

First, only the background of the characters written changes to the color of TextBackground() as you will be able to see from the third line. But we have also managed to convert the whole screen to red. This is a feature of the ClrScr procedure. ClrScr works by writing a blank in every position on the screen. As a result, by setting the background color to red with **TextBackground(Red)** and then calling ClrScr, each blank character that is written sets the background color to red, turning the whole screen red.

Summary

In this chapter you met a variety of features for working with text in Turbo Pascal. The main tool is the string type. This allows you to store lines of characters in variables and then manipulate these strings of characters with a selection of ready-built functions and procedures. The functions and procedures we introduced (among other things) now allow you to join strings, find the length of strings, copy and delete strings within strings, and convert strings to numbers and back.

We also introduced you to the char type. This type is linked closely to the ASCII character set, allowing you to use all the ASCII symbols including control characters in your programs. We showed you how to switch between the symbol itself and the ASCII number using Ord() and Chr().

Finally, we made a brief foray into displaying information on screen. This included using different colors and placing the cursor wherever we want on the screen.

Quiz Questions

1 What will the following program print on the screen?

```
Program Len;
Var
    Str: String[11];
Begin
Str := 'abc';
Writeln(Str, ':', Length(Str), ':', 'x' + Str + Str, ':', Length(Str))
End.
```

2 How would you convert the string '3.14159' to a real value? How would you convert it back again?

3 Write a fragment of Turbo Pascal that will convert a string representation of a time such as '06:00' into two integers.

4 Which of the following is true for Turbo Pascal Strings?

'first' < 'last'
'First' < 'last'
'firsT' > 'Last'
'abcde' <= 'abcd'

5 What is the effect of the following fragment of Turbo Pascal if C1 and C2 (of type char) are guaranteed to contain letters?

```
If C1 >= 'a' Then
    Begin
    C2 := Chr(Ord(C1) - Ord('a') + Ord('A'))
    End
Else
    Begin
    C2 := C1
    End;
```

6 What does the following program do?

```
Program Bobble;
Uses Crt;
Begin
ClrScr;
GotoXY(10, 11);
Write('%');
GotoXY(10, 12);
Write('&');
GotoXY(9, 12);
Write('*');
GotoXY(11, 12);
Write('#')
End.
```

Exercises

1 Write a program which will read a string from the user and then print it vertically down the middle of the screen. (The screen is 80 characters wide). For example, if the input were 'My name is Alice', the output would be:

M
y

n
a
m
e

i
s

A
l
i
c
e

(HINT: You'll need to use a For loop).

2   Write a new version of the string reversing program which, instead of reversing the string on top of itself, uses a second string and the '+' operator.

3   The fact that ReadKey doesn't display the entered character on the screen is very useful for entering passwords. Write a program which asks the user to type in a password, without displaying it on the screen. Assume a fixed length of ten characters. (To check that your program works, you might like to print out the password once you've read it, in some surreptitious manner!).

# CHAPTER 5

Taking Control of Your Programs

In this chapter we will be showing you how to make your programs take decisions and also how to make them repeat similar tasks. For this we will introduce you to the **boolean** type which allows variables to take the value **true** or **false** and we will show you how you can combine such variables to make complex decisions.

To actually implement decisions we use **control structures,** two of which you have already met in earlier chapters - the If statement and the For ... To ... Do loop. In this chapter we will recap how you use these structures and then go on to introduce the other constructs.

In the final part we cover the Goto statement - a control structure from the past (which should have been left there) and we show you how to handle the errant users of your programs.

So in a jam-packed chapter, we'll be covering

- The boolean type
- If statements
- Case statements
- While ... Do loops
- Repeat ... Until loops
- For ... To ... Do loops
- The infamous Goto

Why Take Control?

In programming, as in life, simple tasks can often be solved by making a straightforward list of actions. For example, to make a stiff drink:

1 Take a clean glass.

2 Fill it two-thirds full with your favorite liquor.

3 Top with ice.

If you perform these actions one after another, then you'll get your drink.

However, things are never that simple (especially if it's the third time you've performed this particular algorithm today!). What happens if you're performing step 1 and you discover that there are no clean glasses? Clearly, you can't just proceed to step 2. What if twenty guests have just turned up on your doorstep and you want to make them all a stiff drink (indeed, you might need another one yourself to get over the shock of all these people turning up unannounced)? It would be a pain to have to write out the three steps of your algorithm twenty times - what you *really* want is to be able to keep going back to step 1 until you've made twenty drinks.

A programming language's **control structures** allow you to change the step-by-step execution of your program, so that you can solve really difficult problems as well as those that wouldn't tax a chimpanzee (or a heavy drinker!).

Turbo Pascal's basic control structures fall into these two categories:

1 Deciding what to do next based on current circumstances.

2 Doing something repeatedly. (This is also called **looping** because your program **loops** round the same piece of code several times).

Both types of structure, however, use logic to decide which statement to execute next. In Turbo Pascal programs, logic is represented using boolean variables.

The Boolean Type

The boolean type is similar to the other types we've already met (integer, real, string and so on), in that it defines the range of values that can be stored and the operations that can be performed on any variable of this type.

> Englishman George Boole (1814-1864) spent some time as Professor of Mathematics at Cork University in the south-west of Ireland. He is best remembered for inventing **Boolean algebra**. Take my word for it - not only is Boolean algebra staggeringly useful in such diverse areas as mathematics and philosophy, it's also used by computers in everything they do. Were he around today, Professor Boole would have every right to be thoroughly smug!

Declaring a Boolean Variable - Definition

A boolean variable is declared in the same way as other types:

> Var
>
>   *variable_identifier*: boolean;
>
> where boolean is a reserved word.

The Range of Values: True and False

This is where boolean variables differ from integers and the like. Boolean variables can only take the special values **true** and **false.** This allows you to tell your computer about the outcome of certain events. The machine then makes certain decisions based on these **true** or **false** values. Our brains use an equivalent system. If the statement 'it's raining' is true, then we might decide to take an umbrella. A boolean variable is used to make statements in a similar way.

In a later program we're going to declare a set of boolean variables which will describe a typical day. We'll use a declaration statement similar to the one below:

```
Var
      rained_today,
      walked_to_work,
      drove_to_work,
      umbrella_needed,
      forgot_umbrella,
      boss_was_mad,
      bad_day,
      got_wet:    boolean;
```

We can then assign values to these variables to reflect what has actually happened in the real world. For example, we could assign the following values:

```
rained_today := true;
walked_to_work := false;
```

Operations on Boolean Types

Not

The result of the Not operation flips the value of a boolean variable from **true** to **false** and vice-versa. For example, if you only ever drive or walk to work, then you can calculate **drove_to_work** from **walked_to_work**:

```
drove_to_work := not walked_to_work;
```

If **walked_to_work** has the value **true**, this statement assigns the value **false** to the variable **drove_to_work**. On the other hand, if **walked_to_work** has the value **false**, this statement assigns the value **true** to **drove_to_work**

And

The result of the And operation is the value **true** if both of the operands have the value **true**, and is otherwise **false**. For example, to calculate whether or not you should take your umbrella with you, you could write the statement:

```
umbrella_needed := it's_raining and walking_to_work;
```

Umbrella_needed is only assigned the value **true** if both the other variables have been assigned the value **true**.

Or

The result of the Or operation is the value **true** if **either** of the operands have the value **true**.

```
bad_day := got_wet or boss_was_mad
```

If either of the two operands have been assigned the value **true**, then yep, you had a bad day!

Truth Tables

The following table should help you to remember the results of boolean operations. It's called a **truth table**.

Variables		Results	
A	B	A and B	A or B
True	True	True	True
True	False	False	True
False	True	False	True
False	False	False	False

Putting Them All Together

Boolean operations can be mixed into a single expression. If you do this then the Not operations are evaluated first, followed by the And operations, followed by the Or operations. However, it's very easy to get lost in a long expression so we recommend that you use parentheses to mark each evaluation.

In the statement

```
bad_day := ( umbrella_needed and forgot_umbrella ) or boss_was_mad;
```

it's easy to see what causes us to have a bad day.

We also recommend using intermediate variables instead of writing complex boolean expressions. The last example is improved further by writing it as:

```
got_wet := umbrella_needed and forgot_umbrella;
bad_day := got_wet or boss_was_mad;
```

If you write expressions in this way you will find your programs will be much more readable.

Making Decisions

Now that we have heard about George Boole's contribution to logic, we need to return to the original question - what do you do if there aren't any clean glasses? Turbo Pascal has two control structures to help you choose your program's next move: the If statement and the Case statement.

If It's Not One Thing It's Another: If...Then...Else

The If statement is the most important decision-making construct in Turbo Pascal and is used all over the place. You've already seen it in action in a number of earlier examples.

The If Statement - Definition

The basic form of an If statement is as follows:

```
If condition Then
        Begin
        statement1;
        statement2;

        ...
        statementN
        End
Else
        Begin
        else_statement1;
        else_statement2;

        ...
        else_statementN
        End
```

Where *condition* is an expression which when evaluated has a value **true** or **false** and the *statements* and the *else_statements* are Turbo Pascal instructions.

One point about punctuation: the semi-colon is used in Turbo Pascal to indicate the end of a statement. As you can see above, however, this mark is optional immediately before the reserved word **End** in an **If** statement.

So the If statement allows you to choose whether your program executes the first set of **statements** when **condition** has the value **true** or the set of **Else_statements** when the condition is **false**. For example:

```
If bad_day Then
      Begin
      WriteLn("Sorry to hear you had a bad day.");
      WriteLn;
      WriteLn("I suggest you go and kick the dog")
      End
Else
      Begin
      WriteLn("I suggest you pat yourself on the back")
      End
```

Now if bad_day has the value true, you'll see the following output:

> Sorry to hear you had a bad day.
> I suggest you go and kick the dog

Otherwise you'll see:

> I suggest you pat yourself on the back

Compound Statements

When writing these examples we have used **compound** statements. This is where a block of related statements is enclosed by the reserved words Begin and End. Strictly speaking, if the block of statements only contains one statement, Begin and End can be left out. We've used compound statements (and recommend that you do the same) for two reasons. Firstly, it makes your code more readable. Secondly, at some later date you're almost certain to add an extra statement. At this point you have to remember to add in the Begin and End. If you forget you may get unexpected results. For example:

```
If bad_day Then
    WriteLn('Sorry to hear you had a bad day');
    WriteLn('I suggest you go and kick the dog');
```

will always print 'I suggest you go and kick the dog' whereas

```
If bad_day Then
    Begin
    WriteLn('Sorry to hear you had a bad day');
    WriteLn('I suggest you go and kick the dog')
    End
```

will only suggest kicking the dog when you really *have* had a bad day. This is good news for your program writing, and it's even better news for your dog.

Other Kinds of Condition

The expression in an If statement can be any calculation that, when evaluated, has a value **true** or **false**. This includes comparing values (as in the examples of If statements we've encountered in earlier chapters). The following example illustrates what we mean (assume I is an integer):

```
If ( I > 0 ) Then
        Begin
        WriteLn('I is positive')
        End
 Else
        Begin
        WriteLn('I is negative or zero' )
        End
```

As you can see, the condition $I > 0$ can be either **true** or **false**. Depending on the result, the corresponding statements are executed.

As you might expect, you can mix and match the two styles:

```
If   ( not  raining ) and ( temperature > 30 )   Then
      Begin
      WriteLn('Let's go to the beach!!!');
      End
```

Dropping the Else Part

So what if you don't want to do anything when an If condition is **false**? Simple - just drop the Else part altogether:

```
If  rained_today Then
      Begin
      WriteLn('I hope you remembered your umbrella.')
      End
```

Another important point about punctuation. Because the **Else** part is optional, when you include an **Else** you must never put a semicolon before it. If you do, Turbo Pascal thinks the **Else** is not part of the If statement, but a whole new structure.

What To Do With the Evenings?

Now that we've seen how to use the boolean type to make decisions, we're in a position to write a simple decision-making program. This program will ask a number of questions about how our day went, and use that information to suggest what we should do for the evening.

Informally, what we want our program to do is:

1 Ask for the user's name (so that we can personalize responses).

2 Print a welcome message telling them what we intend to do.

3 If they agree to proceed, then

4   Begin

5   Ask whether they drove to work.

6   Ask whether it rained today.

7   If they should have taken their umbrella then

8   Begin

9   Ask if they did.

10   End

11   Ask whether the boss got mad.

12   Work out whether this was a bad day.

13   Print an appropriate suggestion.

14   End

15 Say good-bye.

In writing this informal definition we have emphasized the control structure using indentation, Begins and Ends.

In the definition we have also included a **nested if** statement. This is where one If statement appears inside another If statement (such as the statement starting in step 7 which is contained by the If statement beginning at step 3). As you can imagine, this can get pretty confusing very quickly, which is why we recommend that you lay out your programs using indentations.

Take a look at **EX_5_1.PAS**

```
Program EX_5_1; { Helps you decide what to do with your evening }
Uses Crt;
Var
   rained_today, drove_to_work, got_wet, boss_was_mad, bad_day: Boolean;
                                      { To describe user's day }
   response: Char;        { Key pressed by the user }
   user_name: String;     { User's name }
Begin
Clrscr;

{ Ask for user's name }
Write('Please tell me your name: ');
ReadLn(user_name);

{ Say hello and explain what we're going to do }
WriteLn('Good evening ', user_name, '.');
WriteLn('My name is Ruth, but you can call me Doctor.');
WriteLn('Just kidding!');
WriteLn('I''d like to ask you a few questions and then');
WriteLn('help you decide what to do with your evening.');

{ Ask if the user would like to proceed }
Write('Is that OK? (type "y" or "n") ');
response := readkey;
WriteLn;

{ If they said yes then ask some questions and make a suggestion }
If ( response = 'y' ) or ( response = 'Y' ) Then
   Begin

   { Decide whether to assign the value true or false to drove_to_work }
   Write('Did you drive to work today? (y/n) ');
   response := readkey;
   WriteLn;
   drove_to_work := ( response = 'y' ) or ( response = 'Y' );

   { Decide whether to assign the value true or false to rained_today }
   Write('Did it rain today? (y/n) ');
   response := readkey;
   WriteLn;
   rained_today := ( response = 'y' ) or ( response = 'Y' );

   { Decide whether to assign the value true or false to got_wet }
   If ( rained_today and (not drove_to_work) ) Then
      Begin
      Write('Did you remember your umbrella? (y/n) ');
      response := readkey;
      WriteLn;
      got_wet := ( response = 'n' ) or ( response = 'N' );
```

```
        End;
    { Decide whether to assign the value true or false to boss_was_mad }
    Write('Did the boss get mad at you? (y/n) ');
    response := readkey;
    WriteLn;
    boss_was_mad := ( response = 'y' ) or ( response = 'Y' );

    { Decide whether to assign the value true or false to bad_day }
    bad_day := got_wet or boss_was_mad;

    { Make a suggestion, depending on whether bad_day is true or false }
    If bad_day Then
        Begin
        WriteLn('Sorry to hear you had a bad day.');
        WriteLn('I suggest you go and kick the dog');
        End
    Else
        Begin
        WriteLn('I suggest you pat yourself on the back');
        End;
    WriteLn('and then put your feet up.');

    End;


{ Say goodbye }
WriteLn('Have a good evening, ', user_name, '!');

End.
```

The main control structure in this program is the first If statement:

```
{ If they said yes then ask some questions and make a suggestion }
If ( response = 'y' ) or ( response = 'Y' )
```

This allows the user to back out before the main question and answer session by typing a character other than 'y' or 'Y'.

We then encounter a series of If statements *inside* this main statement. Based on the user's responses, **true** or **false** values are stored in Boolean variables. For example:

```
    { Decide whether to assign the value true or false to boss_was_mad }
    Write('Did the boss get mad at you? (y/n) ');
    response := readkey;
    WriteLn;
    boss_was_mad := ( response = 'y' ) or ( response = 'Y' );
```

This prompts the user to respond with 'y' or 'n' and sets **boss_was_mad** to **true** or **false** accordingly.

Next, we use the following If statement to ensure that the user is only asked whether or not they took their umbrella if it's necessary to do so (namely, if they walked to work and it was raining):

```
{ Decide whether to assign the value true or false to got_wet }
If ( rained_today and (not drove_to_work) ) Then
   Begin
   Write('Did you remember your umbrella? (y/n) ');
   response := readkey;
   WriteLn;
   got_wet := ( response = 'n' ) or ( response = 'N' );
   End;
```

Finally, we calculate a value for **bad_day** with the following:

```
{ Decide whether to assign the value true or false to bad_day }
bad_day := got_wet or boss_was_mad;
```

Then, based on the result, we can print a suggestion for the user's evening:

```
{ Make a suggestion, depending on whether bad_day is true or false }
If bad_day Then
   Begin
   WriteLn('Sorry to hear you had a bad day.');
   WriteLn('I suggest you go and kick the dog');
   End
Else
   Begin
   WriteLn('I suggest you pat yourself on the back');
   End;
WriteLn('and then put your feet up.');
```

Now if **bad_day** has the value **true** you'll see the following output.

```
Please tell me your name: Clyro
Good evening Clyro.
My name is Ruth, but you can call me Doctor.
Just kidding!
I'd like to ask you a few questions and then
help you decide what to do with your evening.
Is that OK? (type "y" or "n")
Did you drive to work today? (y/n)
Did it rain today? (y/n)
Did you remember your umbrella? (y/n)
Did the boss get mad at you? (y/n)
Sorry to hear you had a bad day.
I suggest you go and kick the dog
and then put your feet up.
Have a good evening, Clyro!
```

Otherwise, you'll see:

```
Please tell me your name: Kilvert
Good evening Kilvert.
My name is Ruth, but you can call me Doctor.
Just kidding!
I'd like to ask you a few questions and then
help you decide what to do with your evening.
Is that OK? (type "y" or "n")
Did you drive to work today? (y/n)
Did it rain today? (y/n)
Did you remember your umbrella? (y/n)
Did the boss get mad at you? (y/n)
I suggest you pat yourself on the back
and then put your feet up.
Have a good evening, Kilvert!
```

Multiple Choice: Case ... Of

The If statement allows you to make a simple decision between 2 choices, but often in life you are faced with several choices from which you must select only one.

Because this kind of multiple choice is so common, Turbo Pascal has a special construct to deal with it: the Case statement.

The Case Statement - Definition

The structure of the Case statement is:

```
Case expression Of
    choice1 :
        Begin
        choice1_statement1;
        ...
        choice1_statementN
        End;
    ...
    choiceN :
        Begin
        choiceN_statement1;
        ...
        choiceN_statementN
        End;
    Else
        Begin
        else_statement1;
        ...
        else_statementN
        End
End
```

Where **expression** can be any calculation that results in a value of integer or character type (or any other ordinal type). Each **choice** must be a single value, and each set of **statements** is a list of Turbo Pascal instructions.

The Case statement works by evaluating **expression** and then selecting the appropriate set of statements depending on the value of the result. If no **choice** matches the result of the **expression**, then the set of statements following the Else is executed.

Ordinal Types

Any type that is a **sequence** of **distinctly ordered** elements, such as char, integer or even boolean is called an **ordinal** type. In the Case statement, you can only use *expressions* that result in values of ordinal type. This is because each *choice* must be a distinct element in a clearly defined group of elements. A letter belongs to the group of elements 'A' through 'Z' and 'a' through 'z', and an integer can be any whole number between -32,768 and 32,767.

String type and **real** type are not ordinal types. **String** type isn't an ordinal type because any sequence of characters can be stored as a string. Therefore, the group of elements isn't clearly defined. **Real** type isn't an ordinal type because the elements are not distinct. In the **real** type, 2 numbers differing by 1×10^{-40} would be considered to be the same

You can see that using the boolean type in a Case statement would be a duplicate of the If statement.

Case Example: Un à Dix

We're off to France next year so we've decided to write a program to display the French words for each number from 0 to 10. This will need to include a Case statement similar to the one below.

```
Case number Of
    0:
            Begin
            Write(number:0, ' in French is zero.');
            End;
    1:
            Begin
            Write(number:1, ' in French is un.');
            End;
    2:
            Begin
            WriteLn(number:2, ' in French is deux.');
            End;

    Else
            Begin
            WriteLn('Help! I can only count up to dix!')
            End
End
```

Sub-Ranges

Unfortunately, we've forgotten the French for 3, 4 and 5. All we have to do is replace the lines for 3, 4 and 5 with the following:

```
      3..5:
        Begin
        WriteLn('Sorry, I''ve forgotten what the French for ', number,
'is.');
        End;
```

The '**3..5**' part is called a **sub-range** and means 'choose any value from 3 through 5 inclusive'. You can use sub-ranges to select part of a sequence of elements. Other valid sub-ranges are:

'P' ... 'Z'   Any character from 'P' through 'Z';

-100 ... 100   Any number between -100 through 100;

'0' ... '9'   Any character from '0' through '9' (As the numbers are
                      enclosed in quotes this signifies we are talking about
                      characters not numbers).

If we had also forgotten the French for nine, we could even include this in the one set of statements. In the Case statement you can use commas to add further values or sub-ranges. The following does the job:

```
3..5, 9:
    Begin
    WriteLn('Sorry, I''ve forgotten what the French for ', number, ' is.');
    End;
```

Translating - The Program

The final program for doing the translation, **EX_5_2.PAS**, looks like this.

```
Program EX_5_2;          { Translates a user's number into French }
Uses Crt;
Var                      { Declare variables }
   number: LongInt;          { Number entered by user }
Begin
    Clrscr;

Write('Please type in a number: ');      { Ask user for a number }
ReadLn(number);                          { Store this in number }

{ Based on value stored in number choose statements to execute }
case number of
```

```
      0:            { If number is 0 }
          Begin
          Write(number:0, ' in French is zero.');
          End;
      1:            { If number is 1 }
          Begin
          Write(number:1, ' in French is un.');
          End;
      2:            { If number is 2 }
          Begin
          WriteLn(number:2, ' in French is deux.');
          End;
      3..5, 9:      { This choice applies to 3, 4, 5 and 9 }
          Begin
          WriteLn('Sorry, I''ve forgotten what the French for ', number, ' is.');
          End;
      6:            { If number is 6 }
          Begin
          WriteLn(number:6, ' in French is six.');
          End;
      7:            { If number is 7 }
          Begin
          WriteLn(number:7, ' in French is sept.');
          End;
      8:            { If number is 8 }
          Begin
          WriteLn(number:8, ' in French is huit.');
          End;
      10:           { If number is 10 }
          Begin
          WriteLn(number:10, ' in French is dix.');
          End;
      Else
          Begin
          WriteLn('Help! I can only count up to ten!')
          End
      End { Case }

End.
```

A Case statement such as this one is easy to formulate if this layout is
followed.

Looping the Loop

Now we come back to the question 'what if twenty guests have just turned up
on your doorstep and you want to make them all a stiff drink?'. The answer is
simple: 'use a **loop**'. A loop is a control structure that can be used to execute
the same sequence of statements any number of times. The actual number can
either be fixed by you when you write the program, or it can be determined
by the conditions that exist when you run it.

There are three kinds of loop in Turbo Pascal:

- While loop.
- Repeat loop.
- For loop.

Let's examine each of them in turn.

Do This Any Number of Times: While ... Do

The While loop is the fundamental loop structure in Turbo Pascal because you can write a While loop to replace a Repeat loop or a For loop. However, it's best suited for those situations when you want to do something **zero or more times**.

The While Loop - Definition

The structure of a While loop is as follows:

```
While condition Do
     Begin
     statement1;
     statement2;
     ...
     statementN
     End
```

Where While, Do, Begin and End are reserved words and *condition* is a calculation that results in a value of boolean type.

Therefore, *while* the condition is **true**, the sequence of statements is executed. If the condition is **false** when the loop is encountered, the sequence of statements won't execute at all. Clearly, if the condition is initially **true**, the sequence of statements must set the value to **false** at some point. If condition remains **true**, you end up in an infinite loop which goes round and round forever!

The following program works out your age by making a guess and then asking you whether it's too high or too low. Before it makes any guesses, however, the computer asks you whether you are willing to abide by the rules of the game. If not, no guesses are made. Because the computer is going to make zero or more guesses, you should automatically realize you need a While loop to solve this problem.

The technique we use to make the guesses needs a little explanation. The program assumes the user's age will be no more than 150 years (a fairly safe bet). For the purposes of this quick demonstration, we'll assume the user's age is 49. The diagram below shows the range of possible values for a person's age and a marker for the age we are considering.

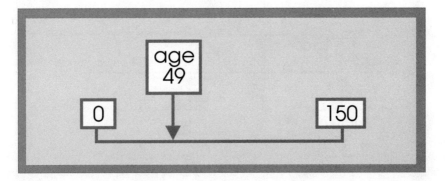

We'll mark the extremes of the range with the variables **low** and **high** and then we make an initial guess half way between the lowest and highest possible values. For the initial guess this is 75, and we store this value in the variable **guess**.

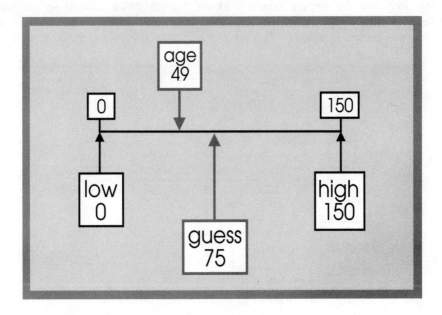

The user will tell us that our guess is too high, so the answer can't be higher than 75, and we can replace the value stored in **high** with this new highest value.

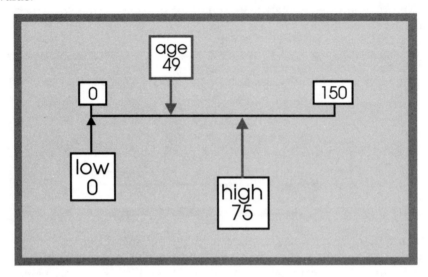

So we need to make a lower guess. We do this by making a second guess *half way* between the current **guess** and the lowest value (stored in the variable **low**). We then replace the value stored in **guess** with this second guess. In this case the second guess is 37: This brings us to the following situation:

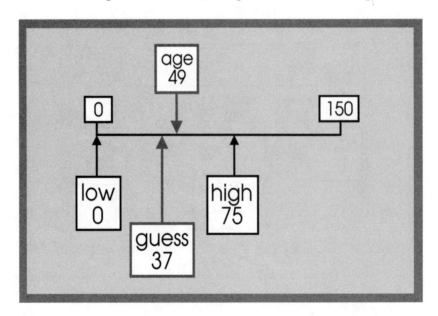

This time, the user tells us that our guess is too low. We need to do the opposite of what we did last time. We make a new guess half way between the current values of **high** and **guess** and replace the value in **low** with the current **guess**. This brings us to the following situation:

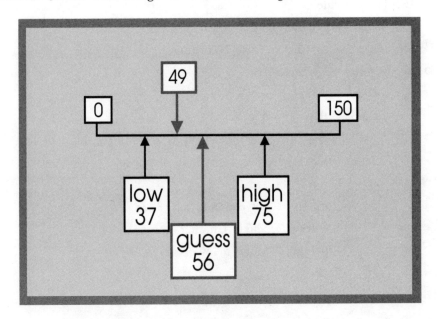

By repeating the above steps we converge on the user's age. According to the theory, we're guaranteed to need no more than 8 guesses to guess correctly.

To make each new guess we use div, because we're only dealing with whole numbers. Then to store the new guesses we use:

```
guess := (low + guess - 1) div 2;
```

or

```
guess := (high + guess + 1) div 2;
```

The '**+ 1**' in the second assignment ensures that, if necessary, **guess** will be able to move from 149 to 150 and the '**- 1**' in the first expression ensures that **guess** will be able to move from 1 to 0.

An informal definition of the program is:

1 Initialize variables

2 Display the rules

3 Ask the user whether they agree to the rules

4 Set **continue** to true or false according to the response.

5 While continue is **true**

6   Begin

7   Display the current guess

8   Ask the user whether the guess is correct, too high or too low.

9   Select what to do based on their response

10   Begin

11   Correct: Set continue to **false**.

12   Too low: Make a higher guess.

13   Too high: Make a lower guess.

14   End

15 End

Steps 9 to 14 are an informal specification of a Case statement (there's no Else part because we're going to ignore invalid responses and just go round again).

The program is as follows:

```
Program Ex_5_3;          { A program to guess the user's age in years }
Uses
   Crt;
Const                    { Declare constants }
   maximum_age = 150;      { Maximum age allowed }
   initial_guess = 75;        { Initial guess }
Var                      { Declare variables }
   high, low, guess: Integer;    { For recording state of game }
   response: Char;             { Key pressed by user }
   continue: Boolean;         { Controls whether program continues }
Begin
Clrscr;
```

```
{Initialize variables }
high := maximum_age;
low := 0;
guess := initial_guess;

{ Display the rules }
WriteLn('I''d like to try and guess your age.');
WriteLn('The rules are:');
WriteLn('   1) I make a guess and you tell me whether it was: ');
WriteLn('         too high or too low or I guessed correctly.');
WriteLn('   2) You''re not older than 150!');
WriteLn('   3) No cheating!!');

{ Ask the user whether they agree to the rules }
Write('Are these rules OK with you? (y/n) ');
response := readkey;              { Record key pressed by user }
Clrscr;

{ Set value of continue to true or false according to response}
continue := (response = 'y') or (response = 'Y');

{ While continue is true execute statements between Begin and End }
While continue Do
   Begin

   WriteLn('I guess ', guess:3, '.');    { Display current guess }

   { Ask user whether guess is correct, too high or too low }
   WriteLn('Please tell me whether:');
   WriteLn('   "c" - I''m correct');
   WriteLn('   "h" - I''m too high');
   WriteLn('   "l" - I''m too low');

   { Select what to do based on user's response }
   response := readkey;
   Case response Of

      'c': { guess is correct }
         Begin
         continue := false; { Set continue to false to exit while }
                            { statement }
         { Say goodbye }
            WriteLn('Thanks for playing. Have a nice day!')
         End;

      'h': { guess is too high }
         Begin
         high := guess;       { Set high point to current guess }
         guess := (low + guess - 1) div 2;    { Make new guess }
         End;
```

```
    '1': { guess is too low }
       Begin
       low := guess; { Set low point to current guess }
       guess := (guess + high + 1) div 2;    { Make new guess }
       End;

     End; { Case }
   WriteLn;
   End { While. Goes back to while statement to check continue }
End.
```

The core of this program is the While loop which executes the enclosed statements again and again while guessing the age. Points to note are that when the While loop is first encountered, it only executes if **continue** is **true**, that is, if the user has agreed to abide by the rules. Thereafter, it will continue to execute while the age is too high or too low. As soon as the age is correct, continue is set to **false** so that the loop will be abandoned next time round.

Do This at Least Once: Repeat ... Until

The Repeat loop is the second most general kind of loop in Turbo Pascal. It's the loop to use when you want to do something **one or more times**.

The Repeat Loop - Definition

The structure of a Repeat loop is:

```
Repeat
     statement1;
     statement2;
     ...
     statementN
Until condition
```

Where Repeat and Until are reserved words and **condition** is a boolean expression.

The sequence of statements is executed repeatedly until **condition** becomes **true**. Because **condition** is checked **after** each execution of the loop, the loop is guaranteed to execute at least once. Typically, **condition** will be **false** when the loop is first encountered, and the loop body will arrange for it to become **true** at some time, so as to terminate the loop. The reserved words Repeat ... Until group the statements, so you don't need to use Begin ... End in this case.

As an example, let's write a sad little program which is always on the lookout for new companions. It's going to keep asking the user to be its friend until they agree. From that description, it should be clear that the question will be asked one or more times, so you should automatically think of a Repeat loop. The algorithm is:

1 Say hello.

2 Repeatedly

3   Ask the user to be friends.

4   Until they agree.

5 Say thank you.

Here's the program:

```
Program Ex_5_4; { Keeps asking the user to be our friend until they agree }
Uses Crt;
Var
    response: Char; { Key pressed by user }
Begin
Clrscr;

{ Introduce ourselves }
WriteLn('Hello. My name''s Polly Paranoid.');

{ Keep asking them to be our friend until they agree }
Repeat
   WriteLn('Please, will you be my friend? (y/n)');
   response := readkey
   Until (response = 'y') or (response = 'Y');

{ Say thank you }
WriteLn('Thank you! You''ve made my day!')
End.
```

This time, we've controlled the program's activities using the Repeat loop. This loop continues to execute its sequence of statements (thereby posing the question), until the user's response is '**y**' or '**Y**'. This then sets the condition:

```
(response = 'y') or (response = 'Y')
```

to **true** and the loop terminates.

Do This for All These Values: For ... To ... Do

A For loop is the least general loop in Turbo Pascal. It should be used for situations when you want to something **for every value in a sequence of values**.

The For Loop - Definition

The structure of a For loop is:

```
For  index := expression1 To expression2 Do
     Begin
     statement1;
     statement2;
     ...
     statementN
     End
```

where For, Do, Begin and End are reserved words and *Index, expression1* and *expression2*   are variables of ordinal type.

The sequence of statements are executed for successive values of **index** from **expression1** to **expression2**. All of **index**, **expression1** and **expression2** must be ordinal types like Integer or Char, because you must be able to work through the values in order, so as to get from **expression1** to **expression2**. Note that if **expression1** is greater than **expression2**, the loop is guaranteed not to execute at all.

Don't change the **index** inside the statements in the loop body, or you'll regret it (maybe not today, maybe not tomorrow, but soon, and for the rest of your life ...).

Take a look at the next program:

```
Program Ex_5_5; { Prints the alphabet using a For loop }
Uses Crt;
Var
    index: Char;    { Index of the For loop }
Begin
    Write('The alphabet is: ');

    { Do the statements between begin...end }
    { with index set to each value from 'a' to 'z' }
    For index := 'a' to 'z' Do
        Begin
        Write(index)
        End { For. Go back to the for statement. }

End.
```

Here, **index** will be set to 'a', 'b', 'c', and so on up to 'z', so the loop will execute 26 times. This kind of loop would be useful for, say, a filing-cabinet style of application where we wanted to do something for every letter of the index. When you run the program you will see the following:

For ... Downto

You can also run over your sequence backwards by replacing the keyword To with Downto. If we do that in Program Ex_5_5 and run it, we should get the following:

```
The alphabet is: zyxwvutsrqponmlkjihgfedcba
```

Rice, Rice and More Rice: Using a For ... To Loop

Let's look at an example that uses an integer index instead of a character index. This example is based on the following story:

In ancient times, a foolish emperor (weren't they all?) was waging war with a foreign king. In fear of losing the fight, he called on a wise old man (weren't they all?) from the local village to advise him.

The emperor told the wise man that if he helped him to win the war he would be paid handsomely. The wise man agreed to give the emperor his best ideas in return for some rice. The emperor, puzzled, asked how much rice the wise man would want. The wise man replied "I would like as much rice as you would get if you put one grain on the first square of a chess board, two on the second, four on the third and so on for every square on the board." The emperor, thinking he was on to a good thing, readily agreed.

Some months later, the wise man's advice had resulted in a crushing defeat for the enemy. Two of the emperor's servants were duly dispatched to the local rice seller, chessboard at the ready. Only when the servants returned two weeks later, with heads bowed, did the emperor realize his terrible mistake ...

So how much rice did the wise old man ask for? In order to work this out we need to calculate a running total for all the squares. We're doing something for every value in a sequence of values so we need to use a For loop. The algorithm is as follows:

1 Initialize total to 0 and **grains_on_square** to 1.

2 For every value in the sequence 1 to 8*8

3   Add **grains_on_square** to total.

4   Multiply **grains_on_square** by 2 (for the next time round the loop).

5 Print total.

The program is as follows:

```
Program Ex_5_6; { Calculates how much rice you'll get if you ask for one }
                { grain on the first square of a chess board, two on the }
                { second, four on the third, ... }
Uses Crt;
Const
   grains_per_gram = 100;        { Estimate of grains in 1 gram of rice }
                                 { (for calculating the total weight) }
Var
   square: Integer;                    { Current square (index of the for loop) }
   grains_on_square, total: Real;  { Number of grains on current square }
                                   { and total }
Begin
Clrscr;

{ Initialize variables }
total := 0;             { Initially no grains }
grains_on_square := 1;  { There's 1 grain on the first square }

{ Do statements between begin...end for every square on the board }
For square := 1 to 8 * 8 Do

   Begin
   total := total + grains_on_square;        { Calculate new total }
grains_on_square := grains_on_square * 2; { Calculate grains on next square }
   End; { For. Go back to the For statement }

{ Print the result }
WriteLn('You will be paid approximately ', total:20:0, ' grains of rice,');
WriteLn('which is about ',
        round(total/grains_per_gram/1000000/1000000/1000):3,
        ' thousand million tons!');

End.
```

Here, the For loop is doing most of the work, executing its two statements 64 times (for every integer value from 1 to 64). Note that we've actually written '8*8' instead of 64. This doesn't slow things down because Turbo Pascal is clever enough to do the calculation when the loop begins and keep a copy of the result.

Notice that the variable **total** has the type Real. We've done this because we suspect that the answer is going to be very large - in fact, far too large for any of the integer types. However, when we come to print the total, we'd like to show it as a whole number. You've seen the functions trunc and round being used before to convert a real number into an integer, but we can't do that in this case. This is because, as we've just pointed out, **total** will be too large. Therefore what we must do is use the following piece of trickery:

```
WriteLn('You will be paid approximately ', total:20:0, ' grains of rice,');
```

The clever part of this WriteLn statement is the expression **total:20:0** which tells Turbo Pascal to print **total** in a field width of twenty characters, *with no digits after the decimal point*. Therefore, to the user it appears as an integer. Try running the program and you'll see this for yourself!

Jumping All Over the Place: The Infamous Goto

Turbo Pascal has a nasty little construct called the Goto statement. It hails from the days when people didn't think that control structures were good enough for writing large powerful programs. However, they *are* powerful enough, and therefore it's fairly easy to come up with rules for using the Goto statement.

Rules for Using the Goto Statement

1 Don't.

2 (For advanced programmers only) Don't either.

Please, please, skip the rest of this section and move straight on to *Error Handling*.

Still here? OK. For the braver readers out there, I'll describe the Goto statement - after all, it *is* fairly entertaining!

The Goto statement allows you to jump all over your program, ignoring any structure that you've carefully built in with Ifs, loops, procedures and so on. The result is code spaghetti. If you really want to use Goto, the first thing you must do is declare some **labels** at the top of your program. These will be used to mark destination code. Turbo Pascal allows you to use identifiers as in the following example:

```
Program Nasty;
Label
        hell_and_dont_come_back;
   ...
```

Then, you have to attach each label to a statement in your program (in this case the **end** which terminates the program):

```
   ...
        hell_and_dont_come_back: end.
   ...
```

Then, when the fancy takes you, you can use Goto to jump to the labeled statement from almost anywhere else in your program:

```
   ...
        Goto hell_and_dont_come_back;
   ...
```

Once you're there, there's no going back! So much for the Goto statement. You're welcome to it. We have written one example of its use in **GOTO.PAS** for your entertainment.

```
Program Ex_5_7; { Allows the user to feel the effects of }
               { the Goto statement }
Uses Crt;
Label
   hell_and_dont_come_back; { Destination for goto }
Var
   response: Char;          { Response from the user }
Begin
    Clrscr;

    { Find out if we have a brave and foolhardy user }
    Write('Would you like to try the GOTO STATEMENT!? (y/n) ');
    response := readkey;
    WriteLn;
```

```
    { If we do have a maverick user, bail out now }
    If (response = 'y') or (response = 'Y') Then
    Begin
    WriteLn('Things are getting HOT!'); { Sound the alarm }
    Goto hell_and_dont_come_back;       { Jump to labeled statement }
    End;

    { If we got here, the user didn't use goto }
    { so congratulate them }
    WriteLn('I don''t blame you!');

hell_and_dont_come_back: end.
```

The interesting part of this program is the If statement:

```
    { If we do have a maverick user, bail out now }
    If (response = 'y') or (response = 'Y') Then
    Begin
    WriteLn('Things are getting HOT!'); { Sound the alarm }
    Goto hell_and_dont_come_back;       { Jump to labeled statement }
    End;
```

If the user agrees to try Goto, your program will print a warning message, leap out of the If statement and land with a bump at the end of the program. No more statements will be executed. If, on the other hand, they don't agree your program will proceed in the normal way and the WriteLn statement following the If is executed.

Error Handling

The world is full of errors, and the programming world is no exception. There are compiler errors, logic errors, user errors, I/O errors, system errors, and so on and so on.

Compiler errors are those annoying ones you get when you first try to run your program, such as Semi-colon expected or Bad type in assignment. You can usually get rid of them by correcting spelling mistakes and making sure your statements are in the right format.

Logic errors are the kind of errors you get when you didn't understand the problem fully, or when you didn't code it correctly. You usually hope to deal with these early on using common sense and the debugger.

But what if your program is running and something out of the ordinary happens? What if a printer breaks down while you're sending a file? What if you get incorrect input? These things happen. Trying to do something appropriate in such circumstances is called **error handling**.

We'll deal more fully with errors and debugging in Chapter 7, but as error handling makes heavy use of control structures, we'll look at it in some detail here. However, before we start it's worth saying that it can be tricky, especially if you want to do it well. It can also significantly increase the size of your programs, which is why we've not attempted to do it thoroughly for most of the simple, illustrative examples in this book.

What we will look at though is how you might begin to handle **user errors** - namely, deciding what to do when a user provides bogus input. This is one of the most important kinds of error handling because users are so unreliable (we're all human after all). If you can manage to verify user input, then your programs will be a lot more robust.

The Untrustworthy User

Consider a program which asks the user to enter a date. We'd like to be able to check that the month is in the range 1 to 12, that the user hasn't assumed there are 29 days in February unless it's a leap year, and so on. This is a deceptively difficult task, but a very important one for almost any record-keeping system.

For simplicity, we'll assume that the user is asked for the day, month and year as separate items. Our program will repeatedly ask the user for a date until they provide a valid one. An algorithm for this is:

1   Repeat
2   Read day, month and year
3   Check day, month and year
4   Until day, month and year are valid
5   Say good-bye.

If we refine this algorithm into a further level before trying to code it, we could get something like this:

1	Repeat
2.1	Read the day.
2.2	Read the month.
2.3	Read the year.
3.1	Check that the year is in the range 0 to 99.
3.2	If the year is valid then
3.3	Begin
3.4	Check that the month is in the range 1 to 12.
3.5	If the month is valid then
3.6	Begin
3.7	Check the day is in range according to the month and year.
3.8	End
3.9	End
4	Until the day, month and year are valid.
5	Say good-bye.

Step 3.7 needs a little more explanation before we look at the code. We need to take into account what month it is, and if it's February, we also need to check whether or not this year is a leap year. A leap year is one which is either:

> divisible by 100 **and** by 400.

or

> divisible by 4 and **not** by 100.

The mod operator can be used to check whether one number is divisible by another. If x **mod** y is 0, x is divisible by y. With all this in mind, we can test for a leap year using the following code:

```
century_year := ( year mod 100 = 0 );
If century_year Then
        Begin
        leap_year := ( year mod 400 = 0 );
        End
Else
        Begin
        leap_year := ( year mod 4 = 0 );
        End
```

The final program for the date-checking problem is below.

```
Program Ex_5_8; { Asks the user to enter a date until they get it right }
Uses Crt;
Var
    day, month, year: LongInt;                      { Day, month and year }
                                                    { entered by user }
    valid_day, valid_month, valid_year: Boolean; { For recording whether }
                                                    { input is valid }
    century_year, leap_year: Boolean;               { For recording whether }
                                                    { year is a century year }
                                                    { and/or a leap year }

Begin
{ Repeat statements up to until}
Repeat

    { Ask the user to enter a date }
    Write('Please enter day: ');
    ReadLn(day);
    Write('Please enter month: ');
    ReadLn(month);
    Write('Please enter year: ');
    ReadLn(year);

    { Year must be positive }
    valid_year := ( year >= 0 );

    { If year is valid, we can proceed to test month }
    If valid_year Then
        Begin

        { Month must be between 1 and 12 }
        valid_month := ( month >= 1 ) and ( month <= 12 );

        { If month is valid, we can proceed to test day }
        If valid_month Then
            Begin

            { Day must be checked against month }
            Case month Of

                { September, April, June and November }
                9, 4, 6, 11:
                    Begin
                    valid_day := ( day >= 1 ) and ( day <= 30 );
                    End;

                { January, March, May, July, August, October, December }
                1, 3, 5, 7..8, 10, 12:
                    Begin
                    valid_day := ( day >= 1 ) and ( day <= 31 );
                    End;
```

```
                    { February }
                    2:
                        Begin
                        { If year is divisible by 100, it's a century year }
                        century_year := ( year mod 100 = 0 );

                        If century_year Then
                            Begin
                            { Year is leap if divisible by 400 }
                            leap_year := ( year mod 400 = 0 );
                            End
                        Else
                            Begin
                            { Year is leap if divisible by 4 }
                            leap_year := ( year mod 4 = 0 );
                            End;

                        If leap_year Then
                            Begin
                            { February has 29 days }
                            valid_day := ( day >= 1 ) and ( day <= 29 )
                            End
                        Else
                            Begin
                            { February has 28 days }
                            valid_day := ( day >= 1 ) and ( day <= 28 )
                            End

                        End

                    End { case month... }
                End { if valid_month... }
            End {if valid_year }

        until valid_day and valid_month and valid_year; { Finished if date valid }

    WriteLn('Thank you.')
    End.
```

Notice how, using nested If statements, we proceed further and further into the validation as parts of the date pass muster - the month is only checked if the year is OK and the day is only checked if the year is OK and the month is OK. Note also the Case statement which, like our example earlier, makes heavy use of lists of alternatives such as:

```
{ January, March, May, July, August, October, December }
1, 3, 5, 7..8, 10, 12:
```

This would have been very fiddly to formulate using If.

The end result of our validation exercise seems complex for such a simple task, but we'll see in the next chapter how we can package code into procedures and functions so we never need to write it twice.

Summary

In this chapter, we've shown you how to control your programs in a structured manner. This allows you to write sophisticated programs for complex tasks.

Turbo Pascal has two basic control structures:

1   You can make decisions with an If statement or, if you have multiple simple choices, with a Case statement.

2   You can execute a set of statements multiple times using a While loop, a Repeat loop or a For loop:

> A While loop should be used when you want to do something zero or more times.

> A Repeat loop should be used when you want to do something one or more times.

> A For loop should be used when you want to do something for every value in a sequence of values.

The While loop is the most general form of loop because it can be used to implement the other two. However, the Repeat and For loops are easier to use for their specialized purposes.

The Goto statement can be used to jump all over your program, producing code spaghetti. It's best avoided.

Error handling is an important goal in programming, but it's tricky to do it well. You should, however, strive to verify user input because it often directs the flow of your programs and because users are very unreliable.

Quiz Questions

1   Given the following declarations:

```
var
        plugged_in, switched_on, is_running: Boolean;
```

what value will **is_running** have after the following three assignments?

```
switched_on := false;
plugged_in := true;
is_running := plugged_in and switched_on;
```

2   Which control structures should you use to make decisions in Turbo Pascal?

3   Which three rules can help you decide what kind of loop to use in a particular situation?

4   When should you use the Goto statement?

5   Can you identify three kinds of error which programs may need to handle?

6   Why is it particularly important to check for user errors?

Exercises

1   Write a program to help with scoring a game of Black Jack. The program should read a card from the user and then print the number of points for that card (aces score one or eleven, 2-10 scores the face value of the card; jacks, queens and kings score ten). For simplicity, ask the user to enter the card value as 'a, 2-10, j, q or k' and then read it as a string. For example, if the user types '10', the output should be:

A 10 scores ten points.

If the user types 'a', the output should be:

An ace scores one or eleven points.

2 Freda the frog has strayed from the pond in search of food. She needs to get back as quickly as possible before she dries out. With an almighty effort, Freda can cover half the distance to the pond with her first hop. After the first hop, she will only have enough puff left to leap half as far again with her second hop. After the second hop, she'll only be able to leap half as far again with her third hop, and so on. When Freda gets to within six inches of the pond, she'll be able to drag herself in.

As an example, if Freda is 100 feet from the pond, she'll need eight hops to get back. Write a program that asks the user how far Freda is from the pond (in feet) and then calculates how many hops it will take her to get back to the pond.

(HINT: use a loop).

3 Write a program which requests a time from the user in the format HH:MM, as in 04:37 or 23:39. Your program should keep asking until the user enters a sensible time in the correct format. For example 25:30 is not sensible and 2:10 is in the wrong format.

(HINT: use the string processing routines Length(), Copy() and Val() in your solution).

Structured and Modular Programming

Now that you're beginning to write more complex programs, you'll find that you often need to use the same group of statements several times in the same program. In Turbo Pascal you use sub-programs to repeat tasks. These are parts of programs that you include in your main program. They are identified and when you wish to run the sub-program you use the identifier to 'call' the sub-program. Calling the sub-program executes the statements in the sub-program and then returns control back to the main program.

In Turbo Pascal there are two kinds of subprograms: **functions** and **procedures**. A function always returns a single value. A procedure can return any number of values including none. In this chapter we'll introduce you to writing these two types of sub-program, and we'll show you how to use them wisely.

In this chapter we'll cover:

- Structured programming
- User-defined functions, formal and actual parameters and recursive functions
- User-defined procedures, value and variable parameters
- Simple modular programming using units

Structured Programming

Faced with a complex problem you will find it's often easiest to break the problem down into smaller tasks that can be solved separately. In Turbo Pascal you can then use sub-programs to solve the individual tasks. This method of dividing a program into separate tasks, is called **structured programming**. By dealing with each task separately you will greatly reduce the complexity of your programs, which will in turn prevent you from making as many mistakes.

Turbo Pascal's Standard Sub-programs

At this point, you may be wondering about all this talk about procedures and functions, vaguely remembering hearing us mention these terms before. Because there are some tasks that every programmer is expected to need at some point, rather than get everyone to re-invent the wheel Borland have fitted out Turbo Pascal with a number of standard sub-programs. These include input and output procedures such as Readkey, Read(), ReadLn(), Write() and WriteLn(), math functions like Sin(), Cos(), Trunc() and Round() and string functions like Length() and Pos(). However, Borland can't think of everything so Turbo Pascal includes the facility for you to write your own functions and procedures.

User-Defined Functions

In Turbo Pascal, **functions** are used to calculate a single value from data you have passed to it, such as joining two or more strings into one. They appear as expressions in assignment statements.

An Example - Power()

Cast your mind back to program **EX_3_2** (alternatively look on the next page). In this program we calculated the money you would have saved given a certain deposit and a certain bank interest rate. The problem is the program can only calculate your savings after one year.

```
Program EX_3_2;
Uses CRT;
{A program to calculate your new savings after 1 year }
Var
   Deposit,          {initial deposit of money}
   Savings,          {To store value of savings after one year}
   Interest          {annual interest rate as a percentage}
                     : Real;
Begin
   ClrScr;
 {Read in values for initial deposit and then interest rate as a percentage}
   Write('Enter your initial deposit: ');
   ReadLn(Deposit);
   Write('Enter the bank''s annual interest rate as a percentage: ');
   ReadLn(Interest);
 {-------------------------------------------------------------------------}
 {Calculate the value of the savings after one year}
   Savings := Deposit + Deposit * Interest / 100;
 {-------------------------------------------------------------------------}
 {Output this new value to the screen}
   Write('After one year you will have ');
   Write(Savings:5:2);
   WriteLn(' in the bank');
End.
```

To calculate your savings after a certain number of years you need to calculate the value of the expression

$$(Deposit + Deposit * Interest/100)^{number\ of\ years}$$

(that is the value of 'Deposit + Deposit * Interest/100' raised to the power of the number of years). Unfortunately, Turbo Pascal doesn't provide a function which can raise a number to a power. Here is where we come to the rescue and write the function ourselves.

Raising a number to a power is simply a question of multiplying the number by itself the number of times equal to the value of the power. The only time this varies is if the power is equal to zero, in which case the result is always one. So our algorithm for the function is quite straightforward. By adding the feature necessary for a function we came up with the code on the next page.

```
Function Power(Factor : Real ; Exponent : Integer) : Real;
Var
    Counter : Integer;
    Temp : Real;
Begin{ Power }
{Any number raised to the power 0 = 1}
    If Exponent = 0
        Then
            Power := 1.0
{Otherwise, multiply factor by itself exponent number of times}
        Else
            Begin
                Temp := Factor;
                For Counter := 2 to Exponent do
                Begin
                    Temp := Temp * Factor;
                End;
            End;
{Assign the value of temp to power}
    Power := Temp;
End{ Power };
```

We'll now take a look at how the function has been put together.

The Function Heading

The first line of a function is called the function **heading** and has the following structure.

⬤ Says that the statements that follow are a function by using the reserved word Function.

⬤ Uses a legal identifier to name the function. (We have chosen **Power** as the name for our function).

⬤ Defines the type of the value to be returned by the function. Functions always return a single value, so you write a colon and the type of the value after the parentheses.

⬤ Inside the parentheses you include a list of variable identifiers and their types. You can include several variables of the same type separated by commas, with a colon between the list and the type. You then separate lists of same type variables with a semi-colon. These variables are called the **parameters** of the function

Parameters

When you use sub-programs, you'll want to pass on specific data for the sub-program to work with. You do this by declaring variable identifiers called **parameters** in the sub-program heading. You then use these identifiers throughout the sub-program. When you call a sub-program you can include specific values between the parentheses, Turbo Pascal takes these specific values and stores them in the parameter variable identifiers you have included in the heading. Wherever the parameter appears in the sub-program Turbo Pascal uses the value stored in it.

In **Power** we have two parameters: **Factor** and **Exponent**.

The Function Body

The function body is the body of statements that do the work of a function and includes:

▶   Declaration statements for units, constants and variables that the function will use. As these are only to be used by the function, they are called **local data**. (In the **Power** function **Counter** and **Temp** are the local variables).

▶   The statements that make up the function. One of these **must** be an assignment statement assigning a value to the function identifier. (In **Power**, there is the the assignment statement **Power := Temp** which defines the value).

Look through the function **Power**. Only the function identifier, **Power**, the parameters **Factor** and **Exponent**, and the variables **Counter** and **Temp** are used in the function body. The function is an independent part of the program which manipulates values using only those variables defined within the function.

A Function's Skeleton

So when you write a function you need to use the following structure:

Function *Function_Ident*   (*Parameter(s):   Type(s)*): *Func_Type;*
{Local declaration statements}
Begin{*Function_Ident*}
{Statements to be executed when the function is calculated}
which must include, at least once,
the statement *Function_Ident* := *expression*}
End{*Function_Ident*};

Where Function is a reserved word and *Function_Ident* is the name of the function. Within the parantheses is a list of parameters of the same type separated by commas followed by a colon and the type. Separating them with semi-colons, you can then include further lists of same type parameters. The final *Func_Type* is the declared type of the result of the function.

Using a Function in a Program

Now that we have seen how to write a function, let's integrate **Power** into our program.

```
Program EX_6_1;
{A program to calculate your new savings }
Uses CRT;
{Declare the variables for the main program}
Var
   Deposit,          {initial deposit of money}
   Savings,          {To store value of savings after one year}
   Interest          {annual interest rate as a percentage}
                     : Real;
 Num_Years : Integer; {Years money to be saved}
 {_____}
{THE FUNCTION}
{The Function Heading}
Function Power(Factor : Real ; Exponent : Integer) : Real;
{Declare the local variables}
Var
   Counter : Integer;
   Temp : Real;
{The Function Body}
Begin{ Power }
{Any number raised to the power 0 = 1}
   If Exponent = 0
     Then
```

```
        Temp := 1.0
{Otherwise, multiply factor by itself exponent number of times}
      Else
        Begin
          Temp := Factor;
          For Counter := 2 to Exponent do
              Begin
              Temp := Temp * Factor;
              End;
        End;
{Assign the value of temp to power}
    Power := Temp;
End{ Power };
{_____}
{THE MAIN PROGRAM}
Begin
   ClrScr;
 {Read values for initial deposit, interest rate and number of years}
  Write('Enter your initial deposit: ');
  ReadLn(Deposit);
  Write('Enter the bank''s annual interest rate as a percentage: ');
  ReadLn(Interest);
  Write ('Enter the number of years you will leave the money in : ');
  ReadLn(Num_Years);
 {-------------------------------------------------------------------}
{Calculate the value of the savings after this number of  years}
Savings :=Deposit * Power (1+Interest/100. Num_Years);
 {-------------------------------------------------------------------}
{Output this new value to the screen}
   Write('After ', Num_Years, ' you will have ');
   Write(Savings:5:2);
   WriteLn(' in the bank');
End.
```

The first thing to notice is the position of the function. When you write a program you write your functions and procedures after you have declared variables and before the main program block.

Also, to call the function we use the function identifier and the actual values we want the function to operate on. The function identifier and the actual data are collectively called the **function designator**. As you can see, we can make these actual values the result of an expression. These actual values are called the **actual parameters**.

Actual Parameters Vs Formal Parameters

The identifiers in the function heading are called the **formal parameters** and the actual values in the function designator that the program must operate on are called the **actual parameters**.

In **EX_6_1** the actual parameters are **Deposit+Deposit*Interest/100** and **Num_Years**. When the program is run Turbo Pascal evaluates the expression **Deposit + Deposit * Interest / 100** and stores the result in the variable **Factor**. It also takes the value stored value in **Num_Years** and copies it into **Exponent**.

A Code of Conduct for Parameters

The number of actual parameters must be equal to the number of the formal parameters and each pair of formal and actual parameters must be of the same type. So you couldn't write the following assignment statement:

```
Result := Power(3.0);
```

because there's only one actual parameter, whereas **Power** has two formal parameters. Moreover, you can't write

```
Result := Power(3.0, 10.0);
```

as 10.0 is real type, but **exponent** must be of integer type.

The order of actual parameters is also very important. The value of the first actual parameter is assigned to the first formal parameter, and so on.

A Code of Conduct for Functions

So to use functions in your program correctly you must abide by the following rules.

1 Somewhere in the function body there must be an assignment statement with the function name in the left part of the assignment statement. In our example this statement

```
Power := Temp;
```

appears as the penultimate statement. This assignment statement defines the value to be returned. If this assignment statement is omitted, the function won't work.

2 A function designator can't be a statement on its own. You must always use it as part of an expression. You can write, for example, the following assignment statement:

```
Result := (A + B) * (C - D) + Power(2.0, 10) * F;
```

3 A function always returns a single value. This must be assigned somewhere, or else used in a calculation.

The Scope of a Variable

In our definition of a function, we described the variables we used within the function as local variables. This refers to the **scope** of the variable - the parts of a program for which a variable is valid.

Each program body is a sequence of statements that perform the task, surrounded by the pair of words Begin and End. This applies to the main program, and to sub-programs. Also, every time you use a variable you should first of all declare it. The **scope** of a variable is the program body that comes after it has been declared, and any enclosed program bodies which don't re-declare it.

Local Vs Global

A variable that is declared in a sub-program can only be used in the sub-program body. This variable only has the **local** scope of this sub-program. If you try to use a local variable in the main program, Turbo Pascal will show the error message:

Error 3: Undefined variable

A variable has **global** scope if it is declared as part of the main program. This variable can then be used within any procedure or function. If you want to use this variable whilst making its meaning specific to the sub-program, you can re-declare the variable.

Only when the program executes the statement which includes the function designator does *that* function's local variables become defined. When the execution of the function is terminated, all local variables become 'undefined' again. Only the result of the function execution is saved. Because of this, we can re-use local variables in different sub-programs.

An Example of Structured Programming: Rewriting the Palindrome Problem

Now that you have seen the basics of the structured programming and how to write functions, we're going to use this knowledge to re-write a program. In Chapter 4 you solved the problem of whether or not an entered string was a palindrome. Now, we're going to rewrite this program using functions.

The task was divided into some simple sub-tasks:

▶ Enter the string

▶ Replace all upper-case letters with lower-case letters

▶ Delete all punctuation marks

▶ Save the transformed string

▶ Reverse the string

▶ Save the reversed string

▶ Compare the transformed string and the reversed string. Only if they are equal is the entered string a palindrome.

To Function or not to Function?

There's no general rule which defines whether or not certain actions are better written as a function. The answer always lies in the particular program.

In this case the task is made up of a number of steps, some of which are trivial, and some of which are far from trivial and need to be solved separately. For example, the sub-task used to replace all upper-case letters by lower-case letters is fairly detailed. To get this function written you must separate out the specific nature of the task and then write a function to perform this particular task. When the function is written, you can forget about the details of the function and use it as a ready-made solution.

You can then concentrate your efforts on solving the next sub-task. In our case, this is to delete all punctuation marks. Whilst you sort out this sub-task, you can forget about the previous sub-tasks which are already solved, and about future sub-tasks to be solved.

In our program we will need to write functions for three sub-tasks. They are:

- Replace all upper-case letters by lower-case letters
- Delete all punctuation marks, and
- Reverse the string

Not Functions

The following sub-tasks are simple processes and can be written as one or two lines in the program:

- Enter the string
- Save the transformed string
- Save the reversed string
- Compare the transformed string and the reversed string. Only if they are equal is the entered string a palindrome.

These sub-tasks merely enter input data, save the intermediate results, and use the data for comparison.

Function to Replace Upper Case Letters

Let's continue the program. As we've already mentioned, you need to write three functions. We've already worked out the algorithm for each function when we wrote the program in Chapter 4. We'll re-use the code here and transform it into a function by adding a heading and declaring the variables.

Transforming into a Function

To replace upper-case letters we use the following fragment:

```
{ replace upper-case letters}
   For I := 1 to Length(Rope) do
      If ('A'<=Rope[I]) and (Rope[I]<='Z')
         Then
            Begin
            Rope[I] := Chr(Ord(Rope[I]) + 32);
            End;
```

To transform this into a function you need to decide the structure of the function heading. You can do this by answering the following questions:

- How many parameters does the function take?

- What type are these parameters?

- What type is the result?

You then need to answer a further question:

- Which local variables need to be declared within the function?

The Function Heading

Analyzing the fragment you can see that the function takes the string **Rope**, processes it, and returns this processed string so that the program can continue. This implies the function has one parameter of string type. The type of the value to be returned is also clear: it must also be of string type. The only thing left is to name the function. You can do this using any meaningful identifier, for example, **Lower_case**. This is the function heading:

```
Function Lower_case(Rope: String) : String;
```

Variables to Declare

The only variable is **I**. We could declare it as either a local or a global variable. Both ways are legal. Which is better?

All variables used solely within the function should be declared as local variables. Any transfer of data between the function and the 'external' program must be done using parameters. Within the function, the variable **I** is used to look through the string, letter by letter. Outside the function, **I** has no meaning so it's a local variable and we must declare it in the function.

Finally, we need to include the assignment statement

```
Lower_case := Rope;
```

at the end of the function. This statement returns the transformed string.

The Function Lower_case

Now, you can write the function `Lower_case()`:

```
Function Lower_case(Rope: String) : String;
Var
   I  : Integer;
Begin{ Lower_case }
   For I := 1 to Length(Rope) do
      If ('A'<=Rope[I]) and (Rope[I]<='Z')
         Then
             Rope[I] := Chr(Ord(Rope[I]) + 32);
   Lower_case := Rope;
End{ Lower_case };
```

Solving the Other Tasks

By a similar analysis we can produce functions for the other sub-tasks.

Deleting Punctuation

In the original program we used the following fragment:

```
   Res_str := '';
{For each character in the string}
   For I := 1 to Length(Rope) do
{Test if character is a letter}
      If ('a'<=Rope[I]) and (Rope[I]<='z')
         Then
{Only if it is  add it to the temporary string}
            Begin
            Res_str := Res_str + Rope[I];
            End;
```

In order to convert this to the function `Del_punct_marks` we need to answer these questions:

▶ How many parameters does the function take?

▶ What type are these parameters?

▶ What type is the result?

▶ Which local variables need to be declared within the function?

The function needs to take a single parameter. It will process a variable of string type and will also return a value of string type, so the function heading is straightforward.

Within the function, two variables are used. **Res_Str** is re-declared, so avoiding any conflict with the main program. **I** must be declared here, as the variable is local to this function. **I** was also declared in the function **Lower_case**, but this function won't be in operation at the same time as **Del_punct_marks** so Turbo Pascal considers the variable undeclared and we can re-use it.

Reversing the String

We will use the following fragment for a Reverse function.

```
Len := Length(Rope);
For I := 1 to Len div 2 do
{Using a temporary variable swap the letters in the string}
   Begin
   Ch := Rope[Len + 1 - I];
   Rope[Len + 1 - I] := Rope[I];
   Rope[I] := Ch
   End;
```

Again, the function takes a single parameter to process a variable string of type and return a value of string type, so the function heading is straightforward. We need to declare three local variables: **I**, **len** and **Ch**.

Is This A Palindrome (With Functions)?

Having written all the functions we can put together the complete program:

```
Program EX_6_2;
Uses Crt;
{Declare the global variables}
Var
   Rope, Res_str, Init_str, Temp : String;
{-------------------------------------------------}
{FUNCTION LOWER CASE}
Function Lower_case(Rope : String) : String;
{Declare local variables}
Var
   I  : Integer;
Begin{ Lower_case }
{For each character in the string}
   For I := 1 to Length(Rope) do
{Test if the character is lower case}
     If ('A'<=Rope[I]) and (Rope[I]<='Z')
{If it is convert it to upper case}
        Then
           Begin
           Rope[I] := Chr(Ord(Rope[I]) + 32);
           End;
```

```
{Assign the converted string to the function identifier}
   Lower_case := Rope;
End{ Lower_case };
{------------------------------------------------}
{ FUNCTION DEL_PUNCT_MARKS}
Function Del_punct_marks(Rope : String) : String;
{Declare local variables}
Var
   Res_str : String;
   I       : Integer;
Begin { Del_punct_marks }
{Initialize the variable}
   Res_str := '';
{For each character in the string}
   For I := 1 to Length(Rope) do
{Test if character is a letter}
      If ('a'<=Rope[I]) and (Rope[I]<='z')
         Then
{Only if it is  add it to the temporary string}
            Begin
            Res_str := Res_str + Rope[I];
            End;
{Assign the converted string to the function identifier}
   Del_punct_marks := Res_str;
End { Del_punct_marks };
{------------------------------------------------}
{FUNCTION REVERSE}
Function Reverse(Rope : String) : String;
{Declare local variables}
Var
   I, Len : Integer;
   Ch     : Char;
Begin{ Reverse }
   Len := Length(Rope);
   For I := 1 to Len div 2 do
{Using a temporary variable swap the letters in the string}
      Begin
         Ch := Rope[Len + 1 - I];
         Rope[Len + 1 - I] := Rope[I];
         Rope[I] := Ch
      End;
{Assign the converted string to the function identifier}
   Reverse := Rope;
End{ Reverse };
{------------------------------------------------}
Begin
   ClrScr;
   WriteLn('Enter any string of letters: ');
   ReadLn(Rope);
   Init_str := Rope;
   Res_str  := Lower_case(Rope);
```

```
    Res_str  := Del_punct_marks(Res_str);
    Temp     := Res_str;
    Res_str  := Reverse(Res_str);
    If Res_str = Temp
       Then
          WriteLn('''', Init_str, '''',' -is a palindrome!')
       Else
          WriteLn('''', Init_str, '''',' -is not a palindrome');
End.
```

The main program now consists of a series of input and output statements.

The Scope of Identifiers in the Program

Look at the following figure:

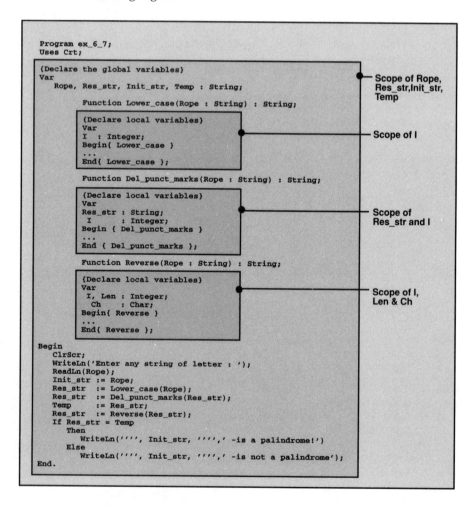

Each region is shown as a rectangle. As you can see, there are no explicit conflicts between variables in the program. However, let's consider the assignment statement:

```
Res_str := Lower_case(Rope);
```

In this situation the variable identifier **Rope** is used twice: once as the formal parameter, and once as the actual parameter.

A more complex situation arises when you use this assignment statement:

```
Res_str := Del_punct_marks(Res_str);
```

Identifier **Res_str** is used three times: as the actual parameter, as the local variable within the function, and as the variable in the left side of the assignment statement. However, there's no conflict here. The variable **Res_str** used in the assignment statement has different meanings in the left and in the right sides of the statement. In the right side it refers to the old value of the variable (that is, *before* the function execution), but in the left side it means the new value (that is, *after* the function execution). Also, though the name **Res_str** is used both for the actual parameter and for the local variable, *within* the function one of them will be renamed. So in this case, there'll be no conflict.

Writing Secret Code

As a second example we are going to write a program to convert your messages into secret code.

The Algorithm

The concept behind our algorithm to code and decode text is to replace each letter with another letter positioned a specified number of characters to the right along a given coding string. The key to our code is that this specified number is the remainder of the length of the string when divided by 26.

The coding string we want to use for lower-case letters is simply the alphabet:

abcdefghijklmnopqrstuvwxyz.

However, the remainder when dividing by 26 can be 0 through 25, so if we used this as our coding string then there won't be a replacement character for 'z' if the key works out as 1 or 'y', and 'z' if the key worked out to 2, and so on. To resolve this we duplicate the string:

abcdefghijklmnopqrstuvwxyzabcdefghijklmnopqrstuvwxyz.

Encoding Lowercase Letters

Now we know what we are trying to achieve we'll consider each separate sub-task and come up with a function for each.

The Function Heading

The first function is to encode the string. This function must take a string and return the coded string. So we start with this function heading:

```
Function Encoding(String_to_encode : String) : String;
```

Encoding is the name of the function, **String_to_encode** is the formal parameter of string type, and the function returns a result of string type.

Selecting Each Character

To encode **String_to_encode** we must encode each character. To access each character in the string we use the index of a string **String_to_encode[I]**. We then work through changing **I** from 1 through to the number of the last character in the string.

To work out which character is at the position **String_to_encode[I]** we need to use the standard function Ord(). Ord(**String_to_encode[I]**) returns the number of the character **String_to_encode[I]** from the ASCII character set. The lower-case letters in the ASCII table are arranged alphabetically so the number of 'a' is the lowest number. To work out the position of **String_to_encode[I]** on our coding string, we then need to find the difference between Ord(**String_to_encode[I]**) and Ord(**'a'**) and add 1 to the result so that

Ord('a') - Ord('a') + 1 = 97 - 97 + 1 = 0 + 1 = 1.

So if **String_to_encode[I]** is the character 'a', our expression evaluates to 1 which is the correct position.

For **String_to_encode[I]** = 'b' and 'z' we also get the correct values:

Ord('b') - Ord('a') + 1 = 98 - 97 + 1 = 1 + 1 = 2.
Ord('z') - Ord('a') + 1 = 122 - 97 + 1 = 25 + 1 = 26.

This gives us the rule which will find the number of the character to be encoded in the coding string.

The Key to the Code

Next, we need to work out how many characters to the right to count. This number is the remainder of the length of the string once it has been divided by 26. We therefore need the following statement:

```
Key := Length(String_to_encode) mod 26;
```

Selecting the Replacement Character

The next thing to do is to find the replacement character you want to insert. The position of the replacement character in the coding string is equal to the expression:

```
Ord(String_to_encode[I]) - Ord('a') + 1 + key
```

If we store the coding string

'abcdefghijklmnopqrstuvwxyzabcdefghijklmnopqrstuvwxyz'

in a variable **Lwr_Coding_Str** we can again use the index for a string.

```
Lwr_Coding_Str[1] = Lwr_Coding_Str[27] = 'a', ¿
```

```
Lwr_Coding_Str[2] = Lwr_Coding_Str[52] = 'z'.
```

So

```
Lwr_Coding_Str[Ord(String_to_encode[I]) - Ord('a') + 1 + Key]
```

will be the replacement character.

Encoding Upper Case Letters

Having worked out how to do this for lower-case letters, we only need a few alterations to do it for upper-case letters.

We use the string

'ABCDEFGHIJKLMNOPQRSTUVWXYZABCDEFGHIJKLMNOPQRSTUVWXYZ'

stored in the variable **Uppr_Coding_Str**. We also use Ord(**'A'**) instead of Ord(**'a'**). As a result, the replacement character is equal to

```
Uppr_Coding_Str[Ord(String_to_encode[I]) - Ord('A') + 1 + Key].
```

The Function Body

The Loop

So that the function **Encoding()** replaces every letter in **String_to_encode**, we use the For loop:

```
For I := 1 to Length(String_to_encode) do ...
```

This loop allows you to process each letter in **String_to_encode** character-by-character.

The Decision

Before we encode the character, we need to establish whether the character is a lower-case letter, an upper-case letter, or a punctuation mark.

In the first two cases you use the strings **Lwr_Coding_Str** or **Uppr_Coding_Str** to replace the letter. In the third case we simply copy the punctuation mark to the output string. This should be stored as another variable **Coded_String**. We will use nested If statements to select the case:

```
Coded_string := '';
{Test whether character is lower case}
If (String_to_encode[I] >= 'a') and (String_to_encode[I] <= 'z')
  Then
    Begin
      Ch := Lwr_Coding_Str[(Ord(String_to_encode[I]) - Ord('a')) + 1 + Key];
      Coded_string := Coded_string + Ch;
    End
  Else
{Otherwise, test whether the character is upper case}
  If (String_to_encode[I] >= 'A') and (String_to_encode[I] <= 'Z')
    Then
      Begin
        Ch := Uppr_Coding_Str[(Ord(String_to_encode[I]) - Ord('A')) + 1 + Key];
        Coded_string := Coded_string + Ch;
      End
{If neither of the above is true assume the character is punctuation}
    Else
      Begin
        Coded_string := Coded_string + String_to_encode[I];
      End
```

It's clear that the string **Coded_string** must initially be empty. Each execution of the loop adds a new character to the string **Coded_string**. As a result, at the end the string **Coded_string** will hold the value of the coded message.

Decoding

The next task is to decode the message. To begin with, let's consider the decoding of the lower-case letters. To decode the message, the string

abcdefghijklmnopqrstuvwxyzabcdefghijklmnopqrstuvwxyz

must be used again. It's also obvious that the same 'distance calculation' must be used. This time, we must search for the required letter to the left of the given letter. The expression

```
Ord(String_to_decode[I]) - Ord('a') + 27
```

gives the values

```
27 <= Ord(String_to_decode[I]) - Ord('a') + 27 <= 52
```

for all lower-case letters. If you subtract the value of the variable **Key** from the expression, then you'll get the correct position of the twin letter. As we only need to get the letter itself we can use the expression as the index for the string variable:

```
Lwr_Coding_Str[(Ord(String_to_decode[I]) - Ord('a')) + 27 - Key]
```

The Complete Program

Without further ado, we can put together the complete program:

```
Program Ex_6_3;
Uses Crt;
{Declare the global variables}
Var
   Input_string, Decoded, Message : String;
   Key        : Integer;
{----------------------------------------------------}
Function Encoding (String_to_encode : String) : String;
{Declaring the variables to use in this function }
Var
   I                                    : Integer;
   T1, T2, Lwr_Coding_Str, Uppr_Coding_Str, Coded_string : String;
   Ch                          : Char;
```

```pascal
Begin{ Encoding }
{Set the inital values of the variables}
 Coded_string   := '';
 T1     := 'abcdefghijklmnopqrstuvwxyz';
 T2     := 'ABCDEFGHIJKLMNOPQRSTUVWXYZ';
 Lwr_Coding_Str := T1 + T1;
 Uppr_Coding_Str := T2 + T2;
 Key :=  Length(String_to_encode) mod 26;
{Convert each character in the string}
For I := 1 to Length(String_to_encode) do
{Test whether character is lower case}
   If (String_to_encode[I] >= 'a') and (String_to_encode[I] <= 'z')
     Then
       Begin
       Ch := Lwr_Coding_Str[(Ord(String_to_encode[I]) - Ord('a')) + 1 + Key];
       Coded_string := Coded_string + Ch;
       End
     Else
{Otherwise, test whether the character is upper case}
       If (String_to_encode[I] >= 'A') and (String_to_encode[I] <= 'Z')
         Then
          Begin
          Ch := Uppr_Coding_Str[(Ord(String_to_encode[I]) - Ord('A')) + 1 + Key];
          Coded_string := Coded_string + Ch;
          End
         Else
  {If neither of the above is true assume the character is punctuation}
          Begin
          Coded_string := Coded_string + String_to_encode[I];
          End;
   Encoding := Coded_string;
End{ Encoding };
{----------------------------------------------------}
Function Decoding (String_to_decode : String) : String;
{Declaring the variables to use in this function }
Var
   I                              : Integer;
   T1, T2, Lwr_Coding_Str, Uppr_Coding_Str, Decoded_str : String;
   Ch                             : Char;
Begin{ Decoding }
 Decoded_str := '';
   T1     := 'abcdefghijklmnopqrstuvwxyz';
   T2     := 'ABCDEFGHIJKLMNOPQRSTUVWXYZ';
   Lwr_Coding_Str := T1 + T1;
   Uppr_Coding_Str := T2 + T2;
   Key :=  Length(String_to_decode) mod 26;
```

```
{Convert each character in the string}
 For I := 1 to Length(String_to_decode) do
{Test whether character is lower case}
  If (String_to_decode[I] >= 'a') and (String_to_decode[I] <= 'z')
    Then
     Begin
     Ch := Lwr_Coding_Str[(Ord(String_to_decode[I]) - Ord('a')) + 27 - Key];
     Decoded_str:= Decoded_str + Ch;
     End
    Else
     {Otherwise, test wether the character is upper case}
       If (String_to_decode[I] >= 'A') and (String_to_decode[I] <= 'Z')
         Then
          Begin
          Ch := Uppr_Coding_Str[(Ord(String_to_decode[I]) - Ord('A')) + 27 - Key];
          Decoded_str:= Decoded_str + Ch;
          End
         Else
{If neither of the above is true assume the character is punctuation}
          Begin
          Decoded_str:= Decoded_str + String_to_decode[I];
          End;
    Decoding := Decoded_str;
End{ Decoding };
{----------------------------------------------------}
{Start the main program}
Begin{ Main }
   ClrScr;
   WriteLn('Enter any string : ');
   ReadLn(Input_string);
   WriteLn('***** Input message *****');
   WriteLn(Input_string);
{----------------------------------------------------}
   Message := Encoding(Input_string);
   WriteLn('***** Coded message *****');
   WriteLn(Message);
{----------------------------------------------------}
   Decoded := Decoding(Message);
   WriteLn('***** Decoded message *****');
   WriteLn(Decoded);
End.
```

Again the main program becomes a series of input and output statements.

Recursion

In the previous cases we called a function from the main program. But a function can be called by itself. This is called **recursion**. This may seem a little strange, but using recursive functions can lead to a more natural style of programming. However, it's not magic - any recursive function could be replaced by a loop.

> When you use a recursive function, the program reaches the function call and then merely executes the statements in the function once again. It remembers where it had reached when it was first reading the function statements, and returns to this statement when it has finished. The secret of recursive functions is knowing when to tell them to stop!

A Recursive Example: Factorial

As an example of a recursive function, consider the calculation of the **factorial** of some hypothetical positive integer called N. (The factorial of a number is the result you get when you multiply together all the numbers from 1 through N.) In mathematics, the factorial of a number is designated by N!, therefore:

```
N! = 1 * 2 * 3 * ... * N.
```

This could be re-expressed as

```
N! = (1 * 2 * 3 * ... * (N -1)) * N.
```

or even as

```
N! = (N-1)! *N
```

So the factorial of N is equivalent to the result of multiplying all the numbers from 1 through (N-1) multiplied by N.

But, how does the recursion end? Without any brakes this statement would just keep on calling itself and no one would be at home ...

However, one of the properties of factorials is that 0! equals 1. So we can calculate 3! as follows:

```
3! = (2!)*3 = ((1!)*2)*3 = (((0!)*1)*2)*3 = (((1)*1)*2)*3 = 1*1*2*3 = 6
```

If we assume we have already written the Turbo Pascal function **Factorial()**, then **Factorial(N)** calculates **N!**, and **Factorial(N - 1)** calculates **(N -1)!** Knowing this you'll be able to see that the recursive call in the function will be as follows:

```
Factorial(N) = Factorial(N - 1) * N;
```

and that eventually this will lead to the statement;

```
Factorial(0) = 1.
```

Now, the function will only need one parameter, the number, which must be an integer. The result will also be an integer, so it's a simple matter to write the heading and the first line:

```
Function Factorial(N : Integer) : Integer;
Begin{ Factorial }
```

We then need to test whether the number is zero, and if it is, assign the value **1** to the parameter.

```
If N = 0
    Then
        Factorial := 1
    Else
```

Then, if the number is not zero we perform the recursive call.

```
        Factorial := Factorial(N - 1) * N;
End{ Factorial };
```

Stepping Through the Program

Let's think about how the function will perform. Let N = 2. To calculate 2! you must write the function designator `Factorial(2)` somewhere in the program. The If statement evaluates the condition (2 = 0) to **false** so the Else part will be executed. This is the assignment statement:

```
Factorial := Factorial(N - 1) * N;
```

It contains the function designator `Factorial(N-1)`. The value of N is 2 so N - 1 = 1. So the function `Factorial(1)` is called.

The If statement evaluates the condition to **false** again, so the Else part is once more executed. As N is now 1 this calls `Factorial(0)`.

Now the If statement evaluates the condition to **true** so the Then part is executed. This is the statement:

```
Factorial := 1
```

So `Factorial(0)` returns a value of 1 to the point we left off in `Factorial(1)` which was the line

```
Factorial := Factorial(N - 1) * N;
```

So N = 1 and this statement now evaluates to 1*1. So Factorial(1) also returns a value 1.

This value is returned to `Factorial(2)` at the same line. Now N = 2 so the statement evaluates 2*1 = 2. So `Factorial(2)` returns the value 2.

An Illustrated Walkthrough

```
Function Factorial(N : Integer) : Integer;
Begin{ Factorial }
If N = 0
    Then
        Factorial := 1
    Else
Factorial := Factorial(N - 1) * N;
End Function
```

Calling Factorial(2)

```
Function Factorial(2 : Integer) : Integer;
Begin{ Factorial }
If N = 0
    Then
        Factorial := 1
    Else
Factorial := Factorial(2 - 1)*2;
```

Calls Factorial(1)

```
Function Factorial(1 : Integer) : Integer;
Begin{ Factorial }
If N = 0
    Then
        Factorial := 1
    Else
Factorial := Factorial(1 - 1) * 1;
```

Calls Factorial (0)

```
Function Factorial(0 : Integer) : Integer;
Begin{ Factorial }
If N = 0
    Then
        Factorial := 1
    Else
Factorial := Factorial(N - 1) * N;
End {Factorial}
```

Which returns a value of 1 and passes control back to the previous call

```
Factorial := 1 * 1;
End {Factorial}
```

Which returns a value of 1 and passes control back to the previous call

```
Factorial := 1 * 2;
End {Factorial}
```

Which gives the answer
Factorial (2) = 2

User-Defined Procedures

There are two kinds of sub-programs in Turbo Pascal - functions and procedures. We've already discussed functions - let's move on to procedures.

The Differences Between Functions and Procedures

These are the four main differences between a function and a procedure:

1 A function returns only one value, whilst a procedure can return any number of values including none.

2 A function call is a part of an expression, whereas a procedure call is an individual statement.

3 A function returns its result through the name of the function; a procedure returns its result only through parameters.

4 Functions can only use **value** parameters; procedures may use **value** and **variable** parameters.

Value Vs Variable Parameters

This last difference needs a bit of explanation.

Both value parameters and variable parameters are kinds of formal parameter (they are used to pass data between the outside program and the sub-program). The difference is that value parameters can only pass information into the sub-program, whereas variable parameters can also pass information out again.

Value parameters are the simplest form of parameters. They allow you to give different starting values for each call of the sub-program. However, they can't return the results from within the sub-program. All parameters in functions are value parameters. The results of a function are stored in the identifier of the function, and returned to the main program through this identifier. This is OK when you have only one single value to pass around, but when you have several you need several variables.

When you write procedures you use variable parameters to pass the results of the procedure to the main program. Variable parameters allow you to modify an external variable from within the procedure.

The example programs will make this clear.

A Procedure's Skeleton

Procedures have similar structures to functions. A procedure declaration has the following skeleton:

Procedure **Proc_identifier** (list of value parameters and their types
                   Var list of variable parameters and their types);
{ Local data declarations }
Begin{ **Proc_identifier** }
{ Statements to be executed }
End{ **Proc_identifier** };

Where Procedure is a reserved word. In the lists of parameters each list of same type variable parameters must start with the reserved word Var. Within the lists parameters are separated by commas, and types are separated by colons from the list of parameters. Same type lists of parameters are separated by semi-colons.

The Procedure Heading

As with a function, a procedure consists of two parts: a procedure heading and a procedure body. In the procedure heading you need to:

▶ State that it is a procedure. (The reserved word Procedure is used).

▶ Identify the name of the procedure with **proc_identifier**.

▶ List the formal **value** parameters and their declared types.

▶ After the reserved word Var list the formal **variable** parameters and their declared types. The keyword Var must be repeated for each new type.

The Procedure Body

The procedure body is the part of a procedure that is executed. It consists of the following:

▶ Declaration statements for all local units, constants and variables used in the procedure.

▶ The statements to be executed, surrounded by Begin and End.

The Procedure Call

To execute a procedure, you just need to write the procedure identifier with the actual parameters. A procedure call, as this is known, can be a statement all on its own.

An Example: the Division Procedure

In this example, we're going to write a procedure that does integer division *using only addition and subtraction*. This is a very important technique in computing, as computers can only really add numbers - this technique is actually how your computer does division!

Firstly, we'll define the terms. We will use **Dividend** as the value being divided and **Divisor** for the value doing the dividing. In the results, **Quotient** is the whole number of times that the divisor divides into the dividend. The **Remainder** is the difference between the dividend and the value of the divisor multiplied by the quotient. So:

Remainder = Dividend - Divisor * Quotient

To work out the algorithm, we'll go backwards. If you look at this fragment of code you will see that it solves our problem.

```
Quotient  := 0;
Remainder := Dividend;
While Remainder >= Divisor do
    Begin
        Remainder := Remainder - Divisor;
        Quotient  := Quotient + 1;
    End;
```

If you feed in 5 as the dividend and 2 as the divisor you get:

Remainder = Dividend = 5, **Divisor** = 2 so **Remainder** is greater than **Divisor** so execute loop
Remainder = 5 - 2 = 3
Quotient = 0 + 1= 1

and control returns to the start of the loop.

Remainder = 3, **Divisor** = 2 so **Remainder** is greater than **Divisor** so execute loop
Remainder = 3 - 2 = 1
Quotient = 1 + 1 = 2

and control is returned to the start of the loop.

Remainder = 1, **Divisor** = 2 so **Remainder** is less than **Divisor** and the loop isn't executed.

So **Remainder** = 1 and **Quotient** = 2, and as 5 = 2 * 2 + 1, this is the correct answer.

Now that we have the heart of our procedure, we need to consider the number, the type and the kind of parameters we need. All the numbers are integers so the type is easily decided.

In this case we're after two things:

1   You must pass two initial integer numbers, the divisor and the dividend, and divide one by the other into the procedure. You therefore need two formal parameters for these two numbers. These numbers are *not* the results of the procedure execution, and they must be declared as value parameters.

2   The result of the procedure execution is two values: the quotient and the remainder. So we need two formal parameters to store the results. They must be variable parameters as they are the results of the procedure.

The final result is the procedure below.

```
Procedure Dvd(Dividend, Divisor : Integer;
              Var Quotient, Remainder : Integer);
Begin{ Dvd }
   Quotient  := 0;
   Remainder := Dividend;
   While Remainder >= Divisor do
   Begin
      Remainder := Remainder - Divisor;
      Quotient  := Quotient  + 1;
   End;
End{ Dvd };
```

To get the same results as above you would need to include the statement

```
Dvd(5,2, Q,R);
```

The values 5 and 2 are then stored in the variables **Dividend** and **Divisor** respectively. After the procedure has executed the value stored in **Quotient** (2) will be stored in **Q** and the value stored in **Remainder** (1) will be stored in **R**. In the rest of the program you can use the variables **Q** and **R** for these results.

An Example: the Procedure Swapping Values

There are cases when a procedure needs only variable parameters. Think about the following.

A common problem in programming is swapping the values in two variables. Analyzing our requirements you would expect because there are two input values you would need two corresponding value parameters. There are also two output values so you would expect to need two corresponding formal variable parameters. So the procedure needs four formal parameters. However, variable parameters allow you to pass a value *into* the procedure, as well as to pass out the result which was calculated within the procedure. Variable parameters have the same property as value parameters, and also the additional property of saving the result.

Because this is the case it is sufficient to declare just two variable parameters.

```
Procedure Swap(Var A, B : Integer);
Var
   Temp : Integer;
Begin{ Swap }
   Temp := A;
   A    := B;
   B    := Temp;
End{ Swap };
```

When you write the procedure call

```
Swap(X, Y);
```

the current values of **X** is passed to **A** and the value of **Y** is passed to **B**. Within the procedure the values are swapped so the value that was in **A** is now in **B** and vice versa. At the end of the procedure the value in **A** is stored back into **X** and the value in **B** is stored back into **Y**. So the values have been swapped - neat isn't it?

Simple Modular Programming

Modular programming is an enhancement of straightforward structural programming with sub-programs. You are now enough of an experienced programmer to be able to write your own sub-programs and you can see the advantages of using your own sub-programs. Now, we come to the disadvantage (there's no such thing as a free lunch). If you want to use the procedure in another program you must copy the text of the procedure into the new program. If you need to use the procedure in yet another program you must copy it into this new program and so on. It's all a bit time-consuming and error-prone.

So Turbo Pascal lets you keep different programs in different 'modules' called **units**. The idea is very simple. You gather all the sub-programs you require into one unit, name it, and compile it. After that, by simply including the name of your unit in the Uses clause of your program, you can use all the procedures and the functions in the program.

We have already met units in Chapter 1. We introduced them there because of a procedure we needed to use called ClrScr. This comes in one of the standard units Borland supply with Turbo Pascal called **Crt**. This includes procedures and functions for handling the monitor through DOS including ClrScr which clears the output screen.

Borland supply other units for other tasks one of which is called the System unit. This is used to store all the most commonly used functions and procedures. Because they are so common Turbo Pascal doesn't even require you to include the name System in the Uses clause.

Now we'll write our own unit containing the functions **Power()** and **Factorial()**, and the procedures **Dvd()** and **Swap()**.

Definition of a Unit

A simple unit has the following general form:

Unit *unit_name*;
Interface
{ The headings of all the sub-programs }
Implementation
{ The bodies of all the sub-programs}
End.

The first line contains the reserved word Unit and the unit identifier. The next statement **must** start with the reserved word Interface after which you write the headings of all the sub-programs which you wish to include in the unit . After the reserved word Implementation you must write the complete sub-programs of the unit. You can see that the headings of the sub-programs must be written twice and they must be identical

The name of your unit and the name of the file where your unit is saved must be the same. For example, you want to name your unit My_lib **(yes you do!). So the first line will be:**

Unit My_lib;

You must save the unit as MY_LIB.PAS.

This is what your first unit should look like:

```
Unit My_lib;
{------------------------------------------------}
Interface
{------------------------------------------------}
Function Power(Factor, Exponent : Integer) : Integer;
Function Factorial(N : Integer) : Integer;
Procedure Dvd(Dividend, Divisor : Integer;
              Var Quotient, Remainder : Integer);
Procedure Swap(Var A, B : Integer);
{------------------------------------------------}
Implementation
{------------------------------------------------}
Function Power(Factor : Real ; Exponent : Integer) : Real;
{Declare the local variables}
Var
   Counter : Integer;
   Temp : Real;
{The Function Body}
Begin{ Power }
```

```
{Any number raised to the power 0 = 1}
   If Exponent = 0
      Then
         Temp := 1.0
{Otherwise, multiply factor by itself exponent number of times}
      Else
         Begin
            Temp := Factor;
            For Counter := 2 to Exponent do
            Begin
               Temp := Temp * Factor;
            End;
         End;
{Assign the value of temp to power}
   Power := Temp;
End{ Power };
{---------------------------------------------------}
Function Factorial(N : Integer) : Integer;
Begin{ Factorial }
{Test wether the number is zero}
   If N = 0
{if so assign the value 1 to the parameter}
      Then
         Begin
         Factorial := 1
         End
      Else
{if the number is not zero do the recursive call}
         Begin
         Factorial := Factorial(N - 1) * N;
         End;
End{ Factorial };
{---------------------------------------------------}
Procedure Dvd(Dividend, Divisor : Integer;
              Var Quotient, Remainder : Integer);
Begin{ Dvd }
   Quotient  := 0;
   Remainder := Dividend;
   While Remainder >= Divisor do
   Begin
      Remainder := Remainder - Divisor;
      Quotient  := Quotient  + 1;
   End;
End{ Dvd };
{---------------------------------------------------}
Procedure Swap(Var A, B : Integer);
Var
   Temp : Integer;
Begin{ Swap }
   Temp := A;
   A    := B;
   B    := Temp;
End{ Swap };
{---------------------------------------------------}
End.
```

Compiling the Unit

When a unit is compiled the compiler produces a **.TPU** file. A unit can't be executed as it contains the resources which are needed in a program, so the extension is not **.EXE**.

When you compile the unit you need to tell Turbo Pascal where to look for **.TPU** files. To do this you select the Options option from the menu bar at the top of the screen using *Alt+O*. You then select the Directories option by typing the letter D. This opens a dialog box. By filling in the full DOS path in the field EXE and TPU directories, you tell Turbo Pascal where your unit files will be stored. Finally, before you compile the unit you must change the Destination option in the Compile menu to Disk.

Now, you can compile the unit. The result will be the file **MY_LIB.TPU**.

Using a Unit

To use a unit in a program you need to write a Uses clause. You've already seen **Uses Crt** - this allows us to use a standard unit which Borland supplies with Turbo Pascal. To use your own unit in a program you need to write the following:

```
Program ...;
Uses My_lib;
...
Begin
   ...
   P := Power(2, 10);
   ...
   Swap(X, Y);
   ...
End.
```

If the Uses clause with the name **My_lib** is written in the program you can use all the sub-programs from the unit in the main part of the program.

Summary

There are two kinds of subprograms in Turbo Pascal - procedures and functions. Procedures and functions are used to:

▶ Decrease the size of the program.

▶ Extract the sub-tasks from the overall task and solve each of them separately.

Using sub-programs your programs will be clear, easier to read and write and will have fewer errors.

The differences between these two kinds of sub-program are:

▶ Functions always return a single value. Procedures may return zero or more values.

▶ A function is called as part of an expression. A procedure call is a statement.

Both sub-programs may be recursive. If the name of the procedure or function is used within the procedure or function itself, then it's recursive.

A collection of sub-programs can be grouped together in a unit. This is an efficient way to organize your own library of commonly used sub-programs. Borland itself uses this method to store programs for working with the display in the unit **Crt**.

Quiz Questions

1 What do you understand by the term 'structured programming'? Why is it useful?

2 What are the four main differences between Turbo Pascal procedures and functions?

3 Paying close attention to the scope of variables, write down what you think will be the output of the following program.

```
Program Foo;
Uses Crt;
Var
    i, j: Integer;
    k: String;
Procedure Bar(k: String);
    Var
        i: Real;
    Begin
    j := 11;
    i := 7.3;
    k[2] := 'o';
    WriteLn(i:4:2);
    WriteLn(j);
    WriteLn(k)
    End;
Begin
ClrScr;
i := 9;
k := 'Bibble';
Bar(k);
WriteLn(i);
WriteLn(j);
WriteLn(k)
End.
```

4 What's the difference between a value parameter and a variable parameter?

5 How do you make a procedure or function recursive?

6 What are the advantages of using modular programming with Turbo Pascal units?

Exercises

1 Write a function to calculate whether a given coordinate is inside the boundaries of the screen (which is 80 characters wide and 25 characters high). The function heading is:

```
Function On_screen(X, Y: Integer): Boolean;
   { Returns True if the given coordinates are inside the }
   { screen area, returns False otherwise }
```

This function will be used extensively in the next two exercises.

(WARNING: the bottom right-hand corner of the screen should be regarded as off-screen, to prevent unwanted scrolling in subsequent examples.)

Write a program which prints the result of calling **On_screen()** with various on and off-screen coordinates.

2 Write a procedure to draw a given character at a given coordinate. The procedure heading is:

```
Procedure Draw_char(X, Y: Integer; A_char: Char);
   { Draws the character A_char at the coordinates (X, Y) }
   { Does nothing if the coordinates are off-screen }
```

Draw_char() should use **On_screen()** to check whether or not to draw the character. **Draw_char()** should also use GotoXY() and Write() to draw the character itself (as described in Chapter 4).

Write a program which uses **Draw_char()** to put the following stick person in the middle of the screen:

```
    h
   h h
    h
aaaaaaa
    l
   l l
  l   l
```

3 Write a procedure to draw a square on the screen. The caller provides the coordinates of the top left corner, the length of the side and the character to use for the border. The procedure heading is:

```
Procedure Draw_square(Origin_x, Origin_y, Side: Integer; Border: Char);
   { Draws a square whose top left corner is at }
   { (Origin_x, Origin_y), whose side is of length }
   { Side, and whose border is comprised of Border }
   { characters. Parts of the square which are off-screen }
   { are clipped. }
```

Draw_square() should use Draw_char() to ensure that only the on-screen parts of the square are displayed.

Write a program that uses Draw_square() to put the following square in the middle of the screen:

```
##########
#        #
#        #
#        #
#        #
#        #
#        #
#        #
#        #
##########
```

4 Move procedures Draw_square(), Draw_char() and On_screen() into a unit called Square (Square will have to have 'Uses Crt' in its interface part). Write some programs which use loops and the square unit to produce patterns such as the following:

```
ZZZZZZZZZZZZZZZZZ
Z               Z
Z ZZZZZZZZZZZZZ Z
Z Z           Z Z
Z Z ZZZZZZZZZ Z Z
Z Z Z       Z Z Z
Z Z Z ZZZZZ Z Z Z
Z Z Z Z   Z Z Z Z
Z Z Z Z Z Z Z Z Z
Z Z Z Z   Z Z Z Z
Z Z Z ZZZZZ Z Z Z
Z Z Z       Z Z Z
Z Z ZZZZZZZZZ Z Z
Z Z           Z Z
Z ZZZZZZZZZZZZZ Z
Z               Z
ZZZZZZZZZZZZZZZZZ
```

```
@
    @@
    @@    @@@
       @ @    @@@@
       @@@    @  @
              @  @   @@@@@
              @  @  @    @  @@@@@@
              @@@@  @    @   @ @@@@@@@
                    @    @  @@   @@@@@@@@
                    @@@@@ @   @@   @    @@@@@@@@@
                          @   @@   @@  @ @   @@@@@@@@@@@
                          @@@@@@ @   @   @@ @  @  @@@@@@@@@@@@
                                 @    @  @@  @ @  @  @        @
                                 @@@@@@@ @@  @ @  @  @        @
                                        @   @@  @ @  @        @
                                        @@@@@@@@ @ @  @  @    @
                                                @ @@  @ @    @
                                                @@@@@@@@@ @  @
                                                       @  @ @    @
                                                       @@@@@@@@@  @
                                                              @   @
                                                         @@@@@@@@@@@@
```

5   The **crt** unit has a procedure called Delay() which tells Turbo Pascal to pause for a specified number of microseconds. Write a program which uses the **Square** unit, declares two integer variables **zoom** and **Square**, and then runs the following loop for some real action!

```
For Zoom := 1 To 6 Do
   Begin
   For Index := 1 To 15 Do
      Begin
      Draw_square(6 * (Index - 1), (Index - 1), (Index - 1), ' ');
      Draw_square(6 * Index, Index, Index, ':');
      GotoXY(1, 25); { Move the cursor out of the way }
      Delay(140)
      End
   End
```

Can you see how this loop works? Experiment with the value passed to Delay() until you get the best setting for your machine.

CHAPTER 7

Debugging

So you've written your program, it compiled successfully and it was error free and gave valid and useful results when you ran it first time. Dream on!

In nearly every case a program will have some bugs. The Turbo Pascal IDE provides you with a set of powerful tools in the Turbo Debugger with which to find errors.

In this chapter, we'll learn about these tools and about the most effective and time-saving ways of finding and removing your bugs. We'll cover:

- The three kinds of program errors
- Monitoring the output
- Stepping through a program
- Watching expressions
- Tracing into a program
- Setting breakpoints

Three Kinds of Program Errors

All errors can be split into three types:

1   Compile-time errors

2   Run-time errors

3   Logic errors

Compile-time errors are the least complex of your bugs and occur when your program doesn't conform to the syntactical rules of Turbo Pascal. For example, if you've misspelled a word or put in two colons instead of one, these are compile-time errors. These errors prevent your program from being compiled, but they are found and highlighted by the compiler. When Turbo Pascal finds such an error it displays an error message at the top of the screen. These give a number and a brief description of the problem. We have included a full list of error messages in Appendix G, with hints on what to look for if the message is a trifle obscure.

Run-time errors are much more unpleasant. These are errors which cause your program to fail while it's running. They can range from trying to open a file that doesn't exist, to trying to divide by zero. Each run-time error also displays a message for you. In Appendix G we have included a list of the most common run-time error messages with a description of what each one means.

Logic errors are the worst of all. These are errors that Turbo Pascal can't spot as they are in the way your algorithm works. This is the type of error when you enter all the right data, the program compiles and runs successfully, but still you get the wrong results. It's with these types of errors that Turbo Debugger can be an excellent assistant. With the support it provides you can watch the values of variables change or watch how control passes from statement to statement within your program. Using the techniques we describe here, you will be able to 'see' where the program is going wrong.

To show you how Turbo Debugger works, we debugged a couple of our programs and took screenshots along the way.

Compile-time Errors

Program **EX_7_1** was supposed to take two integer numbers and calculate their sum and the reciprocal value of that sum. Inputting values for **A** and **B** should have output the values of **(A + B)** and **1 / (A + B)**. Take a look at the code we started with for **EX_7_1**.

```
Program ex_7_1;
Uses Crt;
Var
   A : Integer;
Begin
   Clrscr;
   WriteLn('Enter an integer number : ');
   ReadLn(A);
   WriteLn('Enter an integer number : ')
   ReadLn(A);
   Writeln('Sum=      ', A + B:1);
   Writeln('Inverse= ',1 / (A + B):3:2);
End.
```

The first thing we tried to do was compile the program by pressing *Alt+F9*. This produced the following screen:

```
 File  Edit  Search  Run  Compile  Debug  Tools  Options  Window  Help
=[■]==================== PROG7-1.PAS ====================1=[↕]=
 Error 85: ";" expected.
Uses Crt;
Var
   A : Integer;
Begin
   Clrscr;
   WriteLn('Enter an integer number : ');
   ReadLn(A);
   WriteLn('Enter an integer number : ')
   ReadLn(A);
   Writeln('Sum=      ', A + B:1);
   Writeln('Inverse= ',1 / (A + B):3:2);
End.


   10:4 ==◄□
F1 Help  F2 Save  F3 Open  Alt+F9 Compile  F9 Make  Alt+F10 Local menu
```

At the top of the screen we got the error message

Error 85 : ';' expected

and the cursor was placed on line 10 under the letter R of the word ReadLn:

```
ReadLn(A);
```

The cursor was placed where the compiler expected to find the semicolon. As you can see, it should have been at the end of the previous line, but all the space means nothing to Turbo Pascal (it's just formatting to make the program easier for us to read). In fact, if we'd put the semi-colon there, Turbo Pascal would have been happy. However, for the sake of clarity, we added a semicolon at the end of the previous line:

```
WriteLn('Enter an integer number : ')
```

Having corrected this error and pressed *Alt+F9* to continue compiling the program, we were confronted with the next error message shown below:

```
 File  Edit  Search  Run  Compile  Debug  Tools  Options  Window  Help
┌[■]═══════════════════════ PROG7-1.PAS ══════════════════════1=[↕]┐
│ Error 3: Unknown identifier.                                      ▲
│Uses Crt;                                                          
│Var                                                                
│    A : Integer;                                                   
│Begin                                                              
│    Clrscr;                                                        
│    WriteLn('Enter an integer number : ');                        
│    ReadLn(A);                                                     
│    WriteLn('Enter an integer number : ');                        
│    ReadLn(A);                                                     
│    Writeln('Sum=      ', A + B:1);                                
│    Writeln('Inverse= ',1 / (A + B):3:2);                          
│End.                                                               
│                                                                   
│                                                                   
│                                                                   
│                                                                   
│                                                                   
│                                                                   
│                                                                   
│                                                                   
│                                                                   
│─── 11:29 ──                                                       ▼
F1 Help  F2 Save  F3 Open  Alt+F9 Compile  F9 Make  Alt+F10 Local menu
```

This time we had an unknown identifier in our midst, but trusty old Turbo Pascal placed the cursor where the error occurred - at the first appearance of the letter **B**. Checking the source code you can see that we hadn't declared the identifier **B**. Sheepishly, we rectified the mistake by altering the declaration to:

```
A, B : Integer;
```

and tried to compile the program once more. This time we were in luck and saw the screen below:

```
  File  Edit  Search  Run  Compile  Debug  Tools  Options  Window  Help
┌─[■]───────────────────────── PROG7-1.PAS ──────────────────────1=[‡]─┐
│Program EX_7_1;                                                       ▲
│Uses Crt;                                                             
│Var                                                                   
│   A, B : Integer;                                                    
│Begin                                                                 
│   Clrscr;             ┌───────────── Compiling ─────────────┐        
│   WriteLn('Ent        │                                     │        
│   ReadLn(A);          │ Main file: PROG7-1.PAS              │        
│   WriteLn('Ent        │ Done.                               │        
│   ReadLn(A);          │                                     │        
│   Writeln('Sum        │ Destination:  Disk   Line number:  0│        
│   Writeln('Inv        │ Free memory:  139K   Total lines:  13│       
│End.                   │                                     │        
│                       ├─────────────────────────────────────┤        
│                       │  Compile successful: Press any key   │        
│                       └─────────────────────────────────────┘        
│                                                                      
│                                                                      ▼
├─*─── 4:8 ───◄█▒▒▒▒▒▒▒▒▒▒▒▒▒▒▒▒▒▒▒▒▒▒▒▒▒▒▒▒▒▒▒▒▒▒▒▒▒▒▒▒▒▒▒▒▒▒▒▒▒►┘
 F1 Help │ Compile source file
```

Our program was now free of compile-time errors.

These compile-time errors are easy to correct because the compiler does most of the diagnostic work. It both finds the error and displays remedial information. It's then a relatively simple process to alter your code and continue compiling the program. Finally, when all compile-time errors are corrected, the compiler displays the following message:

Compile successful: Press any key

Once you get this message the program is ready to run.

Logic Errors and Run-time Errors

Having got our program free of compile-time errors, we ran the program by pressing *Ctrl+F9*. We entered the numbers 10 and 20 and got the following results:

```
Enter an integer number :
10
Enter an integer number :
20
Sum=      20
Inverse= 0.05
```

The program actually gave us the wrong results, meaning we must have a logic error in the program. We pressed on with testing the program using the numbers 10 and 0, but this caused a run-time error as well.

```
 File  Edit  Search  Run  Compile  Debug  Tools  Options  Window  Help
[■]========================= PROG7-1.PAS =======================1═[↕]
  Error 200: Division by zero.
Uses Crt;
Var
   A, B : Integer;
Begin
   Clrscr;
   WriteLn('Enter an integer number : ');
   ReadLn(A);
   WriteLn('Enter an integer number : ');
   ReadLn(A);
   Writeln('Sum=      ', A + B:1);
   Writeln('Inverse= ',1 / (A + B):3:2);
End.



    12:1
 F1 Help  F2 Save  F3 Open  Alt+F9 Compile  F9 Make  Alt+F10 Local menu
```

When we used *Alt+F5* to switch to the output screen, we were confronted with the following screen:

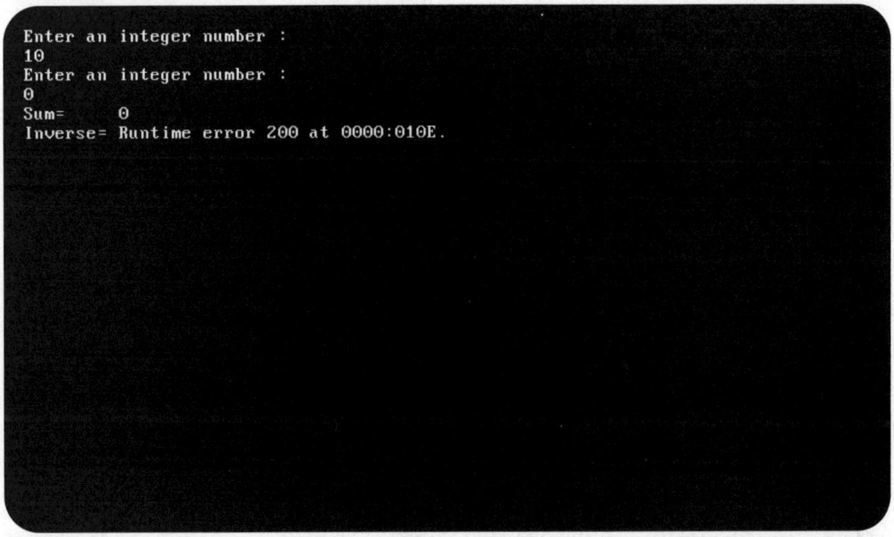

```
Enter an integer number :
10
Enter an integer number :
0
Sum=     0
Inverse= Runtime error 200 at 0000:010E.
```

With logic errors and run-time errors, the program was a dismal failure. The only thing we could do was turn to Turbo Debugger to find the errors and remove them.

Monitoring Output

To assist us when we are debugging we can make some changes to the IDE so that we can monitor the output from programs, without switching backwards and forwards between screens using the *Alt+F5* keys. To see the output of your program, you open an output screen.

▶ Press *F10*, select the Debug menu and then choose Output

As a result, a window called Output will appear at the bottom of the screen:

```
 File  Edit  Search  Run  Compile  Debug  Tools  Options  Window  Help
─────────────────────────── PROG7-1.PAS ───────────────────────1──
Program EX_7_1;
Uses Crt;
Var
    A, B : Integer;
Begin
    Clrscr;
    WriteLn('Enter an integer number : ');
    ReadLn(A);
    WriteLn('Enter an integer number : ');
    ReadLn(A);
    Writeln('Sum=      ', A + B:1);
    Writeln('Inverse= ',1 / (A + B):3:2);
End.

┌─[■]──────────────────── Output ─────────────────2=[↑]─┐
│                                                        │
Luke I:\>tp\bin\turbo
Turbo Pascal  Version 7.0  Copyright (c) 1983,92 Borland Int

 F1 Help  ↑↓←→ Scroll  F10 Menu
```

At startup, the output window displays the last screen from DOS. From now on, all the output data will be displayed in this window, and you'll no longer need to swap screens.

Debugging Techniques

Stepping

To work out what was wrong with our program we began by stepping through the program line by line. To execute a program statement by statement you can do one of two things:

▶ Press *F10*, select the Run menu and then select Step over.

▶ Or press the *F8* key.

In both cases, your program will be compiled and the first **executable** statement in the program is highlighted with a bar.

With our program we got the following result:

```
 File  Edit  Search  Run  Compile  Debug  Tools  Options  Window  Help
┌─────────────────────── PROG7-1.PAS ─────────────────────────1───┐
Program EX_7_1;
Uses Crt;
Var
   A, B : Integer;
Begin
   Clrscr;
   WriteLn('Enter an integer number : ');
   ReadLn(A);
   WriteLn('Enter an integer number : ');
   ReadLn(A);
   Writeln('Sum=     ', A + B:1);
   Writeln('Inverse= ',1 / (A + B):3:2);
End.

┌─[■]──────────────────────── Output ════════════════════════2=[↑]─┐

Luke I:\>tp\bin\turbo
Turbo Pascal  Version 7.0  Copyright (c) 1983,92 Borland International


F1 Help  ↑↓←  Scroll  F10 Menu
```

Pressing *F8* moved the highlight bar to the next statement in the program:

```
 File  Edit  Search  Run  Compile  Debug  Tools  Options  Window  Help
┌─────────────────────── PROG7-1.PAS ─────────────────────────1───┐
Program EX_7_1;
Uses Crt;
Var
   A, B : Integer;
Begin
   Clrscr;
   WriteLn('Enter an integer number : ');
   ReadLn(A);
   WriteLn('Enter an integer number : ');
   ReadLn(A);
   Writeln('Sum=     ', A + B:1);
   Writeln('Inverse= ',1 / (A + B):3:2);
End.

┌─[■]──────────────────────── Output ════════════════════════2=[↑]─┐

Luke I:\>tp\bin\turbo
Turbo Pascal  Version 7.0  Copyright (c) 1983,92 Borland International


F1 Help  ↑↓←  Scroll  F10 Menu
```

This was the procedure ClrScr, which clears the screen. The bar highlights the statement that's about to be executed and the output window still contained the following text:

Luke I:\>tp\bin\turbo
Turbo Pascal Version 7.0 Copyright (c) 1983,92 Borland International

Pressing *F8* again executed the procedure ClrScr and moved the highlight bar to the next statement.

```
 File  Edit  Search  Run  Compile  Debug  Tools  Options  Window  Help
────────────────────────────── PROG7-1.PAS ────────────────────────────1──
Program EX_7_1;
Uses Crt;
Var
   A, B : Integer;
Begin
   Clrscr;
   WriteLn('Enter an integer number : ');
   ReadLn(A);
   WriteLn('Enter an integer number : ');
   ReadLn(A);
   Writeln('Sum=     ', A + B:1);
   Writeln('Inverse= ',1 / (A + B):3:2);
End.

─[■]──────────────────────── Output ──────────────────────────2=[↑]─




─◄►────────────────────────────────────────────────────────────────────►─
F1 Help  ↑↓→← Scroll  F10 Menu
```

As you can see, the output screen cleared.

We pressed *F8* once more:

```
 File  Edit  Search  Run  Compile  Debug  Tools  Options  Window  Help
────────────────────────────── PROG7-1.PAS ────────────────────────────1──
Program EX_7_1;
Uses Crt;
Var
   A, B : Integer;
Begin
   Clrscr;
   WriteLn('Enter an integer number : ');
   ReadLn(A);
   WriteLn('Enter an integer number : ');
   ReadLn(A);
   Writeln('Sum=     ', A + B:1);
   Writeln('Inverse= ',1 / (A + B):3:2);
End.

─[■]──────────────────────── Output ──────────────────────────2=[↑]─
Enter an integer number :




─◄►────────────────────────────────────────────────────────────────────►─
F1 Help  ↑↓→← Scroll  F10 Menu
```

and this time the WriteLn() statement was executed, and the prompt appeared on the output screen. We followed the prompt and entered the number 10, and the screen changed to this:

```
 File  Edit  Search  Run  Compile  Debug  Tools  Options  Window  Help
──────────────────────────── PROG7-1.PAS ──────────────────────────1───
Program EX_7_1;
Uses Crt;
Var
    A, B : Integer;
Begin
   Clrscr;
   WriteLn('Enter an integer number : ');
   ReadLn(A);
   WriteLn('Enter an integer number : ');
   ReadLn(A);
   Writeln('Sum=      ', A + B:1);
   Writeln('Inverse= ',1 / (A + B):3:2);
End.


┌─[■]────────────────────────── Output ─────────────────────────2═[↑]─┐
Enter an integer number :
10



└─◄■────────────────────────────────────────────────────────────────►┘
 F1 Help  ↑↓→← Scroll  F10 Menu
```

We repeated the steps above, pressing *F8* twice and then entering the number 20. The screen changed, as follows:

```
 File  Edit  Search  Run  Compile  Debug  Tools  Options  Window  Help
──────────────────────────── PROG7-1.PAS ──────────────────────────1───
Program EX_7_1;
Uses Crt;
Var
    A, B : Integer;
Begin
   Clrscr;                '
   WriteLn('Enter an integer number : ');
   ReadLn(A);
   WriteLn('Enter an integer number : ');
   ReadLn(A);
   Writeln('Sum=      ', A + B:1);
   Writeln('Inverse= ',1 / (A + B):3:2);
End.


┌─[■]────────────────────────── Output ─────────────────────────2═[↑]─┐
Enter an integer number :
10
Enter an integer number :



└─◄■────────────────────────────────────────────────────────────────►┘
 F1 Help  ↑↓→← Scroll  F10 Menu
```

After Pressing F8

```
 File  Edit  Search  Run  Compile  Debug  Tools  Options  Window  Help
────────────────────────── PROG7-1.PAS ─────────────────────────1───
Program EX_7_1;
Uses Crt;
Var
   A, B : Integer;
Begin
   Clrscr;
   WriteLn('Enter an integer number : ');
   ReadLn(A);
   WriteLn('Enter an integer number : ');
   ReadLn(A);
   Writeln('Sum=      ', A + B:1);
   Writeln('Inverse= ',1 / (A + B):3:2);
End.


─[■]────────────────────── Output ──────────────────────2─[↑]─
Enter an integer number :
10
Enter an integer number :
20



─ ◄                                                         ► ─
 F1 Help   ↑↓→← Scroll  F10 Menu
```

After Entering 20

We pressed *F8* and the WriteLn() statement was executed:

```
 File  Edit  Search  Run  Compile  Debug  Tools  Options  Window  Help
────────────────────────── PROG7-1.PAS ─────────────────────────1───
Program EX_7_1;
Uses Crt;
Var
   A, B : Integer;
Begin
   Clrscr;
   WriteLn('Enter an integer number : ');
   ReadLn(A);
   WriteLn('Enter an integer number : ');
   ReadLn(A);
   Writeln('Sum=      ', A + B:1);
   Writeln('Inverse= ',1 / (A + B):3:2);
End.


─[■]────────────────────── Output ──────────────────────2─[↑]─
10
Enter an integer number :
20
Sum=     20


─ ◄                                                         ► ─
 F1 Help   ↑↓→← Scroll  F10 Menu
```

After we pressed *F8* again we saw the following screen - the results of the second WriteLn() statement.

```
 File  Edit  Search  Run  Compile  Debug  Tools  Options  Window  Help
──────────────────────────── PROG7-1.PAS ──────────────────────────1─
Program EX_7_1;
Uses Crt;
Var
   A, B : Integer;
Begin
   Clrscr;
   WriteLn('Enter an integer number : ');
   ReadLn(A);
   WriteLn('Enter an integer number : ');
   ReadLn(A);
   Writeln('Sum=      ', A + B:1);
   Writeln('Inverse= ',1 / (A + B):3:2);
End.
─[■]───────────────────────── Output ─────────────────────────2=[↑]─
Enter an integer number :
20
Sum=      20
Inverse= 0.05

 F1 Help  ↑↓→← Scroll  F10 Menu
```

The highlight bar had now moved to the final line in the program, to the statement End. Pressing *F8* one final time executed this statement, the program terminated, and we were left with this final screen:

```
 File  Edit  Search  Run  Compile  Debug  Tools  Options  Window  Help
──────────────────────────── PROG7-1.PAS ──────────────────────────1─
Program EX_7_1;
Uses Crt;
Var
   A, B : Integer;
Begin
   Clrscr;
   WriteLn('Enter an integer number : ');
   ReadLn(A);
   WriteLn('Enter an integer number : ');
   ReadLn(A);
   Writeln('Sum=      ', A + B:1);
   Writeln('Inverse= ',1 / (A + B):3:2);
End.
─[■]───────────────────────── Output ─────────────────────────2=[↑]─
Enter an integer number :
20
Sum=      20
Inverse= 0.05

 F1 Help  ↑↓→← Scroll  F10 Menu
```

This shows the second number entered and the results of the program execution. At this point we pressed *Alt+F5* and saw the traditional output screen:

```
Enter an integer number :
10
Enter an integer number :
20
Sum=      20
Inverse= 0.05
```

You've now seen the program running statement by statement, which may have given you some clues as to why we are still getting the wrong result. Before we sort it out, however, we'll show you how to customize your environment even further to help in debugging.

Watching Expressions

The Watch Window

The IDE gives you the ability not only to see the output of the program and the program itself in the edit window, but also to watch the values of the different variables and expressions. To open a **watch window** you do the following:

- ▶ Press *F10*, select the Debug menu and choose Add watch
- ▶ Or press *Ctrl+F7*

Turbo Debugger will open a dialog box where you can type the name of a variable or an expression.

Watching Expressions

In our continuing quest to debug program **EX_7_1,** we decided to use the watch window. Having opened the window the next step was to add the variables to watch. With the window open, we added the variable **A** by typing the letter 'A' in the dialog box. The name of the variable **A** then appears in the window, as shown below:

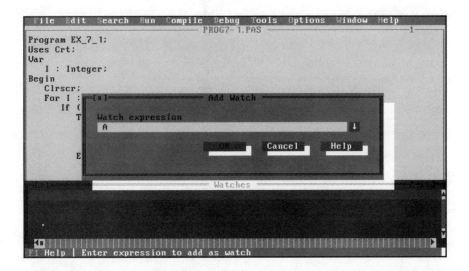

When we pressed *Enter*, the screen changed to show the new Watch window.

The program hadn't been compiled since we opened the watch window, so nothing was known about the variable **A**; therefore the message read Unknown identifier.

With the watch window active, to add another expression you:

▶ Press *Ins.*

The dialog box reappears and you can then type the name of the next variable to watch.

In our program we added the variable **B** and the two expressions **(A + B)** and **1 / (A + B)**:

```
 File  Edit  Search  Run  Compile  Debug  Tools  Options  Window  Help
                      PROG7-1.PAS                              1
 Program EX_7_1;
 Uses Crt;
 Var
    A, B : Integer;
 Begin
    Clrscr;
    WriteLn('Enter an integer number : ');
    ReadLn(A);
    WriteLn('Enter an integer number : ');
    ReadLn(A);
    Writeln('Sum=      ', A + B:1);
    Writeln(' Inverse= ',1 / (A + B):3:2);
 End.

 [■]                         Watches                         2=[↑]
  A: Unknown identifier
  B: Unknown identifier
  A + B: Unknown identifier
  1 / (A + B): Unknown identifier

 F1 Help  F7 Trace  F8 Step  ◄┘ Edit  Ins Add  Del Delete  Alt+F10 Local menu
```

Before we ran the program we could see that both variables and both expressions were marked as Unknown identifiers.

Now that we'd entered all the expressions to watch, we began stepping through the program again. After the first press of the *F8* key, the program compiled, the Begin statement was highlighted, and all the values of the variables and expressions were changed and given default values.

Variables **A** and **B** are of integer type and so they were set to zero. Zero plus zero is zero (no surprises there!) so the expression **(A + B)** is also set to zero. However, it's impossible to divide one by zero so for the time being **1/(A + B)** was described by an appropriate message.

```
  File   Edit   Search   Run   Compile   Debug   Tools   Options   Window   Help
╒═══════════════════════════════ PROG7-1.PAS ══════════════════════════1═══╕
│Program EX_7_1;                                                            │
│Uses Crt;                                                                  │
│Var                                                                        │
│   A, B : Integer;                                                         │
│Begin                                                                      │
│   Clrscr;                                                                 │
│   WriteLn('Enter an integer number : ');                                  │
│   ReadLn(A);                                                              │
│   WriteLn('Enter an integer number : ');                                  │
│   ReadLn(A);                                                              │
│   Writeln('Sum=      ', A + B:1);                                         │
│   Writeln('Inverse= ',1 / (A + B):3:2);                                   │
│End.                                                                       │
│                                                                           │
╒[■]═════════════════════════════ Watches ════════════════════════════2═[↑]═╕
│A: 0                                                                       │
│B: 0                                                                       │
│A + B: 0                                                                   │
│1 / (A + B): Invalid floating point operation                             │
│◄■                                                                       ►│
  F1 Help  F7 Trace  F8 Step  ◄─┘ Edit   Ins Add   Del Delete  Alt+F10 Local menu
```

We continued to step through the program by pressing *F8*. At the first
WriteLn() statement we entered the number **10** and immediately, the values of
the variables changed. **A** now held the value **10**, **B** still held the default value
0 and the expressions **(A + B)** and **1 / (A + B)** were re-evaluated to **10**
and **0.1**.

When we stepped through the next two statements and entered 20 we got a
big clue as to the failing of the program.

```
  File   Edit   Search   Run   Compile   Debug   Tools   Options   Window   Help
╒═══════════════════════════════ PROG7-1.PAS ══════════════════════════1═══╕
│Program EX_7_1;                                                            │
│Uses Crt;                                                                  │
│Var                                                                        │
│   A, B : Integer;                                                         │
│Begin                                                                      │
│   Clrscr;                                                                 │
│   WriteLn('Enter an integer number : ');                                  │
│   ReadLn(A);                                                              │
│   WriteLn('Enter an integer number : ');                                  │
│   ReadLn(A);                                                              │
│   Writeln('Sum=      ', A + B:1);                                         │
│   Writeln('Inverse= ',1 / (A + B):3:2);                                   │
│End.                                                                       │
│                                                                           │
╒[■]═════════════════════════════ Watches ════════════════════════════2═[↑]═╕
│A: 20                                                                      │
│B: 0                                                                       │
│A + B: 20                                                                  │
│1 / (A + B): 0.05                                                          │
│◄■                                                                       ►│
  F1 Help  F7 Trace  F8 Step  ◄─┘ Edit   Ins Add   Del Delete  Alt+F10 Local menu
```

You can see in the Watch window that **A** now holds the value **20**. This is the second number so it should have been assigned to **B**. Of course, when you look closely at the program you can see that the second ReadLn() statement had been written incorrectly. It should have read:

```
Readln(B);
```

So we found the logic error in the program. Correcting it and running it again with A = 10 and B = 20 we got the correct results.

```
Enter an integer number :
10
Enter an integer number :
20
Sum=     30
Inverse= 0.03
```

Dividing by Zero

However, our work wasn't quite finished! We ran the program again and entered zero each time we were asked to enter our integer values. As a result we got the error message on the next page.

```
  File  Edit  Search  Run  Compile  Debug  Tools  Options  Window  Help
┌─[■]──────────────────────── PROG7-1.PAS ══════════════════════1═[↕]─┐
│ Error 200: Division by zero.                                        ▲
│Uses Crt;                                                            ▓
│Var                                                                  ▓
│   A, B : Integer;                                                   ▓
│Begin                                                               
│   Clrscr;                                                          
│   WriteLn('Enter an integer number : ');                          
│   ReadLn(A);                                                      
│   WriteLn('Enter an integer number : ');                          
│   ReadLn(B);                                                      
│   Writeln('Sum=      ', A + B:1);                                 
│_  Writeln('Inverse= ',1 / (A + B):3:2);                           
│End.                                                                ▓
│                                                                    ▼
│══ 12:1 ═══◄▐█████████████████████████████████████████████████▌►═══
└────────────────────────────────────────────────────────────────────┘
  F1 Help  F2 Save  F3 Open  Alt+F9 Compile  F9 Make  Alt+F10 Local menu
```

The program failed because we tried to divide by zero, and Turbo Pascal automatically located the statement that caused the error.

On most occasions the statement

```
Writeln('Inverse= ',1 / (A + B):3:2);
```

will give a valid result, but not when you try to divide one by zero. In this instance Turbo Pascal will halt the program (which isn't much use to us). So to prevent this error we need to include an If statement and test whether A + B = 0. On the next page, we have written the final, robust, and accurate version of the program.

```
Program ex_7_2;
Uses Crt;
Var
   A, B : Integer;
Begin
   Clrscr;
   WriteLn('Enter an integer number : ');
   ReadLn(A);
   WriteLn('Enter an integer number : ');
   ReadLn(B);
   Writeln('Sum=      ', A + B:1);
   If (A + B) = 0
   Then
     Begin
```

```
      Writeln('Zero has no inverse value!');
      End
   Else
      Begin
      Writeln('Inverse= ',1 / (A + B):3:2);
      End;
End.
```

So we successfully debugged our program and removed all three types of error.

Visualizing the Program Execution

Turbo Debugger allows you to see additional information about your program, but it also allows you to see how the control flows through a program. To demonstrate this, type in program **EX_7_3.** This is a simple program which sorts the first ten integer numbers into two groups - odd and even.

```
Program ex_7_3;
Uses Crt;
Var
   I : Integer;
Begin
   Clrscr;
   For I := 1 to 10 do
      If (I mod 2 <> 0)
         Then
             Begin
             WriteLn(I:1,' is odd number');
              End
          Else
             Begin
             WriteLn(I:1,' is even number');
             End;
End.
```

Windows in a Programming World

To gain the full benefit of Turbo Debugger we need to prepare our working environment. As well as the standard editing screen, you should open the output window and the watch window.

To recap, to open an output window:

> Press *F10*, select the Debug menu and then choose Output.

To open a watch window:

> Press *F10*, select the Debug menu and then select Watch.

Selecting and Moving Windows

```
  File  Edit  Search  Run  Compile  Debug  Tools  Options  Window  Help
 ══════════════════════════ PROG7-3.PAS ═══════════════════════════1═
 Program EX_7_3;
 Uses Crt;
 Var
    I : Integer;
 Begin
    Clrscr;
    For I := 1 to 10 do
       If (I mod 2 <> 0)
          Then
             Begin
             WriteLn(I:1,' is odd number');
             End
          Else
             Begin
             WriteLn(I:1,' is even number');
 ═[■]══════════════════════ Watches ═══════════════════════3═[↑]═
                                                                  █
                                                                  █
                                                                  █
                                                                  █
                                                                  █
 ◄█▒▒▒▒▒▒▒▒▒▒▒▒▒▒▒▒▒▒▒▒▒▒▒▒▒▒▒▒▒▒▒▒▒▒▒▒▒▒▒▒▒▒▒▒▒▒▒▒█►█
 F1 Help  F7 Trace  F8 Step  ◄─┘ Edit  Ins Add  Del Delete  Alt+F10 Local menu
```

When you first open the watch window it will hide the output window and both these windows will hide the bottom of the program. So before you start the program, simply rearrange the windows.

Selecting

To move a window you must first **select** it. In the top right-hand corner of each window there is a number. In the IDE, you use this number to select a window by pressing *Alt*+number. To select the edit window press *Alt+1*.

```
  File  Edit  Search  Run  Compile  Debug  Tools  Options  Window  Help
 ═[■]═══════════════════════ PROG7-3.PAS ═══════════════════════1═[↕]═╗
 Program EX_7_3;
 Uses Crt;
 Var
    I : Integer;
 Begin
    Clrscr;
    For I := 1 to 10 do
       If (I mod 2 <> 0)
          Then
             Begin
             WriteLn(I:1,' is odd number');
             End
          Else
             Begin
             WriteLn(I:1,' is even number');
             End;
 End.



 ══ 1:1 ══◄█▒▒▒▒▒▒▒▒▒▒▒▒▒▒▒▒▒▒▒▒▒▒▒▒▒▒▒▒▒▒▒▒▒▒▒▒▒▒█►█
 F1 Help  F2 Save  F3 Open  Alt+F9 Compile  F9 Make  Alt+F10 Local menu
```

Selecting the edit window brings it to the front of the screen and the lines at the edge become doubled. You need to select the Watch window, so press *Alt+3*.

Moving

This is how you move a window you have selected:

> ▶ Press *F10*, select the Window menu then select Size/Move

> ▶ Or press *Ctrl+F5*.

As a result, the lines at the edge become single and yellow. You then use the arrow keys ← ↑ → ↓ to move the window in whichever direction you want. When you are happy that the window is in the right place, press *Enter* to fix the window in that position.

In order to watch program **EX_7_3** we arranged the windows as below:

```
  File   Edit   Search   Run   Compile   Debug   Tools   Options   Window   Help
─────────────────────────── PROG7-3.PAS ───────────────────────────────1──
Program EX_7_3;
Uses Crt;
Var
   I : Integer;
Begin
   Clrscr;
   For I := 1 to 10 do
      If (I mod 2 <> 0)
         Then
            Begin
            WriteLn(I:1,' is odd number');
            End
         Else
            Begin
            WriteLn(I:1,' is even number');
──────────────────────────── Out ┌─[■]══════════════════════════ Watc
 Luke I:\>tp

 Luke I:\>i:\tp\bin\turbo
 Turbo Pascal  Version 7.0  Copyright (c
                                        ◄►░░░░░░░░░░░░░░░░░░░░░░░░░░░░░░░
 F1 Help  F7 Trace  F8 Step  ◄┘ Edit  Ins Add   Del Delete   Alt+F10 Local menu
```

Watching Control

You now need to add the variables to the watch window. The program only contains one variable, **I**, so having selected the watch window, press *Ins* and type I. Your environment should now be setup to watch the program as it runs.

Press *F8* and the program should compile successfully. The first window that will change is the watch window - as soon as we start the program **I** is assigned an arbitrary value. The highlight bar also moves over the reserved word Begin.

When we press *F8* again, we begin the program. The bar moves on down the list of statements and the watch window changes again. This time **I** is given the default value of zero.

```
  File  Edit  Search  Run  Compile  Debug  Tools  Options  Window  Help
──────────────────────────── PROG7-3.PAS ──────────────────────────1──
Program EX_7_3;
Uses Crt;
Var
   I : Integer;
Begin
   Clrscr;
   For I := 1 to 10 do
      If (I mod 2 <> 0)
         Then
            Begin
            WriteLn(I:1,' is odd number');
            End
         Else
            Begin
            WriteLn(I:1,' is even number');
─────────────────────── Out[■]─────────────────────────────────Watc
                                  I: 0
Luke I:\>tp\bin\turbo
Turbo Pascal  Version 7.0  Copyright (c
                                 ◄□▐████████████████████████████████
 F1 Help  F7 Trace  F8 Step  ◄┘ Edit  Ins Add  Del Delete  Alt+F10 Local menu
```

When we press *F8* again the output screen clears as the ClrScr procedure has been called. The highlight bar now sits on the For statement:

```
  File  Edit  Search  Run  Compile  Debug  Tools  Options  Window  Help
─────────────────────────── PROG7-3.PAS ────────────────────────1───
Program EX_7_3;
Uses Crt;
Var
   I : Integer;
Begin
   Clrscr;
   For I := 1 to 10 do
      If (I mod 2 <> 0)
         Then
            Begin
            WriteLn(I:1,' is odd number');
            End
         Else
            Begin
            WriteLn(I:1,' is even number');
─────────────────── Out ─[■]──────────────────────── Watc
                         I: 0

                         ◄□▓▓▓▓▓▓▓▓▓▓▓▓▓▓▓▓▓▓▓▓▓▓▓▓▓▓▓▓▓▓▓▓▓
 F1 Help  F7 Trace  F8 Step  ◄─┘ Edit  Ins Add  Del Delete  Alt+F10 Local menu
```

Now if we press *F8* this changes the value of the variable **I** to 1 as the program starts the For loop. The next time we press *F8*, the program will be controlled by the If statement and the first task the If statement performs is the test. As I = 1,

```
I mod 2 = 1 <> 0
```

so the statement is true. As a result, the program moves to the first WriteLn() statement.

```
  File  Edit  Search  Run  Compile  Debug  Tools  Options  Window  Help
─────────────────────────── PROG7-3.PAS ────────────────────────1───
Program EX_7_3;
Uses Crt;
Var
   I : Integer;
Begin
   Clrscr;
   For I := 1 to 10 do
      If (I mod 2 <> 0)
         Then
            Begin
            WriteLn(I:1,' is odd number');
            End
         Else
            Begin
            WriteLn(I:1,' is even number');
─────────────────── Out ─[■]──────────────────────── Watc
                         I: 1


                         ◄□▓▓▓▓▓▓▓▓▓▓▓▓▓▓▓▓▓▓▓▓▓▓▓▓▓▓▓▓▓▓▓▓▓
 F1 Help  F7 Trace  F8 Step  ◄─┘ Edit  Ins Add  Del Delete  Alt+F10 Local menu
```

Pressing *F8* again we see the bar move to the End in the Then part of the If statement. The WriteLn() statement has been executed, so the output window changes as well.

```
File   Edit   Search   Run   Compile   Debug   Tools   Options   Window   Help
─────────────────────────── PROG7-3.PAS ─────────────────────────1──
Program EX_7_3;
Uses Crt;
Var
   I : Integer;
Begin
   Clrscr;
   For I := 1 to 10 do
      If (I mod 2 <> 0)
         Then
            Begin
            WriteLn(I:1,' is odd number');
            End
         Else
            Begin
            WriteLn(I:1,' is even number');
─────────────────────────── Out ──[■]────────────────── Watc
1 is odd number                      I: 1


                                   ◄□▒▒▒▒▒▒▒▒▒▒▒▒▒▒▒▒▒▒▒▒▒▒▒▒▒▒
F1 Help   F7 Trace   F8 Step   ◄┘ Edit   Ins Add   Del Delete   Alt+F10 Local menu
```

The next *F8* key press moves the bar to the End; in the Else part.

```
File   Edit   Search   Run   Compile   Debug   Tools   Options   Window   Help
─────────────────────────── PROG7-3.PAS ─────────────────────────1──
      If (I mod 2 <> 0)
         Then
            Begin
            WriteLn(I:1,' is odd number');
            End
         Else
            Begin
            WriteLn(I:1,' is even number');
            End;
End.




─────────────────────────── Out ──[■]────────────────── Watc
1 is odd number                      I: 1


                                   ◄□▒▒▒▒▒▒▒▒▒▒▒▒▒▒▒▒▒▒▒▒▒▒▒▒▒▒
F1 Help   F7 Trace   F8 Step   ◄┘ Edit   Ins Add   Del Delete   Alt+F10 Local menu
```

Press *F8* again, and the highlight bar moves back to the If statement and the value of **I** changes to **2**. This is the For loop 'controlling' the program, making it repeat for each value from 1 to 10. The next step is to test the If statement again.

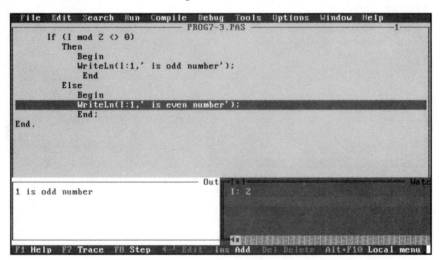

```
File  Edit  Search  Run  Compile  Debug  Tools  Options  Window  Help
                        PROG7-3.PAS                                1
        If (I mod 2 <> 0)
            Then
                Begin
                WriteLn(I:1,' is odd number');
                End
            Else
                Begin
                WriteLn(I:1,' is even number');
                End;
End.
                                Out     [ ]                    Watc
1 is odd number                         I: 2


F1 Help  F7 Trace  F8 Step  ← Edit  Ins Add  Del Delete  Alt+F10 Local menu
```

Now when we test the If statement, I = 2 and

```
I mod 2 = 0
```

so the statement is false. As a result, the highlight bar jumps to the second WriteLn() statement in the Else part.

```
File  Edit  Search  Run  Compile  Debug  Tools  Options  Window  Help
                        PROG7-3.PAS                                1
        If (I mod 2 <> 0)
            Then
                Begin
                WriteLn(I:1,' is odd number');
                End
            Else
                Begin
                WriteLn(I:1,' is even number');
                End;
End.
                                Out     [ ]                    Watc
1 is odd number                         I: 2


F1 Help  F7 Trace  F8 Step  ← Edit  Ins Add  Del Delete  Alt+F10 Local menu
```

When F8 is pressed again, the WriteLn() statement is executed, changing the output screen. The bar moves to highlight the End; statement.

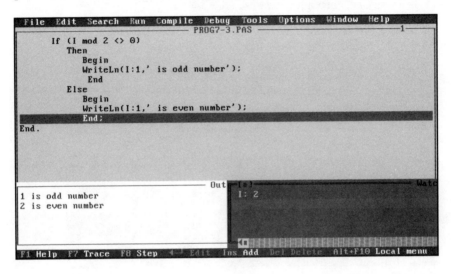

Press *F8* again and the highlight bar moves back to the If statement, the value of **I** changes to **3**, and we begin the whole process again.

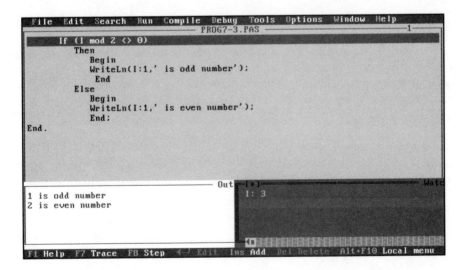

If we keep stepping through the program using F8, the process continues to be repeated. Control jumps between the Then statements and the Else statements as I is increased through to 10.

```
 File  Edit  Search  Run  Compile  Debug  Tools  Options  Window  Help
                          PROG7-3.PAS                                 1
         If (I mod 2 <> 0)
           Then
               Begin
               WriteLn(I:1,' is odd number');
                End
           Else
               Begin
               WriteLn(I:1,' is even number');
               End;
  End.

                               Out  [■]                          Watc
  7 is odd number                    I: 10
  8 is even number
  9 is odd number
  10 is even number

 F1 Help  F7 Trace  F8 Step  ◄┘ Edit  Ins Add  Del Delete  Alt+F10 Local menu
```

As you can see, this gives a very clear indication of which statements are being executed at any one time. This can be invaluable for solving complex logic or run-time errors.

Zooming Windows

It is useful to have all three windows open, but it's difficult to get a good idea of the whole program just seeing the parts of the output screen as we have done in this example. Now that we have finished the program, it would be useful to see the final result. Borland, of course, has thought ahead on this one!

You can use the ↑↓ keys to move up and down through the data in each window. This is all very well, but to be able to see all the output at once, the IDE allows you to zoom a window to full size. To zoom the selected window to full size:

▶ Press *F10*, select the Window menu and then select Zoom

▶ Or press *F5*

```
 File  Edit  Search  Run  Compile  Debug  Tools  Options  Window  Help
═[■]══════════════════════════════Output══════════════════════════2═[↕]═╗
 1 is odd number                                                         █
 2 is even number                                                        
 3 is odd number                                                         
 4 is even number                                                        
 5 is odd number                                                         
 6 is even number                                                        
 7 is odd number                                                         
 8 is even number                                                        
 9 is odd number                                                         
 10 is even number                                                       
                                                                         
                                                                         
                                                                         
                                                                         
                                                                         
                                                                         
                                                                         
                                                                         
                                                                         
 F1 Help  ↑↓→← Scroll  F10 Menu
```

A window can be either zoomed or 'unzoomed' and these keystrokes toggle the state of the window back and forth. To 'unzoom' the window you repeat the same keystrokes:

▶ Press *F10*, select the Window menu and then select Zoom

▶ Or press *F5*

Closing Windows

Remembering the 'any fool can fly but it takes an expert to land' theory, we think it's appropriate that you know how to close windows! This is how you do it:

▶ Press *F10*, select the Window menu and then select (wait for it) Close

▶ Or press *Alt+F3*

And don't forget the Close all option! This does exactly what you would imagine.

Using Breakpoints

You've now seen how you can use Turbo Debugger to check your programs statement by statement, whilst watching the values of the variables change and seeing the output as the program executed the statement. For a long program, or when you are certain that one part of the program is secure, to step through each statement can be as much fun as gargling with hat pins. To deal with this, Turbo Debugger has a further trick up its sleeve - it can set **breakpoints** in your program.

A breakpoint is a designated statement in the program. When you run the program it will stop when control reaches the designated statement. All the previous statements in the program are executed up to, but not including, the designated statement.

We ran program **EX_7_4** to demonstrate this technique. The program asks you to input a number between 1 and 10 and outputs the English word. The program repeats this request until you input a value outside the range.

```
Program ex_7_4;
Uses Crt;
Var
   Number : Integer;
   Error  : Boolean;
Begin
   ClrScr;
   Repeat
      Error := True;
      Write('Enter an integer number from 1 to 10 : ');
      ReadLn(Number);
      Write(Number, ' is ');
      Case Number of
         1  : Write('one');
         2  : Write('two');
         3  : Write('three');
         4  : Write('four');
         5  : Write('five');
         6  : Write('six');
         7  : Write('seven');
         8  : Write('eight');
         9  : Write('nine');
         10 : Write('ten');
         Else
```

```
        Begin
            Write('Wrong data! ');
            Error := False;
        End;
    End {Case};
    If not Error
        Then
            Begin
            WriteLn('Enter again! ');
            End;
    Until Error;
    WriteLn;
End.
```

To set a breakpoint in a program you need to move the cursor to the statement you want to break at, then:

▶ Press *Ctrl+F8*

▶ Or press *F10*, select Debug and then select the Add breakpoint option

Choosing the keystroke will highlight the line marking it as a breakpoint. Choosing the menu item will open a dialog box with 4 further options Condition, Pass Count, File Name and Line Number.

1 In the Condition box you can set a condition which must be true for the breakpoint to take effect.

2 In the Pass Count box you can enter a number for the number of times the condition must be true before the breakpoint takes effect.

3 In the File Name box you can enter a different file name. This will always default to the current file.

4 In the Line Number box you can enter a number for the line where you want to set the breakpoint. This defaults to the current line.

In our program we wanted to stop control before the final test If statement so we set a breakpoint on the statement

```
If not error
```

This statement is now highlighted:

```
File  Edit  Search  Run  Compile  Debug  Tools  Options  Window  Help
[■]============================ PROG7-4.PAS =====================1=[‡]=
          3  :  Write('three');
          4  :  Write('four');
          5  :  Write('five');
          6  :  Write('six');
          7  :  Write('seven');
          8  :  Write('eight');
          9  :  Write('nine');
          10 :  Write('ten');
          Else
             Begin
                Write('Wrong data! ');
                Error := False;
             End;
        End {Case};
        If not Error
        Then
             WriteLn('Enter again! ');
     Until Error;
     WriteLn;
End.

===== 30:7 =====◄■
F1 Help  F2 Save  F3 Open  Alt+F9 Compile  F9 Make  Alt+F10 Local menu
```

To help us watch the execution of the program we also opened the output window and the watch window, rearranged the windows, and added the two variables **number** and **error** to watch.

We then ran the program by pressing *Ctrl+F9* and entered the value 12. The program continued to run until it reached the breakpoint.

```
File  Edit  Search  Run  Compile  Debug  Tools  Options  Window  Help
============================ PROG7-4.PAS =====================1=
          3  :  Write('three');
          4  :  Write('four');
          5  :  Write('five');
          6  :  Write('six');
          7  :  Write('seven');
          8  :  Write('eight');
          9  :  Write('nine');
          10 :  Write('ten');
          Else
             Begin
                Write('Wrong data! ');
                Error := False;
             End;
        End {Case};
        If not Error
                                    = Outpu=[■]============= Wa
  12 is Wrong data!                   Number: 12
                                      Error: False


                                    ◄■
F1 Help  F7 Trace  F8 Step  ◄┘ Edit  Ins Add  Del Delete  Alt+F10 Local menu
```

So instead of repeatedly pressing *F8* you can mark a particular statement and the program will stop when it reaches this breakpoint. When the statement is reached the program stops and Turbo Debugger becomes active again and you can continue your debugging session. For example, you could select the edit window and then press *F8* to step over the last part of the program. Alternatively, you could stop the debugging session altogether by pressing *Ctrl+F2*.

> Pressing *Ctrl+F2* can be done at any point in the session and it resets all debugging so that your next stepping will begin from the first executable statement of the main program.

Clearing a Breakpoint

Once you are satisfied with your program, you'll want to clear the breakpoint. To do so, position the cursor on the breakpoint statement and press *Ctrl+F8* again. You'll notice that the marked line is no longer highlighted.

> There is only one rule in using a breakpoint. You can set a line as a breakpoint if and only if it contains an executable statement. You can't set a line as a breakpoint if it contains a comment, a blank, or a declaration.

Tracing into Program

Up to this point we've considered programs without procedures and functions. The process of debugging programs with sub-programs has its own specific requirements.

Program **EX_7_5** includes a version of the procedure Swap with some errors.

```
Program ex_7_5;
Uses Crt;
Var
   First, Second : Integer;
Procedure Swap(Var A, B : Integer);
Begin{ Swap }
   A     := B;
   B     := A;
End{ Swap };
{──────────────────────────}
Begin
   Clrscr;
   Write('Enter first integer  : ');
   ReadLn(First);
```

```
      Write('Enter second integer : ');
      ReadLn(Second);
      WriteLn('*****Before swap*****');
      WriteLn(First:4, Second:4);
      WriteLn('*****After  swap*****');
      Swap(First, Second);
      WriteLn(First:4, Second:4);
End.
```

We ran the program using the two integer numbers 10 and 20 as input data.

```
Enter first integer  : 10
Enter second integer : 20
*****Before swap*****
  10  20
*****After  swap*****
  20  20
```

You can see that the program gave an incorrect result so we set about debugging the program.

Using the techniques we have learnt so far you would choose the Step Over option for debugging. However, this only allows you to watch the execution of the main program. The execution bar only moves within the main program.

It's fairly clear that the errors are in the procedure, and therefore Turbo Debugger gives you the option of watching the execution of procedures and functions when they are called. This technique is called **tracing**. The difference between stepping and tracing is that tracing moves the execution bar within a procedure or a function when the particular sub-program has been called.

To use tracing:

▶ Press *F10*, select the Run menu and then choose Trace Into

▶ Or press F7

Tracing into Swap

We traced into program **EX_7_5** to debug it. We set up the environment as before and entered the variables **A** and **B** in the watch window.

```
  File  Edit  Search  Run  Compile  Debug  Tools  Options  Window  Help
───────────────────────────── PROG7-5.PAS ─────────────────────────1───
Program EX_7_5;
Uses Crt;
Var
    First, Second : Integer;
Procedure Swap(Var A, B : Integer);
Begin{ Swap }
    A    := B;
    B    := A;
End{ Swap };
{──────────────────────────────────────────────────}
Begin
    Clrscr;
    Write('Enter first integer  : ');
    ReadLn(First);
    Write('Enter second integer : ');
─────────────────────────────── Out
Luke I:\>i:\tp\bin\turbo                 A: Unknown identifier
Turbo Pascal  Version 7.0  Copyright (c  B: Unknown identifier



F1 Help  F7 Trace  F8 Step  ◄┘ Edit  Ins Add  Del Delete  Alt+F10 Local menu
```

We then traced into the program by pressing *F7*. This stepped through the program as though we were pressing *F8*. When program execution reached the procedure call, however, the execution bar 'jumped' into the procedure.

```
  File  Edit  Search  Run  Compile  Debug  Tools  Options  Window  Help
───────────────────────────── PROG7-5.PAS ─────────────────────────1───
Program EX_7_5;
Uses Crt;
Var
    First, Second : Integer;
Procedure Swap(Var A, B : Integer);
Begin{ Swap }
    A    := B;
    B    := A;
End{ Swap };
{──────────────────────────────────────────────────}
Begin
    Clrscr;
    Write('Enter first integer  : ');
    ReadLn(First);
    Write('Enter second integer : ');
─────────────────────────────── Out[■]──────────────────────── Wat
Enter second integer : 20              A: 10
*****Before swap*****                  B: 20
   10  20
*****After   swap*****


F1 Help  F7 Trace  F8 Step  ◄┘ Edit  Ins Add  Del Delete  Alt+F10 Local menu
```

Pressing *F7* we stepped through each statement in the procedure and watched the values of **A** and **B** change.

```
 File  Edit  Search  Run  Compile  Debug  Tools  Options  Window  Help
┌──────────────────────── PROG7-5.PAS ───────────────────────────1───┐
│Program EX_7_5;                                                      │
│Uses Crt;                                                            │
│Var                                                                  │
│    First, Second : Integer;                                         │
│Procedure Swap(Var A, B : Integer);                                  │
│Begin{ Swap }                                                        │
│    A    := B;                                                       │
│    B    := A;                                                       │
│End{ Swap };                                                         │
│{─────────────────────────────────────────────────────────}         │
│Begin                                                                │
│    Clrscr;                                                          │
│    Write('Enter first integer  : ');                               │
│    ReadLn(First);                                                   │
│    Write('Enter second integer : ');                               │
├─────────────────────────────────────── Out ┌─[■]────────── Watc──┐ │
│Enter second integer : 20                    │A: 20                │ │
│*****Before swap*****                        │B: 20                │ │
│    10  20                                   │                     │ │
│*****After  swap*****                        │                     │ │
│                                             ◄■▓▓▓▓▓▓▓▓▓▓▓▓▓▓▓▓▓▓▓▓▓│
└────────────────────────────────────────────┴─────────────────────┘ │
 F1 Help  F7 Trace  F8 Step  ◄┘ Edit  Ins Add  Del Delete  Alt+F10 Local menu
```

You can see that once the statement

```
A := B;
```

has been executed, the values of **A** and **B** are the same and we have lost the value **10**. This is a trivial error in the program, and can be easily remedied by using the additional variable **Temp** to save one of the values.

Having reached this point we stopped tracing into the program (*Ctrl+F2*), selected the edit window (*Alt+1*), and made the necessary changes.

Summary

This chapter has shown the various different errors that you can get in programs, and then shown you various debugging techniques in Turbo Debugger that you can use to correct them.

The three kinds of errors in a program are compile-time, run-time, and logic errors. Compile-time errors are the simplest kind of errors and you can correct them very easily with the help of the Turbo Pascal compiler. Run-time errors will cause your program to crash and as a rule they arise as a result of logic errors in your program. The Turbo Pascal compiler can't help you find these errors, but you'll find the Turbo Debugger will be invaluable.

The Turbo Debugger allows you to step over and trace into programs. Using the step process you can execute the statements of the main program statement by statement. In the same manner the trace process lets you execute not only the statements of the main program, but statements within sub-programs. You can also set breakpoints in programs which allow you to run a program to a certain point.

In addition, the Turbo Debugger allows you to open the output window and the watch window. With these open you can observe the output results and the changes of the given variables as the program executes.

All these add up to a powerful toolbox for fixing programs.

Quiz Questions

1   What are the differences between the three types of program error? Which errors are guaranteed to disappear by the time your program runs?

2   How does Turbo Pascal behave when it encounters a run time error?

3   How do you step through your program as it runs?

4   How could you set up the IDE to keep an eye on the value of interesting variables as you step through your program?

5   What are breakpoints? How are they used?

6   How would you step through a sub-program?

Exercises

It would be almost impossible to provide real exercises for this chapter. We could provide you with buggy programs. However, if you tried to debug them on paper, you wouldn't be using all the neat interactive debugging facilities we've just shown you. If you were to type them in, you would be likely to introduce further bugs (this is nothing personal - it's just a fact of programming life). Worse still, you could spot one or more of the intentional errors as you typed.

What we will do, though, is to encourage you to use the facilities described in this chapter - they really do make programming simpler. For the time being, we suggest that you try the following three pseudo-exercises:

1, **2** and **3**   Use Turbo Pascal's debugging tools to debug your next three buggy programs!

CHAPTER
8

Managing Real World Data

Data types are fundamental to Turbo Pascal. They provide you with a powerful method of maintaining control of your data, and of manipulating that data. We've already met several of the standard simple data types such as integer, real, boolean and char. These allow you to declare variables for most situations involving either numbers or characters, but that ain't all there is to life! Turbo Pascal provides two main ways that you can use types to manage real world data.

The first way is to define your own types in Turbo Pascal. You can define them using the standard types that come with Turbo Pascal. This allows you to be much stricter about the data you are handling and makes your programs much clearer.

The second way that you can model the real world more efficiently in Turbo Pascal is by using **structured** types. Integer, real, boolean and char types are called simple types because variables of these types can only hold a single value at any one time. Variables of structured type can hold several values at any one time. In this chapter we'll introduce you to two structured types: array and record. An array is a collection of values each of the same type, and a record can contain values of different types.

In this chapter we'll cover:

- Defining your own type, including ordinals, sub-ranges and enumerated types

- Arrays, including multi-dimensional arrays and sorting and searching arrays

- Records, including the With statement

- Constant arrays and arrays of records

Defining Your Own Type

Below is a picture of a standard program showing the structure of a Turbo Pascal program. In this first section we're concerned with the one section we have not yet introduced - type definition.

Program Heading
Program   *Prog_Identifier;*

Uses Clause
Uses
        unit_Identifier(s);

Label Declaration
Label
            Label_Identifier(s);

Constant Declaration
Const
        Const_Identifier(s) = Value(s);

Type Definition
Type
        Type_Identifier(s) = Type_Definition(s);

Variable Declaration
Var
        Variable_Identifier(s) : Type_Identifier(s);

Procedures and Functions
Procedure *Procedure_Identifier;*

Procedure Body

Function *Function_Identifier;*

Function Body

Begin

Main Program Block

End.

Type - Definition

To define a new type you add a section to your program with the following structure:

```
Type
    Type_Identifier  =  Type_Definition
```

Where Type is the reserved word, *Type_identitifer* is a legal identifier and *type_definiton* is an expression that defines the new type.

You define the new type using Turbo Pascal's standard types and any types you have already defined in your program. The data you can store in your new type and the operations you can perform on it are then derived from the standard types upon which they are based. Once you've defined a new type, you use the new type identifier when you declare variables of this new type.

The simple example below defines a new type **whole_number**. This has all the same properties as the type integer.

```
Program Ex_8_1;
Uses CRT;
{Define the new type}
Type
    Whole_Number = Integer;
Const
    Divisor = 2;
Var
    Dividend : Whole_Number;
Begin
    Write('Enter a whole number: ');
    Readln(Dividend);
{Use an operation for the base type}
    If (Dividend mod Divisor = 0)
            Then
                Begin
                Writeln('You entered an even number');
                End
            Else
                Begin
                Writeln('You entered an odd number');
                End;
End.
```

You'll often use this new technique to define **enumerated** types or **sub-range** types. Both of these rely on simple **ordinal** types. Having introduced three new concepts in one sentence we'll now explain what we mean!

Ordinal Types

As we said in Chapter 5, a type is ordinal if it is a **sequence** of **distinct ordered** elements. Char, boolean and integer are all ordinal types.

➤ The values of char type are all ASCII characters. These can be arranged in order, according to their ASCII value.

➤ The values of boolean type are simply **true** and **false** (which are quite distinct in computing).

➤ The values of integer type are the whole numbers from -32,768 through 32,768.

Because they are distinct and ordered, you can associate each element of an ordinal type with a whole number by arranging all the elements in sequence. This whole number is called the **ordinal** value of that element. In Turbo Pascal, except for integers, the first element has the ordinal value 1, the second element has the ordinal value 2, and so on. For integers, the ordinal value is the number itself. To find the ordinal value of an element you use a function you already know - ord()

Sub-Ranges - Definition

A sub-range is a range of values from an ordinal type.

> You define a sub-range by specifying the smallest and largest value of the sub-range, separated by 2 periods.
>
> *Lowest_Value .. Highest_Value*

As we saw in Chapter 5, you can use sub-ranges in the Case statement, and there are other occasions when they come in handy, as we'll see later in the chapter. One common use is to define a type when you want to place restrictions on the data that can be stored in a particular variable. In the fragment of a program below, sub-ranges are used to define a type for the musical scale (the characters A through G) and to define the values of the type **age_range** to be any number from 0 through 150.

```
Type
    Musical_Scale = 'A' .. 'G';
    Age_Range = 0 .. 150;
Var
    Note : Musical_Scale;
    Exact_Age, Guessed_age : Age_Range;
```

Since we have defined the variable **note** to be of type **musical_scale**, it can only be assigned the characters '**A**' through '**G**'. As this type is based on the char type, variables of **musical_scale** type can be operated on by any function that would take char type variables.

Exact_age and **Guessed_age** are both of type **age_range** so they are limited to the values 0 through 150. They can be used wherever an integer type variable could be used.

Enumerated Types

Enumerated types are a real strength of Turbo Pascal. They allow you to collect together a series of related elements and define them as a type.

Enumerated Types - Definition

To define an enumerated type you declare the complete list of values, between parentheses and separated by commas.

```
Type
    Type_Identifier  = (Value_1, ..., Value_n);
```

Enumerated types are ordinal types and the ordinal value of any element is defined by its position in the list.

Example: Days of the Week

Enumerated types can be used to make your programs more readable and understandable. You can also have stricter control over the values stored in variables. As an example, declaring **days_of_week** as a type allows us to make the later Case statement much more readable.

```
Type
    Days_of_week = (Monday, Tuesday, Wednesday, Thursday, Friday, Saturday,
                    Sunday);
Var
    Day : Days_of_week;
```

Later in the program you can use this type to select which message to output.

```
    Case Day of
        Monday .. Friday
            Begin
            Writeln('Go to Work!');
            End
```

```
        Saturday, Sunday
            Begin
            Writeln('Put your feet up');
            End
```

> When you use enumerated types, you'll encounter one significant drawback
> fairly quickly. The values defined for enumerated types can't be used in
> WriteLn() or ReadLn() statements. In the above example **WriteLn(Day)**
> would cause a compile-time error because the value stored in **Day** is not a
> string and can't be output.

Structured Data Types

We have already used a number of simple data types such as integer, real,
boolean and char. These are called simple types because they can only take a
single value at any one time. To deal with situations where you wish to handle
similar types of data, Turbo Pascal includes structured data types. We will now
look at two of these types - array and record.

When you use structured types you should define a new type based on the
structured type and then declare variables of this new type. This will make
your programs more robust, and will also allow you to pass variables into
procedures.

Arrays

Arrays are a structured data type, and as such can hold more than one value,
but the question is: why do we need them?

The Value of Arrays

Arrays are useful if you need to handle a collection of similar items of data.
Imagine you'd collected the average temperatures for each month for the last
year in your native city. You'd have twelve real values. To get anything like the
average, or the maximum, you'd want to be able to manipulate all 12 values.
You could easily declare twelve variables of real type:

```
Var
    Temp_1, Temp_2, Temp_3, Temp_4, Temp_5, Temp_6,
    Temp_7, Temp_8, Temp_9, Temp_10, Temp_11 , Temp_12 : Real;
```

Each variable can hold only one value, and having assigned the values to each variable you can then manipulate them. This may sound a bit arduous, but it's still possible. However, imagine if you had 10 years worth of data with 120 values, or similar data for 10 other cities, or similar data plus the average rainfall for each month. Arrays provide you with a much better way of handling this sort of data.

The Structure of an Array

The basic structure of an array is akin to that of a table. For the moment we'll consider a table with just one row.

	Jan	Feb	Mar	Apr	May	June	July	Aug	Sep	Oct	Nov	Dec
Temperature												

Each cell stores one value, whilst the array name refers to the whole table.

Array - Definition

To define an array type in Turbo Pascal you use the following structure:

```
Type
   Array_Type_Ident =Array (lower_limit . Upper_limit ) Of type_Ident;
Var
     Array_ident_1, Array_Ident_2 : Array_Type_Ident;
```

Where Array is a reserved word, *Array_Type_Ident* is the name for the new type, and *Type_Ident* is the type of the values. *lower_limit* ..
Upper_limit can be any sub-range. *Array_ident_1, Array_Ident_2* are the identifiers for any variables of the new array type with the identifier *Array_Type_Ident..*

The sub-range defines the number of items in the array. This number is fixed in the definition and can't be changed during the program execution. Also notice that *Type_Ident* is the type for all the items of the array. All items in an array have the same type.

> The number of items in an array is equal to **Upper_limit** - **Lower_limit** + 1

Using Individual Items of an Array

To identify an individual item in an array, you write the array identifier followed by the number of the position of the item enclosed by square brackets. This number is called the **index** of the item.

For instance having defined **Weather** as an array type, and then declared **Temp** as an array of **weather** type as below:

```
Type
     Weather = Array[1 .. 12] of Real;
Var
     Temp : Weather
```

the temperature in month 6 is identified by the variable **Temp[6]**.

Don't get carried away though. You can only access values **Temp[1]** through **Temp[12]**. Looking for **Temp[13]** will get you nowhere - nor would looking for **Temp['A']**. Both these will give you compile-time errors

How to Input and Output Arrays

Before using an array you must assign values to each of the items. You can use assignment statements to do this. For an array such as this one:

```
Type
    ArrayType = Array[1..10] of Integer;
Var
    ArrayName: ArrayType;
```

you could write a sequence of assignment statements such as this:

```
ArrayName[2] := 21;
ArrayName[1] := 5;
ArrayName[10] := 7;
```

However, this is a bit of a tedious method!

A much more efficient way of assigning values is to use a For statement and use the index to select the individual item.

```
For I := 1 to 10 do
Begin
   Write('Enter item ', I:1, ' of the array : ');
   ReadLn(ArrayName[I]);
End;
```

The loop above stores each newly entered value into the next item of the array. As the value of I increases from 1 through 10 each item of the array is assigned a value.

Manipulating Information in Arrays

When you've input the data in your array you'll need to do something with the information. Two of the most common ways you will manipulate values in arrays are **searching** and **sorting**.

Searching for a Specific Value

The following example shows you how to find an item in an array which has a certain property. In this case, the certain property we're looking for is the item with the hottest value.

Example: Finding the Maximum Temperature

To find the hottest month this year in our city using the array, we start by making the assumption that the first item of the array holds the maximum value in the array. As a result of this assumption we can copy the value in **Temp[1]** into another variable called **Hottest**.

We can then test this assumption by comparing the value of the next item of the array with the value in **Hottest**. There are two possibilities:

1 The value in **Hottest** is greater than the value of the next item and our assumption is valid.

2 The value in **Hottest** is less than the value of the next item and our assumption is invalid.

In the first case we don't need to do anything. But in the second case we need to make the fresh assumption that this next item is the maximum temperature and so copy this new value into **Hottest**.

If we repeat this process for all the elements in the array, at the end the value in **Hottest** will be the maximum temperature. Program **EX_8_2** implements these ideas.

```
Program Ex_8_2;
Uses Crt;
Type
    Weather = Array[1..12] of Real;
Var
    Temp    : Weather;
    Cmpnent : Integer;
    Hottest : Real;
Begin
    ClrScr;
    For Cmpnent := 1 to 12 do
        Begin
        Write('Enter temperature ', Cmpnent, ': ');
        ReadLn(Temp[Cmpnent]);
        End;
    Hottest := Temp[1];
    For Cmpnent := 2 to 12 do
        If Temp[Cmpnent] > Hottest
            Then
                Begin
                Hottest := Temp[Cmpnent];
                End;
WriteLn('Hottest temperature is ', Hottest:5:2);
End.
```

Firstly, we input the temperatures and store them as separate items of an array. The Write() statement uses the index of each item to ask for the temperatures in order. We then assign the value of the first item to **Hottest** (this was our original assumption) and then test the next 11 items. Notice that the For loop only runs from items 2 through 12, as we don't have to re-test the first value.

Example: Is There Anybody in There?

Let's look at how to search an array for a specific value. (You could use this program if you'd stored your friends' names in an array and you wanted to check whether you'd already entered Bob's name.)

Clearly, the first thing to do is to look through all the items (names) in the array and check whether the value of each item is **Bob**. Therefore, we can include the following statement:

```
If Names[I] = 'Bob'
```

We need to repeat this test until we find Bob's name, or until we come to the end of the items in the array. This requires a Repeat ... Until statement with the final condition testing two clauses in the statement:

```
Until (Names[Index] = 'Bob') or (Index = 10);
```

We've assumed only 10 names, but that's because we're lonely people. In the Repeat loop we'll need to go through each item in the array. To do this we will have to step the index up by one for each pass through the loop.

```
Repeat
      Index := Index + 1;
Until (Names[Index] = 'Bob') or (Index = 10);
```

We should give the user a message when the process is successful, and it would also be useful to tell them the index of the item which contains Bob's name. To do this we can use an If statement:

```
Repeat
      Index := Index + 1;
      Found := (Names[Index] = 'Bob');
      If Found
         Then
            Begin
            Bob_index := Index;
            End;
Until (Found) or (Index = 10);
```

We've also replaced the expression

```
(Names[Index] = 'Bob')
```

with a new variable **Found** so that we can record whether we were successful in our search. **Found** is of boolean type, so it can have the values **True** or **False**.

By adding a section to accept your input the program becomes **EX_8_3** below.

```
Program Ex_8_3;
Uses Crt;
Type
   NamesType          = Array[1..10] of String;
Var
   Names              : NamesType;
   Index, Bob_index   : Integer;
   Found              : Boolean;
Begin
{Initialize the variables}
   Index := 0;
   Found := False;
{Enter a list of 10 names}
   ClrScr;
   Write('Enter 10 names ');
   For Index := 1 to 10 do
      Begin
      ReadLn(Names[Index]);
      End;
{Reset the counter to zero}
   Index := 0;
{Test each value to find Bob's name}
   Repeat
      Index := Index + 1;
      Found := (Names[Index] = 'Bob');
{If Bob's name is found save the index}
      If Found
         Then
            Begin
            Bob_index := Index;
            End;
Until (Found) or (Index = 10);
{Let the user know what the result was}
If Found
      Then
         Begin
         Writeln('Bob''s your uncle ');
         Writeln('Bob is number ', Bob_Index:2,  ' in your list');
         End
      Else
         Begin
         Write('Wot, No Bob! ');
         End
End.
```

Sorting Arrays

Sorting the data in an array makes finding information a much quicker process. As your programs progress you'll find yourself sorting and re-sorting data very frequently. Because of the importance of sorting you'll find there are many different algorithms associated with the process. We're going to consider just two of them. In each case, we'll use an algorithm to sort the array into descending order with the largest value first and the lowest value last.

Selection Sorting

The first method we'll use will find the maximum value within an array and swap this value with the first item of the array. We then disregard the first item of the array which now has the highest value. The next step is to swap the second highest value with the existing second item, and so on.

In order to write the program, assume that some swaps have already been done and consider the items of the array numbers K through N. From our program above we know how to find the maximum value from these items. We assume the Kth item is the current maximum value and initialize the index to K:

```
Max := A[K];
Ind := K;
```

From here you can find the maximum value and the number of the item which contains that maximum value:

```
For I := K + 1 to N do
   If Max < A[I]
      Then
         Begin
         Max := A[I];
         Ind := I;
         End;
```

The last step is to swap the value of the Kth item with value of `A[Ind]` which now holds the maximum value:

```
Temp   := A[Ind];
A[Ind]:= A[K];
A[K]   := Temp;
```

As a result you get the following program fragment:

```
Max := A[K];
Ind := K;
For I := K + 1 to N do
   If Max < A[I]
     Then
        Begin
        Max := A[I];
        Ind := I;
        End;
   Temp   := A[Ind];
   A[Ind]:= A[K];
   A[K]   := Temp;
```

So this makes the value in the Kth position of the array the maximum value of the Kth through the Nth values. Now if we repeat this process for K equal to 1 through N-1 we will complete the process, so it's a simple step to create the outer For loop. The part we've already written can simply be inserted into the body of the outer loop. As a result you'll get the following fragment of program:

```
For K := 1 to N - 1 do
   Begin
   Max := A[K];
   Ind := K;
   For I := K + 1 to N do
     If Max < A[I]
        Then
           Begin
           Max := A[I];
           Ind := I;
           End;
   Temp   := A[Ind];
   A[Ind]:= A[K];
   A[K]   := Temp;
   End;
```

So the complete version of the program is:

```
Program Ex_8_4;
Uses Crt;
Const
   N = 10;
Type
   IntArray = Array[1..N] of Integer;
Var
   A                     : IntArray;
   I, K, Max, Temp, Ind : Integer;
Begin
   ClrScr;
{ Input array }
   WriteLn('***** Input  array *****');
   For I := 1 to N do
      Begin
      Write('Enter component ', I:1, ' of the array : ');
      ReadLn(A[I]);
      End;
   WriteLn('***** Entered  array *****');
   For I := 1 to N do
      Write(A[I]:4);
   WriteLn;
   WriteLn('***** Intermediate arrays *****');
   For K := 1 to N - 1 do
      Begin
      Max := A[K];
      Ind := K;
      For I := K + 1 to N do
         If Max < A[I]
            Then
               Begin
               Max := A[I];
               Ind := I;
               End;
      Temp  := A[Ind];
      A[Ind]:= A[K];
      A[K]  := Temp;
      For I := 1 to N do
         Write(A[I]:4);
      WriteLn;
   End;
{ Output array }
   WriteLn('***** Sorted array *****');
   For I := 1 to N do
      Write(A[I]:4);
   WriteLn;
End.
```

The program not only prints out the original array and the sorted result, but it also shows you the intermediate states of the array so you can watch how the array is changed step-by-step.

```
Enter component 1 of the array : 69
Enter component 2 of the array : 93
Enter component 3 of the array : 70
Enter component 4 of the array : 61
Enter component 5 of the array : 86
Enter component 6 of the array : 90
Enter component 7 of the array : 88
Enter component 8 of the array : 57
Enter component 9 of the array : 39
Enter component 10 of the array : 40
***** Entered   array *****
  69  93  70  61  86  90  88  57  39  40
***** Intermediate arrays *****
  93  69  70  61  86  90  88  57  39  40
  93  90  70  61  86  69  88  57  39  40
  93  90  88  61  86  69  70  57  39  40
  93  90  88  86  61  69  70  57  39  40
  93  90  88  86  70  69  61  57  39  40
  93  90  88  86  70  69  61  57  39  40
  93  90  88  86  70  69  61  57  39  40
  93  90  88  86  70  69  61  57  39  40
  93  90  88  86  70  69  61  57  40  39
***** Sorted array *****
  93  90  88  86  70  69  61  57  40  39
```

Bubble Sorting

Our second means of sorting uses a different method. Assume we have the following values:

3, 5, 2, 6, 8.

To these values we are going to apply the simple rule:

'If the value of an item is less than its right neighbor, swap values. Otherwise do nothing'.

We then go back to the beginning of the values and repeat this rule. We keep on doing this until no values change places.

Let's see what happens with the values above. The first value is less than the second so swap them:

5, 3, 2, 6, 8.

Now compare the second and the third values. The second value is greater than third so do nothing and move on to compare the third and fourth values. These should be swapped and we get the values below:

5, 3, 6, 2, 8.

Now the fourth is less than the fifth value so we need to swap. At the end of this first application the values have become:

5, 3, 6, 8, 2.

Applying the rule above the values change as follows:

5, 6, 3, 8, 2
5, 6, 8, 3, 2.
6, 5, 8, 3, 2
6, 8, 5, 3, 2
8, 6, 5, 3, 2.

You can see that after each repetition of the process, the current smallest value is set in the right-most position. The process of numbers moving through the body of other numbers is likened to a bubble in liquid - hence the name.

Implementing the Algorithm

Let's implement the method. The processes of comparisons and swaps can be written as follows:

```
For I := 1 to N - 1 do
   If A[I] < A[I + 1]
      Then
         Begin
         Temp       := A[I];
         A[I]       := A[I + 1];
         A[I + 1]  := Temp;
         End;
```

The For statement executes these processes for all pairs of numbers. The process must now return to the beginning of the list, and be repeated at most N - 1 times. This creates the outer For loop:

```
For K := 1 to N - 1 do
Begin
   For I := 1 to N -1 do
      If A[I] < A[I + 1]
         Then
            Begin
            Temp       := A[I];
            A[I]       := A[I + 1];
            A[I + 1]   := Temp;
            End;
End;
```

The complete program is shown below. Again, it's also designed to output the intermediate information.

```
Program Ex_8_5;
Uses Crt;
Const
   N = 10;
Type
   IntArray = Array[1..N] of Integer;
Var
   A                 : IntArray;
   I, K, Temp, Ind : Integer;
Begin
   ClrScr;
{ Input array }
   WriteLn('***** Input  array *****');
   For I := 1 to N do
      Begin
      Write('Enter component ', I:1, ' of the array : ');
      ReadLn(A[I]);
      End;
{Show the entered values first}
   WriteLn('***** Entered  array *****');
   For I := 1 to N do
      Begin
      Write(A[I]:4);
      End;
   WriteLn;
{Heading for the intermediate output}
   WriteLn('***** Intermediate arrays *****');
{The Bubble Sort}
   For K := 1 to N - 1 do
```

```
   Begin
     For I := 1 to N -1 do
       Begin
        If A[I] < A[I + 1]
           Then
              Begin
              Temp       := A[I];
              A[I]       := A[I + 1];
              A[I + 1]   := Temp;
              End;
       End;
       {During the sort output the intermediate values}
       For I := 1 to N do
          Begin
          Write(A[I]:4);
          End;
       WriteLn;
   End;
{ Output array }
   WriteLn('***** Sorted array *****');
   For I := 1 to N do
      Begin
      Write(A[I]:4);
      End;
   WriteLn;
End.
```

Multidimensional Arrays

Arrays aren't restricted to just one-dimension. If, for instance, you had collected the figures for rainfall as well as temperature for each month then you can visualize an array with the structure opposite to store the information.

Weather	Jan	Feb	Mar	Apr	May	June	July	Aug	Sep	Oct	Nov	Dec
Temperature												
Rainfall												

To declare a two-dimensional array type **data** you need to define the second dimension using another sub-range between the [ ] as below

```
Type
     Data = Array [1..2, 1..12] of real;
Var
     Weather : Data;
```

You can see from the table that the type has 2 rows and 12 columns. To identify an individual item you now need to write two coordinates. For example, if you write

```
Weather[2,4]
```

the reference is to the fourth item in the second row (April rainfall). The first index refers to the first range and the second index refers to second range so if you tried to write

```
Weather[4,2]
```

or

```
Weather[2,-4]
```

Turbo Pascal would give you compile-time errors.

Multi-dimensional Processing

To process a multi-dimensional array you need to use nested For statements. For example, if you need to input the items of the **Weather** array you would need to use the following code:

```
For First_Index := 1 to 2 do
   For Second_index := 1 to 12 do
      Begin
      Write('Enter Weather[', First_Index:1, ',', Second_index:1, '] : ');
      ReadLn(Weather[First_Index,Second_index]);
      End;
```

This fragment of program allows you to enter the items of the array row by row.

The way the nested loop works is to set the first value of the loop parameter **First_index** as **1** and then execute the whole of the nested loop. As a result **Second_index** steps through the values from **1** to **12** and the following items will be entered **Weather[1,1]**, **Weather[1,2]**, ..., **Weather[1,12]**. After that, the nested loop finishes and the loop parameter **First_index** increases its value to **2**. From here, the process of the items being entered continues with the second row being input.

Records

Arrays Vs Records

An array is a very useful data structure. But it has an obvious disadvantage. All items of an array must be of the same type. In real life, you'll want to describe groups of related items of different types. In describing a person, for example, their name would be a string type, whilst their age needs to be stored as an integer type.

A record is a structured data type that allows you to mix 'n' match types. This is the essential difference between arrays and records. You could say that records are a more general version of arrays.

Cutting a Record - Definition

To declare variables based on your record type you need the structure below:

```
Type
    Record_Ident = Record
        Field_Ident_1 : Type_ident_1;
        ...
        Field_Ident_n : Type_ident_n;
    End;
Var
    Var_Ident_1, Var_Ident_2 : Record_Ident;
```

Where Record is a reserved word, Record_ident and the Field_idents are valid identifiers and the type_idents are valid types. Field is the term used to describe the 'internal' items in a record. To declare fields of the same type, the Field_idents should be seperated by commas. To finalise the declaration of a record type, you must include an End; statement (complete with semi-colon).

Var_Ident_1 and Var_Ident_2 are declared as variables of Record_ident type.

An Example Record

As an example, to declare a record type for addresses you could write the following:

```
Type
   Address = Record
      House_number : Integer;
      Street_name, City_name : String;
      State_name    : String[2];
      Zip_code      : Integer;
   End;
```

House_number, **Street_name**, **City_name**, **State_name**, and **Zip_code** are all fields of the record type **Address**.

Field Designators

If, later in the program, we wrote:

```
Var
     Bob_address, Mary_address : Address;
```

then both of the variables **Bob_address** and **Mary_address** would be of **address** type. This would allow us to store the complete details of each address in the record fields.

To indicate each field for each variable you use **field designators**:

```
Bob_address.House_number := 27;
Bob_address.Street_name   := 'Headline Road';
Bob_address.City_name     := 'Santa Monica';
Bob_address.State_name    := 'CA';
Bob_address.Zip_code      := 93247;
```

A field designator consists of the variable identifier, followed by a period, followed by the field identifier as in **Variable_ident.Field_Ident**.

This is useful if you want to identify an individual field, but can be cumbersome when trying to manipulate the whole record. As an alternative, Turbo Pascal provides you with the With ... Do statement.

The With Statement

The structure of a With ... Do statement is as follows:

With *Rec_Var_ident* Do
Begin
   Statement_1;
   ...
   Statement_n;
End;

Where *Rec_Var_ident* is the identifier for the record variable and With, Do, Begin and End are reserved words. The statements can be any legal Turbo Pascal statements.

Assigning Values to Records

By using the With ... Do statement you can rewrite the above assignment statements in a more convenient way.

```
With Bob_Address do
Begin
   House_number  := 27;
   Street_name   := 'Headline Road';
   City_name     := 'Santa Monica';
   State_name    := 'CA';
   Zip_code      := 93247;
End;
```

Constant Arrays and Records

If you have a collection of similar constant values you can store those constant values as a single array (if the values are all of the same type) or record (if the values are of different type).

For instance, having defined the array or record type **struc_type** with *n* items or fields you then declare the constant as follows:

Const
  Const_Ident : *Struc_type* = (*Const_value_1*, ... , *Const_value_n*);

Const is the reserved word and *Const_Ident* is the identifier for the constant array (or record) and *Const_value_1* to *Const_value_n* is the list of values.

Example Program

Let's write a program to calculate the number of days between two dates in the twentieth century. We'll ask the user to enter two dates as a string in the form MM-DD-YY.

The first step is to convert the string into integer values. Next, we need to calculate the number of days from 1 January 1900 to the entered date. This is then repeated for the second date. The difference between these two values is the number we're looking for.

To store the dates we need to define **DateType** as a record type with three fields: **Day**, **Month**, and **Year** each of integer type. We then need to declare two variables: **Date1** and **Date2**:

```
Type
    DateType = Record
                  Day   : Integer;
                  Month : Integer;
                  Year  : Integer;
              End;
Var
      Date1, Date2 : DateType;
```

And, of course, we also need a string variable in the program:

```
Str_1 : String;
```

Now we're set up ready to perform the first step, converting a date from string format to record format. We do this using the string procedure Val() and a With statement:

```
With Date1 do
   Begin
      Val(Copy(Str_1, 1, 2), Month, Error_code);
      Val(Copy(Str_1, 4, 2), Day,   Error_code);
      Val(Copy(Str_1, 7, 2), Year,  Error_code);
   End; { With }
```

After the conversion the fields **Date1.Month**, **Date1.Day**, and **Date1.Year** will hold the corresponding integer values, and you can then manipulate them. The variable **Error_code** is redundant in this program.

Now we need to calculate the number of days from 1 January 1900 to the first entered date and assign this value to the variable **No_days_1**. Let's divide this step into some sub-steps.

1   You know the whole number of years from 1900 to the entered year. This is the value of the variable **Date1.Year**. Each year contains 365 days so:

```
With Date1 do
   Begin
   No_days_1 := Year * 365;
   End;
```

But we also need to consider leap years so we add the statements:

```
With Date1 do
If Month <= 2
   Then
      Begin
      Year := Year - 1;
      End;
No_days_1 := No_days_1 + Year div 4;
```

If the month in **Date1.month** is January or February we need to discard the current year. The additional days caused by a leap year are only added after February is over. The last statement in the sequence calculates the number of leap years among any given number of years which will also be the extra number of days, and adds this value to the previously calculated value in the variable **No_days_1**.

2   Now we need to look at the variable **Date1.Month**. To calculate the number of days which must be added to **No_days_1** you need to define the following constant array:

```
Type
 MonthType = Array[1..12] of Integer;
Const
 Curr_Day : MonthType = (0, 31, 59, 90, 120, 151, 181,212, 243, 273, 304, 334);
```

The list of values is the number of days from the beginning of any year to the end of any given month. For example, if the value of the variable `Date1.Month` is `3`, then January and February have been and gone and you can add 59 days (31 days in January and 28 days in February) to the sum. So, `Curr_Day[Month]` = `CurrDay[3]` = `59.`

The assignment statement

```
With Date1 do
Begin
No_days_1 := No_days_1 + Curr_day[Month];
End;
```

adds the corresponding number of days to the variable `No_days_1`.

3 Now we need to process the variable `Date1.Day`. This is easy-peasey. Simply add the value of this variable to the value of the variable `No_days_1`:

```
With Date1 do
Begin
No_days_1 := No_days_1 + Day;
End;
```

So this gives the number of days from 1 January 1900 to the first date. We can repeat the same process for the second date. The last step then is to print out the number of days between the two dates.

```
Write('The number of days between two dates : ');
WriteLn(No_days_2 - No_days_1);
```

And that's it! The complete program is shown in Program `EX_8_6`.

```
Program ex_8_6;
Uses Crt;
Type
   DateType = Record
               Day   : Integer;
               Month : Integer;
               Year  : Integer;
            End;
   MonthType = Array[1..12] of Integer;
Const
Curr_Day : MonthType = (0, 31, 59, 90, 120, 151, 181, 212, 243, 273, 304,334);
```

```
Var
   Str_1                              : String;
   Error_code, No_days_1, No_days_2  : Integer;
   Date1, Date2                       : DateType;
Begin
   ClrScr;
   Write('Enter first  date (MM-DD-YY) : ');
   ReadLn(Str_1);
   With Date1 do
      Begin
      Val(Copy(Str_1, 1, 2), Month, Error_code);
      Val(Copy(Str_1, 4, 2), Day,   Error_code);
      Val(Copy(Str_1, 7, 2), Year,  Error_code);
      No_days_1 := Year * 365;
      If Month <= 2
        Then
           Begin
           Year := Year - 1;
           End;
      No_days_1 := No_days_1 + Year div 4;
      No_days_1 := No_days_1 + Curr_day[Month];
      No_days_1 := No_days_1 + Day;
      End;{ With }

   Write('Enter second date (MM-DD-YY) : ');
   ReadLn(Str_1);
   With Date2 do
      Begin
      Val(Copy(Str_1, 1, 2), Month, Error_code);
      Val(Copy(Str_1, 4, 2), Day,   Error_code);
      Val(Copy(Str_1, 7, 2), Year,  Error_code);
      No_days_2 := Year * 365;
      If Month <= 2
        Then
           Begin
           Year := Year - 1;
           End;
      No_days_2 := No_days_2 + Year div 4;
      No_days_2 := No_days_2 + Curr_day[Month];
      No_days_2 := No_days_2 + Day;
      End;{ With }
   Write('The number of days between two dates : ');
   WriteLn(No_days_2 - No_days_1);
End.
```

The program can be used to calculate your age in days, if ever you found yourself in need of such information.

Arrays of Records

An array doesn't just have to have numerical type items, they can have any type items including record type. This produces an array of records. For example, you could write the follow declarations:

```
Type
    Person_Rec_Type = Record
               Name : String;
               Age  : Integer;
            End;
    Person_Arr_Type = Array[1..5] of Person_Rec_Type;
Var
    Person : Person_Arr_Type;
```

Each item of the array Person is a record, so each item of the array has two fields, **Name** and **Age**. Each item in the array is designated by

```
Array_Identifier[Index].Field_Identifier.
```

and you can use a combination of With statements and For statements to assign values:

```
For I := 1 to 5 do
   With Person[Index] do
   Begin
      Write('Enter a name : ');
      ReadLn(Name);
      Write('Enter an age : ');
      ReadLn(Age);
   End;{ With}
```

This fragment of the program allows you to enter names and ages to all items of the array.

How To Find an Item Within an Array of Records

An array of records is an array *in its nature*. So all actions for 'pure' arrays are available for arrays of records. For example, you might want to find a given name among the items of an array, and print out the age of the person with this name. Assuming you'd already entered the array take a look at the following fragment of program:

```
Write('Enter a name to be found : ');
ReadLn(Search_Name);
Index := 0;
Repeat
     Index := Index + 1;
     Found := (Person[Index].Name = Search_Name);
     If Found
        Then
           Begin
           Found_index := Index;
           End;
Until (Found) or (Index = 5);
```

Having entered the name of a person we use the same processes to find an item as before. As we're now using an array of records the following statement is used:

```
Found := (Person[Index].Name = Search_Name);
```

To output the age of the person with the given name we need to add the following:

```
If Found
   Then
      Begin
      Write(Search_Name,' age is ');
      WriteLn(Person[Found_index].Age : 2);
      End
   Else
      Begin
      WriteLn('Name is not found. ');
      End
```

The complete program then looks like this:

```
Program ex_8_7;
Uses Crt;
Type
    Person_Rec_Type = Record
                Name : String;
                Age      : Integer;
             End;
    Person_Arr_Type = Array[1..5] of Person_Rec_Type;
Var
```

```
   Person              : Person_Arr_Type;
   Index, Found_Index : Integer;
   Search_Name         : String;
   Found               : Boolean;
Begin
   ClrScr;
   For Index := 1 to 5 do
     With Person[Index] do
        Begin
        Write('Enter a name : ');
        ReadLn(Name);
        Write('Enter an age : ');
        ReadLn(Age);
        End;
   WriteLn('***** Entered data *****');
   For Index := 1 to 5 do
     With Person[Index] do
        Begin
        Write(Name, ' ');
        Write(Age);
        WriteLn;
        End;
   Write('Enter a name to be found : ');
   ReadLn(Search_Name);
   Index := 0;
   Repeat
     Index := Index + 1;
     Found := Person[Index].Name = Search_Name;
     If Found
        Then
           Begin
           Found_Index := Index;
           End;
   Until Found or (Index = 5);
   If Found
     Then
        Begin
        Write(Search_Name,' age is ');
        WriteLn(Person[Found_Index].Age : 2);
        End
     Else
        Begin
        WriteLn('Name is not found. ');
        End;
End.
```

Summary

In Turbo Pascal you can define your own types. This lets you define types based on a sub-range of values from a larger range of values. This is dependent on the larger range of values being an ordinal type. Turbo Pascal also lets you define a type based on an ordered group of data. These are called enumerated types.

The two structured data types in Turbo Pascal are arrays and records. Unlike other basic Turbo Pascal data, types arrays and records have an internal structure. Both are used to store collections of similar data. It is recommended that when you use these structures you define a new type based on the structure of the array or record and then declare variables of this type. You can use either structure to store a collection of similar constants.

Each element in an array is of the same type. To denote a certain item of an array you use the indexed variable. This is the array name followed by an index in square brackets.

A record is a more general data type. A record contains fields which can be of different types. A field designator is used to identify a specific field. This is the record name, followed by a period and the name of the field.

Quiz Questions

1 In the declaration

```
Var
    Dollars: ???;
    Cents:   ???;
```

Dollars and **Cents** will be used to record the price of some article. Declare appropriate types for **Dollars** and **Cents** to reflect their possible values.

2 Given the declaration

```
Var
    Temperature: (Freezing, Normal, Hot, Sizzling);
```

write a Case statement to print the String 'Go to the beach' or 'Watch TV' on the screen according to the value of **Temperature**.

3 What kind of loop would you use to process all the components of an array?

4 When performing a bubble sort, if no exchanges are made on a particular pass along the array then the array must be sorted and we can stop straight away. How would you go about incorporating this optimization in Program **EX_8_5**?

5 Declare Record types suitable for representing squares and circles, as might be used in a graphics program.

6 Declare a record type that might be used by the Internal Revenue Service to record information about an individual.

Exercises

1 Write a modified version of **EX_8_2** which uses an enumerated type to represent months (instead of the integers 1 through 12).

(HINT: You may find the following type and constant definitions useful in your solution:)

```
Type
    { Enumerated type to represent the months }
    Month = (Jan, Feb, Mar, Apr, May, Jun, Jul, Aug, Sep, Oct, Nov, Dec);
    { An array of Real numbers corresponding to each month }
    Weather = Array[Month] of Real;
Const
    { A constant array for converting the enumeration }
    { into a readable string }
    Month_strings: Array[Month] Of String = (
        'January',
        'February',
        'March',
        'April',
        'May',
        'June',
        'July',
        'August',
        'September',
        'October',
        'November',
        'December'
        );
```

2 Write a program which will read five car descriptions from the user. Each description should describe the car's make, model, average fuel consumption (in miles per gallon) and price. The make and model should be recorded as a single string while the fuel consumption and price should be recorded as reals.

Once the descriptions have been read, your program should search through them to find the most expensive car and print the corresponding make, model and fuel consumption.

3   Record types provide very useful abstractions of application entities, leading to a more natural style of programming. Consider the **Draw_square()** family of procedures from the exercises in Chapter 6. These all take a separate X and Y coordinate as parameters. We could, instead, have defined a record type called **Coord** to represent these two related values.

Take a copy of one of your square-drawing applications from Chapter 6 (preferably one of those using the unit) and modify it to use a **Coord** type throughout.

Does the new program work? Which program would be easier to write from scratch? Which is easier to read?

# CHAPTER 9

Filing For Beginners

In all the programs so far we've used the keyboard to input data and the screen to output the results. As a result, all our data was lost when the program finished. To enable you to permanently store data, Turbo Pascal incorporates functions and procedures which manipulate **files**. In this chapter we'll introduce you to these functions and go into detail about using files to store your data.

In this chapter we'll cover

> ▶ Simple data files
>
> ▶ Creating, opening and closing files
>
> ▶ Sequential access to files
>
> ▶ Random access to files
>
> ▶ Text files
>
> ▶ Processing text files

Simple Data Files

In Turbo Pascal, File is a structured data type. The structure is a linear sequence of items (similar to an array). Simple data files are a sequence of items of the same type.

Declaring a File

This is how you declare a file of items of the same type:

```
Var
    Internal_File_Identifier : File of Type_Identifier;
```

where Var, File and of are reserved words. *Internal_File_Identifier* is the variable identifier for the file and *Type_Identifier* is a valid type.

Unlike an array, a file has no fixed length. The number of items in a program can vary during the run-time of a program. When you first declare a file it's empty, and you then add and remove items as and when you want to.

External and Internal File Names

Before using a file in a program, you need to set up a link between the Turbo Pascal program and the file to be processed. Within the program, you need to use a legal identifier. This identifier is the file's **internal** name. Outside the program, you must use a DOS filename. This is called the file's **external** name. The internal and external names must be different to each other, and to be able to use an external file within a program, you need to establish a link using the Assign() procedure.

According to the rules of DOS, each filename has a limit of 8 characters, followed by a period, followed by a maximum of 3 characters. The final 3 characters are called the file extension. You don't have to use all of these characters, but 8 or 3 respectively is the maximum.

Assign()

The structure of the function Assign() is as follows:

> Assign(*Internal_File_Identifier* , *'External_name'*)
>
> where **External_name** is the DOS file name and extension. It's written as a string and enclosed in quotes and can include the full path of the file. If you don't use the full path for the file, Turbo Pascal will create the file in the current directory.

As an example, if you wrote the following statements:

```
Var
    My_file        : File of Integer;
Begin
Assign (My_File, 'C:\File_1.Dat');
```

you would have assigned the identifier **My_file** to the external file **FILE_1.DAT** in the C:\ directory. Throughout the program you need to use the identifier **My_file.** Any operations you perform on **My_file** affects the items in **FILE_1.DAT**. If you wanted to perform any operations on the file in DOS, you'd use the name **FILE_1.DAT**.

Creating a File - Rewrite()

Having linked the internal and external names, the next step is to create the file. To do this you use the following procedure:

> Rewrite(**Internal_File_identifier**);

This creates the file with the external name you have assigned to the **Internal_File_identifier**.

So the statements:

```
Var
    My_file        : File of Integer;
Begin
Assign (My_File, 'C:\File_1.Dat');
Rewrite(My_file);
```

create an empty external file with the name **FILE_1.DAT**.

Closing a File - Close()

You've only just created a file and we're telling you how to close it! This does seem odd, but remembering to close files in Turbo Pascal is important for a couple of reasons:

1 If you don't close all files before the program ends, none of the operations you've performed on the files will take effect.

2 You must close a file before you can switch between operations. For instance, after writing items to a file you must close it and then open it again before you can read any items.

If a file is closed, your program can't access its data until you re-open the file.

To close a file you use the following procedure

```
Close(Internal_File_Identifier);
```

So the statements:

```
Var
    My_file         : File of Integer;
Begin
Assign (My_File, 'C:\File_1.Dat');
Rewrite(My_file);
Close(My_file);
```

now closes our newly created **FILE_1.DAT**.

Example: An Open and Shut Program

Adding a program header and an End. statement gives us the simple program below.

```
Program Ex_9_1;
Var
    My_file         : File of Integer;
Begin
    Assign(My_file, 'C:\FILE_1.DAT');
    Rewrite(My_file);
    Close(My_file);
End.
```

This program creates a new file **FILE_1.DAT** in the C:\ directory, as you can see from the following screenshot.

```
AUTOEXEC BAT           461 21/07/94   10:28
CONFIG   SYD           367 20/07/94   10:04
CONFIG   BAK           379 20/07/94   12:40
AUTOEXEC BAK           422 20/07/94   12:40
WINWORD      <DIR>         20/07/94   12:59
NEC_IDE  SYS        21,669 20/07/94   13:39
AUTOEXEC SYD           444 21/07/94   10:21
CONFIG   SYS           370 20/07/94   13:39
PAINT        <DIR>         20/07/94   14:28
CH_7     PIC <DIR>         20/07/94   17:17
CH-5     PIC <DIR>         20/07/94   17:18
PROG7-1  PAS           271 20/07/94   18:07
PROG7-3  PAS           317 13/07/94   20:10
PROG7-4  PAS           812 13/07/94   22:45
PROG7-5  PAS           517 21/07/94   10:48
COLLDOS      <DIR>         22/07/94   10:34
CH-2     PIC <DIR>         25/07/94   15:00
CH-9     PIC <DIR>         25/07/94   17:28
SHOTS    ONE <DIR>         26/07/94   10:14
CH-7     SCR <DIR>         28/07/94   16:50
FILE_1   DAT             0 30/07/94   17:36
        41 file(s)         116,699 bytes
                       396,386,304 bytes free

Luke C:\>
```

Sequential Access to Files

Because of the sequential structure of a file you can write/read each item in sequence. You only have access to one item of a file at a time, and when you've written or read an item, you are moved on to the next item. You can only add or examine one item of a file at a time, starting at the beginning of the file. Finally, you can't alter an item in a file.

With these words of dire warning ringing in your ears, we'll go on to look at reading and writing data to your file.

Adding Data to Your File - Write()

To add items to your new, empty file, you use a procedure we know well - Write(). To make sure you write to your file rather than to the screen, you make the first parameter of the procedure the internal name of the file. So the structure is:

Write(*Internal_File_Identifier*, *Expression*);

where the result of *Expression* is a value or a variable of the same type as the values in the file.

The following statements are an example of using Write()

```
Assign(My_file, 'C:\File_1.Dat');
Rewrite(My_file);
Write(My_file, Temp);
```

If they were executed, you would create a file **FILE_1.DAT** in the C:\ directory with one item in it - the value of the variable **Temp**.

To add a series of values to the file you can use a Repeat loop. In the loop, you use the variable **Temp** as a temporary resting place for each new value. As we work through the loop, the value is read from the screen and stored in **Temp**. In the next statement, this value is written to the file. As the loop comes round again, the value stored in **Temp** changes to the new value.

```
Repeat
   Write('Enter an integer : ');
   ReadLn(Temp);
   Write(My_file, Temp);
   Write('Continue? Reply Y or N : ');
   ReadLn(Ch);
Until (Ch = 'n') or (Ch = 'N');
```

The user decides how many items to add to the file using the loop and the condition.

Don't attempt to use WriteLn() to write to simple data files. WriteLn() writes an end of line character after each value. This character is of char type and so will cause an error when writing to a file of integer type.

Opening the File - Reset()

To examine the items in a file you must first open it. To open an **existing** file you use the following procedure:

Reset(*Internal_File_Identifier*) ;

Don't try to use the procedure Rewrite() to open an existing file. Rewrite() creates files, and so would overwrite the existing file with a new empty file of the same name.

> Equally, don't try to Reset() a file until you've created it with Rewrite(). If the file doesn't exist, Turbo Pascal will display a run-time error message and halt your program.

Reading the Contents - Read()

To read an item in a file you use the following procedure:

> Read(*Internal_File_Identifier,   Variable_Identifier*);
>
> As with Write() the first parameter must be the internal identifier for the file.

The value of the item in the file is stored in the variable whose identifier is the second parameter.

Scraping the Bottom of the Barrel - Eof()

Once you have read a value from the file, Turbo Pascal skips to the next item. If you execute the statement again, the next value is read and stored in the variable, and so on.

But how many times can you read the file items? The length of the file is unknown because it may contain any number of items. To check whether the end of the file has been reached, the function Eof() is used. Eof is an abbreviation of 'End of file'. The function call

> Eof(*Internal_File_Identifier*)

returns the value **True** if the current position is beyond the last item of the file *Internal_File_Identifier*. Otherwise, it returns **False**.

We can then use Eof() to stop Turbo Pascal reading beyond the last item in a file.

```
While (not Eof(My_file)) Do
   Begin
   Read(My_file, Item);
   <assignment statement>
   End;
```

You can replace **<assignment statement>** with a statement or series of statements to assign each value from the file. We have used a While loop to cover the possibility that the external file is empty. If this is the case, there's nothing to read and the program skips the loop.

309

Example: Be Positively Average

The following example asks you to enter a series of positive and negative integers from the keyboard, and divides them into two files: positive numbers in one file, negative numbers in the other. We then want to calculate the average for the positive numbers.

Let's create some subtasks to break the problem down.

1 Create the two files. We want to use our own file names so we'll enter the names as strings. We can then read these strings into a variable and use this variable in the assign statement.

```
WriteLn('Enter a file name for positive values : ');
ReadLn(Ext_Pos_Name);
Assign(Int_Pos_Name, Ext_Pos_File);
Rewrite(Int_Pos_Name);
WriteLn('Enter a file name for negative values : ');
ReadLn(Ext_Neg_File);
Assign(Int_Neg_Name, Ext_Neg_File);
Rewrite(Int_Neg_Name);
```

2 Read in the numbers. As they are entered, we need to write the positive numbers to one file and the negative numbers in another file. We can use a Repeat loop to do this. Having created our file and entered some data, we then need to close the files. This allows us to switch to reading the files.

```
Repeat
   Write('Enter an integer : ');
   ReadLn(Item);
   If (Item > 0)
      Then
        Begin
         Write(Int_Pos_Name, Item);
         End
      Else
         Begin
         Write(Int_Neg_Name, Item);
         End;
   Write('Continue? Reply Y or N : ');
   ReadLn(Ch);
Until (Ch = 'n') or (Ch = 'N');
Close(Int_Pos_Name);
Close(Int_Neg_Name);
```

3 Calculate the average for the positive numbers. It's important to remember the sequential nature of files. Each item must be processed as soon as you read it, because the procedure Read() moves on to the next item straightaway. You can't return to an item if you've already read the next item.

To calculate the average, you need to know the sum of all the items, divided by the number of items. Let's use two variables, **Counter** and **Sum**, both of Integer type. As we read each item from the file, we increase **Counter** by one and add the value of the item to the value of **Sum**. To obtain the average, we then divide **Sum** by **Counter** and output this to the screen. To make sure we only use the values in the file, we initialize these two variables before we use them.

```
Reset(Int_Pos_Name);
Counter := 0;
Sum    := 0;
While (not Eof(My_file)) Do
   Begin
   Read(Int_Pos_Name, Item);
   Counter := Counter + 1;
   Sum     := Sum + Item;
   End;
Until Eof(Int_Pos_Name);
Close(Int_Pos_Name);
Average := Sum / Counter;
WriteLn('Average for positive values is ', Average:5:2);
```

Putting all these subtasks together we come up with the program below.

```
Program Ex_9_2;
Uses Crt;
Var
   Int_Pos_Name, Int_Neg_Name        : File of Integer;
   Ext_Pos_File, Ext_Neg_File, S : String;
   Item, Counter, Sum : Integer;
   Ch               : Char;
   Average          : Real;
Begin
   Clrscr;
   WriteLn('Enter a file name for positive values : ');
   ReadLn(Ext_Pos_File);
   Assign(Int_Pos_Name, Ext_Pos_File);
   Rewrite(Int_Pos_Name);
   WriteLn('Enter a file name for negative values : ');
   ReadLn(Ext_Neg_File);
```

```
   Assign(Int_Neg_Name, Ext_Neg_File);
   Rewrite(Int_Neg_Name);
   Repeat
      Write('Enter an integer : ');
      ReadLn(Item);
      If Item > 0
         Then
            Write(Int_Pos_Name, Item)
         Else
            Write(Int_Neg_Name, Item);
      Write('Continue? Reply Y or N : ');
      ReadLn(Ch);
   Until (Ch = 'n') or (Ch = 'N');
   Close(Int_Pos_Name);
   Close(Int_Neg_Name);
   Reset(Int_Pos_Name);
   Counter := 0;
   Sum     := 0;
   Repeat
      Read(Int_Pos_Name, Item);
      Counter := Counter + 1;
      Sum     := Sum + Item;
   Until Eof(Int_Pos_Name);
   Close(Int_Pos_Name);
   Average := Sum / Counter;
   WriteLn('Average for positive values is ', Average:5:2);
End.
```

Random Access to Files - Seek()

Files are usually accessed sequentially. Turbo Pascal also provides another method of access known as **random access**. Random access allows you to select the particular item in the file which you want to process, by specifying the number of the position of the item.

As items in a file are arranged in sequence, Turbo Pascal assigns a number to the position of each item in a similar fashion to the index in an array. The numbering starts with zero, so the position of the first item is zero, the position of the second item is 1, and so on.

The Procedure Seek()

To access the item in this way, use the procedure Seek(). This procedure moves the current position to the position which has the new number. The procedure has the following structure:

> Seek(*Internal_File_identifier, Postion_Number*);
>
> *Postion_Number* can be any expression or variable that yields a positive integer number.

As an example, if you include the procedure calls

```
Seek(My_file, 5);
Write(My_file, Variable);
```

Turbo Pascal moves the current position to the sixth item in the file (remember that the first item is position zero) and then writes the value in **variable** into this position in the file.

How Big Is My File?

As the size of a file can vary, Turbo Pascal has a function to track the size. The following function call

> FileSize(*Internal_File_Identifier*)

returns the number of items in the file *Internal_File_Identifier*.

Because the first position is zero, the number of items in a file is one greater than the last position in the file. As a result the following procedure call

```
Seek(Internal_FIle_identifier, FileSize(Internal_File_Identifier));
```

is often used to move the current position to just past the last item in the file.

Where Am I - FilePos()

As your files get bigger and bigger you may want to know where you are in a file. You can find this out by using the function FilePos()

> FilePos(*Internal_File_Identitfier*)

This returns the number of the current position in file *Internal_File_Identifier*.

Example: Creating a Personal Information System

You can use all these processes to build a personal information system. This could hold the names of all your friends, their dates of birth and their telephone numbers.

Structure of the System

Let's use a record to store the information about each of your friends. We want to be able to save the information independently from the program, and not to have to access each item sequentially. To do this we need a file of records.

We'll then need to write different operations to write and read items, to find specific names, and to change fields of a record.

Defining the Structure

The first thing to do is define a new type based on a record and then to declare a file of records.

```
Type
    Rec_type = Record
                    Name              : String;
                    Date_of_birth     : String;
                    Telephone_number  : String;
                End;
Var
    My_file        : File of Rec_type;
    Rec_var        : Rec_type;
```

My_file is a file of **Rec_type**, and we have also declared another variable **Rec_var** which is just a single record of **Rec_type**. We can use **Rec_var** to store individual records from the file.

Creating the External File

Next we need to create the external file and link it to the internal variable **My_file:**

```
External_name := 'File_1.rec';
Assign(My_file, External_name);
Rewrite(My_file);
```

We now have a shiny, new, empty file.

Writing in the Data

Now we want to fill the file with records:

```
Repeat
   Write('Enter a name : ');
   ReadLn(Rec_var.Name);
   Write('Enter a date of birth : ');
   ReadLn(Rec_var.Date_of_birth);
   Write('Enter a telephone number : ');
   ReadLn(Rec_var.Telephone_number);
   Write(My_file, Rec_var);
   Write('Continue? Reply y/n : ');
   ReadLn(Ch);
Until (Ch = 'n') or (Ch = 'N');
```

The ReadLn() procedures store the entered strings in the fields of **Rec_var.**

Then the procedure

```
Write(My_file, Rec_var);
```

writes the values in the fields of **Rec_var** into the file.

So, to start the new system we use Program **EX_9_3**

```
Program Ex_9_3;
Uses Crt;
Type Rec_type = Record
                    Name              : String;
                    Date_of_birth     : String;
                    Telephone_number  : String;
                End;
Var
   My_file      : File of Rec_type;
   Rec_var      : Rec_type;
   Ch           : Char;
Begin
   Clrscr;
   Assign(My_file, 'File_1.rec');
   Rewrite(My_file);
   Repeat
     Write('Enter a name : ');
     ReadLn(Rec_var.Name);
     Write('Enter a date of birth : ');
     ReadLn(Rec_var.Date_of_birth);
     Write('Enter a telephone number : ');
```

```
      ReadLn(Rec_var.Telephone_number);
      Write(My_file, Rec_var);
      Write('Continue? Reply y/n : ');
      ReadLn(Ch);
   Until (Ch = 'n') or (Ch = 'N');
   Close(My_file);
End.
```

Adding to the File

Having set up the system, you'll soon want to add some new names. The new record must be input after the last item of the existing file. We can use the Seek procedure, coupled with the FileSize function, to do this in one statement:

```
Seek(My_file, FileSize(My_file));
```

As we count the positions from zero, the file size is one more than the last position. This is where we would want to add new records.

The program to add a new record is then the simple one below.

```
Program Ex_9_4;
Uses Crt;
Type Rec_type = Record
                   Name               : String;
                   Date_of_birth      : String;
                   Telephone_number   : String;
                End;
Var
   My_file      : File of Rec_type;
   Rec_var      : Rec_type;
Begin
   Clrscr;
   Assign(My_file, 'File_1.rec');
   Reset(My_file);
   Seek(My_file, FileSize(My_file));
   Write('Enter a name : ');
   ReadLn(Rec_var.Name);
   Write('Enter a date of birth : ');
   ReadLn(Rec_var.Date_of_birth);
   Write('Enter a telephone number : ');
   ReadLn(Rec_var.Telephone_number);
   Write(My_file, Rec_var);
   Close(My_file);
End.
```

As we mentioned earlier, a file must have been created before you try to reset it. If you wish to run this program you should run **EX_9_3** first.

Searching for an Item

Having set up this information system, we need to know how to get at the individual items. First of all the program needs to elicit the name to be found, so we use the following statements:

```
Write('Enter the name of the person you are looking for : ');
ReadLn(Sought_Name);
```

The program must then look through all the items and compare the value in the field **Name** of each record, with the name we are looking for. If the name is found then we must write all the fields on the screen. If it isn't found, we need to produce a message saying nothing was found. The algorithm used in this search is the same one we used to search an array.

```
Counter := 0;
Repeat
   Seek(My_file, Counter);
   Read(My_file, Rec_var);
   Found := (Rec_var.Name = Sought_Name);
   If Found
      Then
         Begin
         Found_ind := Counter;
         End;
   Counter := Counter + 1;
Until (Found or Eof(My_file));
```

If a matching name is found, then the boolean variable Found will hold the value **True** and the variable **Found_ind** will hold the position of the name. Otherwise, it will hold the value **False**. We therefore choose which message to display, depending on the value of Found.

We've used the **counter** variable to move us step-by-step through the file rather than relying on the Read() procedure. **Counter** is increased by one after each step through the loop. As Seek() uses the value of **counter** as the position it is to move to, this advances Seek() item by item through the file.

We increase **counter after** the If statement so that the value of **Found_Ind** is the position of the matching record. We can then add the statements below to complete the algorithm.

```
If Found
   Then
      Begin
         Seek(My_file, Found_ind);
         Read(My_file, Rec_var);
         WriteLn(Rec_var.Name);
         WriteLn(Rec_var.Date_of_birth);
         WriteLn(Rec_var.Telephone_number);
      End
   Else
      Begin
      WriteLn('Name is not found. ');
      End;
```

The complete program to search for an item in a file is shown below.

```
Program Ex_9_5;
Uses Crt;
Type Rec_type = Record
                   Name              : String;
                   Date_of_birth     : String;
                   Telephone_number  : String;
                End;
Var
   My_file       : File of Rec_type;
   Rec_var                    : Rec_type;
   Sought_Name          : String;
   Found                      : Boolean;
   Found_ind, Counter  : Integer;
Begin
   Clrscr;
   Assign(My_file, 'File_1.rec');
   Reset(My_file);
   Counter := 0;
   Write('Enter a name to be found : ');
   ReadLn(Sought_Name);
   Repeat
      Seek(My_file, Counter);
      Read(My_file, Rec_var);
      Found := Rec_var.Name = Sought_Name;
      If Found
         Then
            Begin
```

```
                Found_ind := Counter;
             End;
        Counter := Counter + 1;
   Until (Found or Eof(My_file));
   If Found
      Then
         Begin
            Seek(My_file, Found_ind );
            Read(My_file, Rec_var);
            WriteLn(Rec_var.Name);
            WriteLn(Rec_var.Date_of_birth);
            WriteLn(Rec_var.Telephone_number);
         End
      Else
         Begin
         WriteLn('Name is not found. ');
         End;
   Close(My_file);
End.
```

Amending an Item

When someone moves house you might want to change their telephone number in your database. So you'd need to find the item and then change the value in the field. We already know how to find an item, so the next step is to read the record from the file. You then enter the new telephone number into the existing field. Having done this, you then write the same record (which now has the changed information) back to the same position in the file. You can do this by altering the three WriteLn() statements in the second If statement in **EX_9_5** to the four lines shown in italics below:

```
   If Found
      Then
         Begin
            Seek(My_file, Found_ind );
            Read(My_file, Rec_var);
            Write('Enter new telephone number : ');
            ReadLn(Rec_var.Telephone_number);
            Seek(My_file, Found_ind );
            Write(My_file, Rec_var);
         End
      Else
         Begin
         WriteLn('Name is not found. ');
         End;
```

The full program to amend a field is below.

```
Program Ex_9_6;
Uses Crt;
Type Rec_type = Record
                    Name               : String;
                    Date_of_birth      : String;
                    Telephone_number   : String;
                  End;
Var
   My_file        : File of Rec_type;
   Rec_var                   : Rec_type;
   Sought_Name            : String;
   Found                     : Boolean;
   Found_ind, Counter   : Integer;
Begin
   Clrscr;
   Assign(My_file, 'File_1.rec');
   Reset(My_file);
   Counter := 0;
   Write('Enter a name to be found : ');
   ReadLn(Sought_Name);
   Repeat
      Seek(My_file, Counter);
      Read(My_file, Rec_var);
      Found := Rec_var.Name = Sought_Name;
      If Found
         Then
            Begin
            Found_ind := Counter;
            End;
      Counter := Counter + 1;
   Until (Found or Eof(My_file));
   If Found
      Then
         Begin
            Seek(My_file, Found_ind );
            Read(My_file, Rec_var);
            Write('Enter new telephone number : ');
            ReadLn(Rec_var.Telephone_number);
            Seek(My_file, Found_ind );
            Write(My_file, Rec_var);
         End
      Else
         Begin
         WriteLn('Name is not found. ');
         End;
   Close(My_file);
End.
```

Text Files

In Turbo Pascal, text is a type used to define files. Instead of just a sequence of values of one particular type, files declared as text are structured into **lines** of characters. Each line ends with a special symbol, an end-of-line marker. Using this type of file allows us to model the real-world more closely. However, you can only access text files **sequentially**. You **can't** use Seek() with text files.

Declaring a Text File

To declare a file of text type you need to write the following:

```
Var
    File_Identifier : Text;
```

Text is a reserved word and *File_Identifier* is a legal identifier.

External & Internal Filenames for Text Files

The same rules apply to text files as to simple data files. As a result, you must still use the procedure Assign to link an internal and external name.

If you'd declared **Txt_File** as a variable of text type, and you wanted to use the DOS file **FILE.TXT**, you'd need to write the following statement:

```
Assign (Txt_File, ' FILE.TXT ');
```

Throughout the program you would then use the identifier **Txt_File**.

Rewrite() & Reset() with Text Files

You also use the procedures Rewrite() and Reset() to perform the same processes on files of text type as you do for the simpler sequential files.

To open the new text file **Txt_File** you write

```
Rewrite(Txt_File_1);
```

To open an existing text file **Txt_File_2** you write

```
Reset(Txt_File_2);
```

Writing to a Text File

Because text files are structured in lines, you can write values to a text file using both Write() and WriteLn(). The structure is the same as for simple sequential files

```
WriteLn(Internal_File_Identifier,   Expression);
```

WriteLn() adds an end of line marker to the end of the characters which you are adding to the file. Write() just adds the characters in the expression to the file. After adding values with WriteLn() you move to the next line, whereas after adding values with Write() you remain on the same line. You'll keep adding to the same line with Write() until an end of line marker is written with WriteLn()

Reading from a Text File

The use of Write() and WriteLn() is paralleled by the use of both Read(),and ReadLn() to read values from a text file. The structure is the same:

```
ReadLn(Internal_File_Identifier,   Variable_Identifier);
```

with the next value stored in the *Variable_Identifier*.

Depending on the type of the variable, starting from the current position, Read() will read until it reaches the next illegal character for that type. Read() stops there and any subsequent call of Read() will start from this position. For example, if the variable were of integer type, Read() would ignore all blanks and then read until it reached the next non-numeric character.

ReadLn() works the same way, **except** that when it has stopped reading, it moves beyond the end of line marker.

```
If Read() encounters the end of line marker it moves on to the next line
and continues reading the value from there.
```

End of Line Marker - Eoln()

As with simple sequential files, the Eof() function provides information about whether the end of file has been reached. In parallel with this, Turbo Pascal includes the Eoln() function. The function call is as follows:

```
Eoln(Internal_Identifier)
```

and becomes **True** if the end of line marker is reached. Otherwise, it returns the value **False**.

Example: Viewing a Text File

As an uncompiled program, **EX_9_1.PAS** is just a text file. We used Turbo Pascal to copy **EX_9_1.PAS** on to the screen and to count the number of 'a's in the program.

To count the number of 'a's we must test each character and see if it is the letter 'a'. If it is, then we add one to a variable **Counter**. Of course, the initial value of the variable **Counter** needs to be zero.

To copy one line of the text file you must read each character from the file and then write each character to the screen. To read each character we use a variable of type char. This enables us to store all the ASCII characters. The Line Feed code is ASCII character 10, so we can use Read() to input the whole of the file if we so wish. However, we can better control the display if we use ReadLn() and WriteLn().

So, to input each line we need to read each character (as long we are not at the end of the line). The following statements also include the test of whether or not the character is an 'a':

```
While not Eoln(Txt_File) do
   Begin
      Read(Txt_File, Ch);
      Write(Ch);
        If Ch = 'a'
      Then
           Begin
           Counter := Counter + 1;
           End;
   End;
```

To jump to the next line in the file you need the following statement:

```
ReadLn(Txt_File);
```

To move to the next line on the screen we need to use the WriteLn; statement.

These statements process each line. Naturally, we need to process each line as long as we're not at the end of the file. The following statements, placed around our existing statements, guard against this:

```
While not Eof(Txt_File) do
Begin
   < Processing of the line >
End;
```

The complete program is shown below.

```
Program Ex_9_7;
Uses Crt;
Var
   Txt_File      : Text;
   Path_String   : String;
   Ch            : Char;
   Counter       : Integer;
Begin
   Clrscr;
   Write('Enter the path  for file Ex_9_1.pas : ');
   ReadLn(Path_String);
   Assign(Txt_File, Path_String + 'Ex_9_1.pas');
   Reset(Txt_File);
   Counter := 0;
   While not Eof(Txt_File) do
      Begin
      While not Eoln(Txt_File) do
         Begin
            Read(Txt_File, Ch);
            Write(Ch);
            If Ch = 'a'
               Then
            Begin
                Counter := Counter + 1;
            End;
         End;
      ReadLn(Txt_File);
      Writeln;
      End;
   WriteLn('The letter ''a'' occurs ', Counter:1,' times');
   Close(Txt_File);
End.
```

The following screenshot shows you the output from the program.

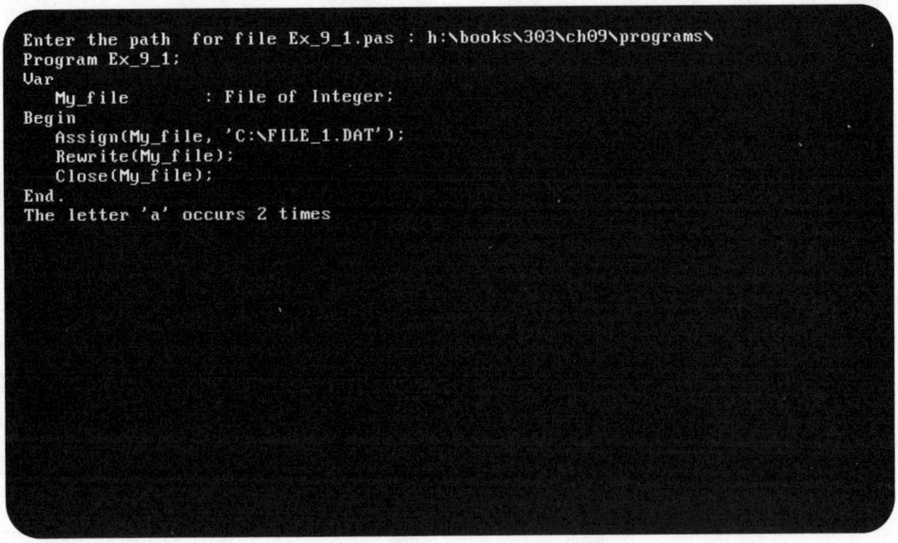

```
Enter the path  for file Ex_9_1.pas : h:\books\303\ch09\programs\
Program Ex_9_1;
Var
    My_file       : File of Integer;
Begin
    Assign(My_file, 'C:\FILE_1.DAT');
    Rewrite(My_file);
    Close(My_file);
End.
The letter 'a' occurs 2 times
```

Summary

Files are the only data structure in Turbo Pascal which allows you to store your data on permanent storage media. Using other data structures your data is lost once the program terminates. There is no restriction on the size of a file - they can have any number of items. They can also vary in size whilst the program is running.

When you use files, there are 3 operations you must perform. They are:

1   Set up the link between your program and the file you are going to process.

2   Open the file to allow processing.

3   Close the file when the processing is finished.

There are two different kinds of files: **simple data** files and text files. Simple data files are a sequence of items of the same type. Text is a type in Turbo Pascal. Files declared as text type are a sequence of lines. Each line can be made up of several different characters. Each line finishes with an end-of-line marker. The end of both kinds of file is marked by an end-of-file marker.

There are also two different methods of accessing data stored in files: **sequential** and **random**. Sequential access processes item by item. This is the only method available for text files. Random access uses the Seek() procedure. In this procedure you can specify the position of the item.

Quiz Questions

1 Arrays and files have a similar structure, but can you list three differences?

2 What are the differences between sequential and random access to files?

3 What is special about text files?

4 Write down a general nested loop for processing a text file.

5 Write a single Pascal statement which will move to the end of a non-text file called Fred (so that a new item can be appended).

6 Why is it important to close a file before your program finishes?

Exercises

1 Write a program which reads a text file and writes it out on the screen with every line reversed. For example, a file containing

> I'm a very forward looking person!
> Although you may not think so...

would come out as

> !nosrep gnikool drawrof yrev a m'I
> ...os kniht ton yam uoy hguohtlA

2 According to legend, the designer of the QWERTY keyboard (those with 'QWERTY' as the first six letters on the top row), based the layout of the letters on the frequency of occurrence of each letter in literature - the most common characters were actually placed in hard-to-reach locations! The idea was that typists had to be slowed down because early typewriters were too clumsy to cope with high typing speeds. Write a program which will measure the frequency of occurrence of each of the letters in an arbitrary text file, printing the results on the screen.

(HINT: You may find the following types useful in your program:)

```
Type
    Letters = 'a'..'z';
    Letter_array = Array[Letters] Of LongInt; { An array for storing }
                                              { the totals for each
character }
```

3   Write a program, based on exercise 3 of Chapter 8, which uses a 'File
    of Car' to store the car descriptions, instead of an array. Your program
    shouldn't restrict the number of cars which the user can enter (but for
    simplicity, you can force them to enter at least one).

# CHAPTER 10

Letting the Data Run Free

By now, we've seen lots of ways of storing data in Turbo Pascal, from simple integer variables right the way up to files. A simple type like real stores a single value. A structured data type such as array stores multiple values in a structured format. In this chapter, we're going to introduce you to a whole new way of storing data with **dynamic data structures** which will make our programs even more powerful.

Dynamic data structures can be tricky to master, but you'll find them indispensable when you begin to tackle more challenging programming problems. So rather than trying to show you all the ins and outs, we'll take you on a guided tour so that you can get an idea of what's possible. By the end of the chapter, you will have seen how a couple of simple procedures and a dynamic data structure can be used to sort any amount of data of any type, in a very fast and elegant way!

We'll cover the following topics:

- The special **pointer** type used in all dynamic data structures

- The added value of dynamic data structures

- The different varieties of dynamic data structure - **lists**, **trees** and **graphs**

- How to use a tree to sort data

- How to use simple **recursive rules** to grow or climb a tree

- How to represent a tree using pointers

- How to translate recursive rules into **recursive procedures**

Pointer Types

Dynamic data structures make extensive use of special types called **pointer types**. We haven't come across them so far, so we'll kick off this chapter with a short introduction. All the other variables in Turbo Pascal are used to store data *directly*, that is at the memory location identified by the variable itself. A **pointer variable** is different - it *points at* data which is stored *somewhere else* in memory. This allows us to get hold of storage when our program is running, as and when the need arises.

Declaring a Pointer Variable - Definition

In Turbo Pascal, a pointer variable is declared like this:

> Var
>
>   **Pointer_Identifier** : ^**Type_Identifier**;
>
> where Var is the reserved word. This says that **Pointer_Identifier** can point to a value of type **Type_Identifier**. The ^ (or caret) symbol indicates that **Pointer_Identifier** is of pointer type. It was selected for this purpose because it looks a bit like an arrow *pointing* upwards.

Let's look at a concrete example. You're already familiar with a Real variable declared like this:

```
Var
          A_real: Real;
```

We declare a *pointer to* a Real thus:

```
Var
          A_real_ptr: ^Real;
```

Adding **_ptr** to the end of the variable name is a common convention used by programmers. The figure below shows the difference between the variables **A_real** and **A_real_ptr**. The variable **A_real** identifies a memory cell which actually contains a Real value. In contrast, **A_real_pointer** identifies a memory cell which *points at* a Real value which is stored somewhere else.

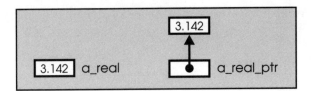

Initializing a Pointer Variable

When a program starts all variables contain garbage. Turbo Pascal provides the special **nil** value for initializing pointer variables. For example:

```
A_real_ptr := nil;
```

indicates that **A_real_ptr** has the value 'not pointing at anything'. In our graphical representation we can draw this as a shaded box as below.

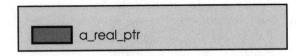

We can also test for the **nil** value just like we can test for any other value:

```
If A_real_ptr = nil Then
          Begin
          WriteLn('A_real_ptr isn't pointing anywhere')
          End;
```

The body of this If statement will only be executed if **A_real_ptr** isn't pointing anywhere.

Dynamic Memory

Usually, pointer variables are used to point at **dynamic memory**. This is memory which is grabbed from the RAM on your PC during the run-time of your program. Using dynamic memory we don't have to decide how much data our programs can handle before we run them, so our programs can adapt themselves to different circumstances.

We can ask Turbo Pascal for a new piece of dynamic memory with the new procedure.

```
New(Pointer_Identifier);
```

This reserves a memory cell and makes **Pointer_Identifier** point to it. The size of the piece of memory reserved depends on the type that **Pointer_Identifier** is pointing to. So the statement

```
New(A_real_ptr^);
```

reserves a memory cell large enough to store a real value.

Dereferencing a Pointer Variable

Having claimed a memory cell, we need to be able to refer to the value being 'pointed-at'. Getting at the pointed-at value is called **dereferencing** and you dereference a pointer variable to do this. To dereference a pointer variable you use the same caret symbol (^) that we used to declare the variable, but place the symbol at the end of the variable. For example, to store the value **3.142** in memory cell we claimed above, we write

```
A_real_ptr^ := 3.142;
```

and if we wanted to print out the value, we would write the following:

```
WriteLn(A_real_ptr^);
```

Discarding Dynamic Memory

Once we've finished with a dynamic memory cell, it's good practice to return it to the system. This makes it available for use elsewhere in our program. To discard dynamic memory, we use the dispose procedure:

```
dispose(Pointer_Identifier);
```

So the statement

```
dispose(A_real_ptr);
```

makes the memory cell which held the value **3.142** available for re-use while **A_real_ptr** once again contains garbage.

If you want to use **A_real_ptr** again later on, then it's a good idea to mark it as 'not pointing at anything' again, just as we did earlier:

```
A_real_ptr := nil;
```

Note that we don't need to dispose of dynamic memory if our program is about to finish, because when that happens all dynamic memory is returned to the system anyway.

A Simple Example

The following program shows a pointer variable being used to perform a simple task - storing and dereferencing a Real pointer variable - using the techniques that we've discussed in this section. As an aid to comparison, a Real variable is used alongside the pointer one.

```
Program Ex_10_1;
{ A program which shows a Real pointer variable }
{ being used alongside an ordinary Real variable }
Uses Crt;
Var
          A_real: Real;
          A_real_ptr: ^Real;
Begin
Clrscr;
{ Initialize }
A_real := 0;
A_real_ptr := nil;
{ Store a value }
A_real := 3.142;
New(A_real_ptr); { Get some dynamic memory first }
A_real_ptr^ := 3.142;
{ Compare the values }
If  A_real = A_real_ptr^ Then
 Begin
 WriteLn('Everything''s OK')
 End
Else
     Begin
     WriteLn('If you see this, we have a major problem!')
     End;
{ Discard the dynamic memory }
dispose(A_real_ptr)
{ Didn't need to do that because the program's about to finish,}
End.
```

Static Vs Dynamic

Up until this chapter, we've used simple types like Integer and Real to store single values. Simple types are useful for doing calculations, recording user responses, and so on. We've also used structured data types like Array, Record and File, which store multiple values of the same type. Structured data types allow us to handle large amounts of related data. Because their shape (and usually their size) is fixed when the program is compiled, Array, Record and File are referred to as **static data structures**. Below is an illustration of static data structures.

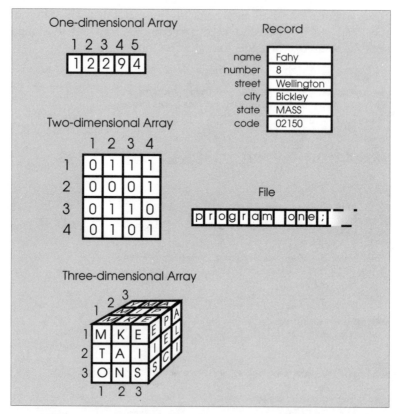

In this chapter, we're going to examine **dynamic data structures** which, like structured data types, can be used to store multiple values. The added value of dynamic data structures is that their size and shape can be changed while the program is running, so helping the program adapt to the real task at hand. Used properly, dynamic data structures can also be very efficient and are often able to make difficult problems in programs significantly easier to solve.

Dynamic Data Structures — Lists, Trees and Graphs

The illustration below shows an example of each of the three main varieties of dynamic data structure:

▶ **Lists**

▶ **Trees** and

▶ **Graphs**

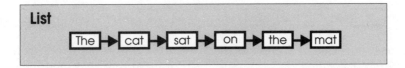

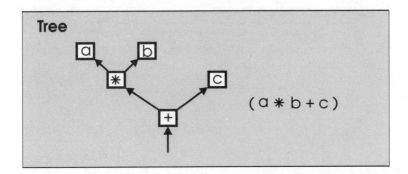

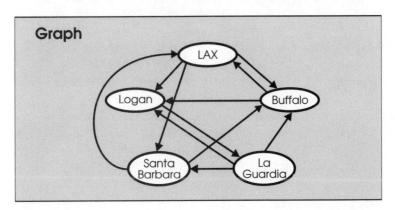

Each of these structures consists of **items** (pieces of data) connected by **links** (arrows) to other items. Looking at each structure in turn, we'll see how to change their size and shape.

Lists

The **list** shows the sentence 'the cat sat on the mat' broken down into individual word items linked from left to right.

If we want to add a word to the end of the sentence, we simply attach it to the end with a new link and a new item. For example, adding 'yesterday' would result in the new list in the figure below

It's easy to insert a word too. If we want to insert 'squarely' before 'on', we just detach the link between 'sat' and 'on' and slot in a new item as shown

The → cat → sat → squarely → on → the → mat → yesterday

We can also delete words easily. For instance, to delete 'squarely', we detach 'sat' from 'squarely' and make it point to 'on' instead.

Trees

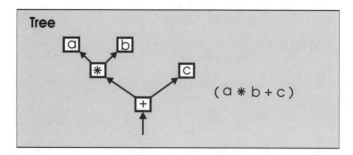

Tree

$(a * b + c)$

Links and items can be used to create other useful structures too. One of them is the **tree** shown above. (OK, it doesn't have bark and leaves, but when drawn like this, the links do look a bit like branches!).

Just like lists, trees are easy to modify. If we want to change the expression in the first picture to **(a * b + c + d)**, we simply add a couple of extra links and items, and to get the picture below.

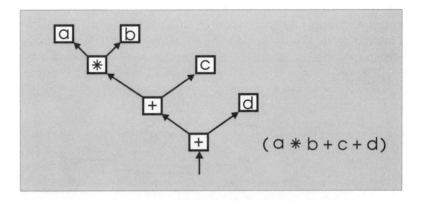

$$(a * b + c + d)$$

Graphs

We're not restricted to lists and trees when we're using links and items. We can build web-shaped structures called **graphs**. Our first example was pinched from an airline booking system. It shows today's connecting flights between various airports. For instance, there's a flight from Buffalo *to* Logan (indicated by the direction of the link). Also, it's possible to fly today from LAX to La Guardia, via a connecting flight to Logan.

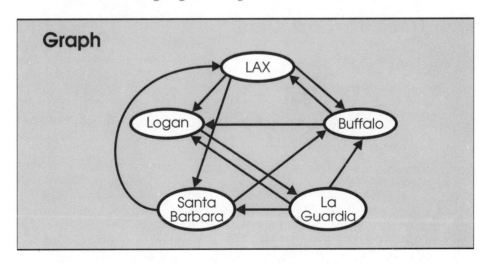

Other graphs similar to this one can be used to calculate the quickest or the cheapest route from one airport to another, or the fewest connections - just the kind of thing an airline booking system needs to be able to do to keep customers happy!

Again, it's simple to manipulate a structure like this. If an extra flight is chartered from Logan to Buffalo, we simply add a new link, to produce the new graph

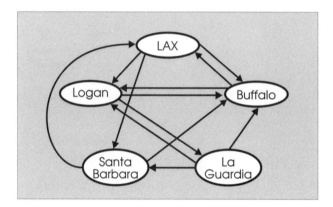

We can also show the changing state of the flights. As each flight departs, we can remove it from the booking system by deleting the corresponding link.

Using Trees to Sort Data

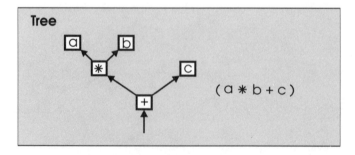

In this section we're going to see how to use a tree data structure like the one above to sort data efficiently. There is no programming in this section. We're just going to define some simple rules for growing and climbing trees. We'll see how to turn the rules into Turbo Pascal later in the chapter.

Trees like this are called **binary trees**, because every fork has at most *two* branches coming out of it.

Growing a Tree

This is the tree we're going to try and build

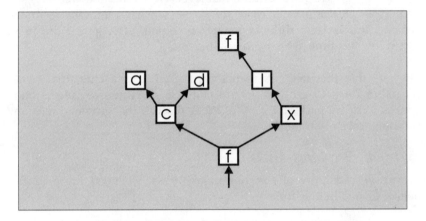

Think of it as a real living tree with a letter nestled in each fork. Each fork has up to two branches growing upwards from it. For example, the fork containing 'c' has a branch emerging to its left and one to its right. The fork containing 'x' has a single branch growing to its left. And, the fork containing 'a' has no branches. There is a single trunk at the bottom (a special branch which happens to be vertical and thicker than the rest).

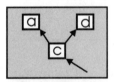

This tree has some important properties. Firstly, we already know that the structure *looks* like a tree. But, if we chop through the branch below 'c', we get something that *also* looks like a tree.

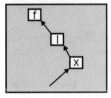

If we chop below 'x' instead, we get *another* tree (although this one has no right branches). No matter where we chop, we still get a tree. This is because the tree structure **recurs** from the trunk to the topmost branches. Because of this, we refer to it as a **recursive** data structure.

Remember from our dealings with chars and strings that we can think of the letters of the alphabet as ordered values ('a' < 'b' < 'c' and so on). This allows us to talk about another important property of our tree. If you look at the fork containing 'c', you'll notice that every character higher up the tree to its *left* (in this case the single character 'a') is *less than* 'c' itself. And, every character up the tree to its *right* ('d') is *greater than or equal to* 'c'. If we go down a level to the fork containing 'f', we can see that every letter up the tree to *its* left ('a', 'c' and 'd') is *less than* 'f' and that every letter up the tree to its right ('x', 'l' and 'f') is *greater than or equal to* 'f'. So, we have another recursive property, namely **'left is less, right is greater or equal'**. The letters are in some sense sorted by the time we've grown the tree.

The fact that this tree has recursive properties is a clue that we should use **recursive rules** to grow it and to climb it. A recursive rule is one which applies *itself* as part of the rule. We'll discuss the growing rule and the climbing rule separately.

A Recursive Growing Rule

Before we can grow one of our binary trees, we need the collection of letters below to put in the forks.

We'll grow the tree by taking each letter in turn and inserting it into its correct position

> This kind of sorting is called an **insertion sort.** The bubble sort in Chapter 8 is an **exchange sort**

In order to grow the tree, we take each letter in turn and apply the following recursive rule:

If there's no branch, grow a new branch and put our letter in the new fork at the top
    OTHERWISE, climb to the fork at the top of this branch ...
        If the letter here is greater than ours, apply the rule to the left branch
            OTHERWISE, apply the rule to the right branch

This rule is best demonstrated by stepping through the example.

1   Initially, we have a collection of letters and no tree. If we take the first letter ('f') and apply the rule, we have no branches, so we grow one and put 'f' in the new fork at the top. This first branch forms the trunk of the tree.

2   We then take 'x' to the bottom of the tree and apply the rule. This time, there is a branch (the trunk) so we climb up to the fork containing 'f'. 'x' is greater than 'f', so we apply the whole rule again to the right branch. When we apply the rule this time, we have no branch, so we grow a new one and put 'x' in the new fork at the top.

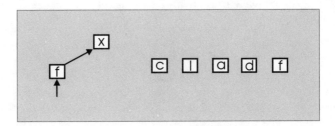

3   We now pick up 'c' and take that to the bottom of the tree. There is a branch so we climb to the fork containing 'f'. 'c' is less than 'f' so we apply the rule to the left branch. There's no branch here, so we grow one and put 'c' in the new fork at the top.

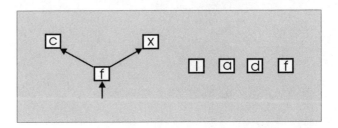

4 Taking 'l' to the tree and applying the rule, we climb to the fork containing 'f'. We find that 'l' is greater than 'f', so we apply the rule to the right branch. There is a branch here so we climb to the fork at the top. This time, we find that 'l' is less than 'x', so we apply the rule to the left branch. Now there's no branch, so we grow one and put 'l' in the new fork at the top.

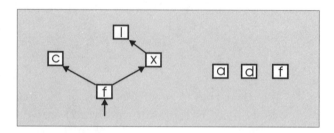

Informally, the last few steps become:

5 Taking 'a', we climb to the left of 'f', then to the left of 'c', then grow a branch and put 'a' at the top

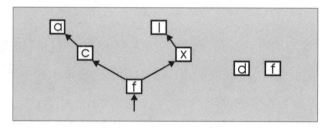

6 Taking 'd', we climb to the left of 'f', then to the right of 'c', then grow a branch and put 'd' at the top

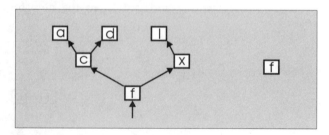

7   Finally, we take 'f' to the tree. This time, we find that 'f' is *equal* to the letter at the top of the branch so, we climb to the right. We then move to the left of 'x', to the left of 'l', grow a branch and put 'f' at the top. We've now safely installed a *second* 'f' in the tree, and the final result is shown below

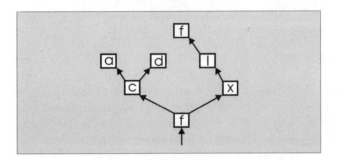

Phew! That was hard work. But remember what we've done. We've taken an arbitrary collection of letters, and applying a simple recursive rule, we've grown a recursive tree which has the 'left is less, right is greater or equal' property. Objective achieved!

There is a definite 'Aha!' factor here. If you haven't already said to yourself "Aha! I see how this works", try growing the tree again by stepping through the description above. Then, take the letters and the rule and try it for yourself on paper (without peeking at the solution!). Once you've mastered the technique, you'll be ready to climb the tree.

Climbing a Tree

So now we know how to grow a tree with the desired properties. Our next objective is to climb it, writing down the letters in alphabetical order in our handy notebook!

A Recursive Climbing Rule

Instead of trying to work out exactly *how* to visit the letters in order, we should be able to formulate another recursive rule which exploits the way we grew the tree. If we follow this new rule to the letter (!) at every fork and branch, the sorting will be done for us. We've actually done most of the work by growing the tree according to the first rule, so the climbing rule is even simpler:

If there is a branch, climb to the fork at the top of the branch ...
   Apply the rule to the left branch.
   Write down the letter at this fork.
   Apply the rule to the right branch.

Intuitively, because of the way we grew the tree, this ought to work. At any particular fork, all the letters to the left are less than the letter *at* the fork so they should be written down *before* it. Similarly, all the letters to the right are greater than or equal to the letter at the fork, so they should be written down *after* it; in between, we should write down the letter at the fork. Obviously, if there's no branch, we should do nothing.

We'll illustrate by climbing the tree in the previous figure. So that you can

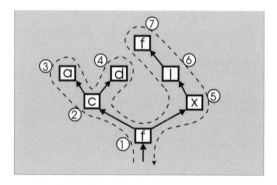

follow the progress of our climb we have illustrated it below
And we have written a step-by-step description here:

1   We start by going to the base of the tree. There is a branch here (the trunk), so we climb to the fork at the top of it (point 1 in the diagram). According to the rule, we must now apply the whole rule *again* to the left branch before we do anything else ...

2   There's a branch here, so we climb to the fork at the top of it (point 2) and apply the whole rule to the left branch ...

3   There's a branch here, so we climb to the fork at the top of it (point 3) and apply the whole rule to the left branch ...

4   Now, there's no branch so we do nothing. This completes the current application of the rule and we 'return to' point 3 ...

5   We now apply the second part of the rule that we started at point 3, writing down the letter at this fork. So, our notebook now has 'a' emblazoned on it. We now apply the third part of the rule, thus applying the whole rule again to the right branch. ...

6   Again, there's no branch so we do nothing. We've completed another application of the rule, so we 'return to' point 3 ...

7   We've now applied all three parts of the rule at point 3, so we return to point 2 ...

8   At point 2, we apply the second part of the rule and write down 'c'. Our notebook now has 'a' and 'c' written on it. We now apply the third part of the rule, thus applying the whole rule again to the right branch (bringing us to point 4) ...

Dropping the jargon again:

9   There's no left or right branch at point 4, so we just write down 'd'. Our notebook now contains 'a', 'c', 'd' and we return to point 2 ...

10   We've now applied all parts of the rule at point 2, so we return to point 1 ...

11   We write down 'f' (so our notebook contains 'a', 'c', 'd', 'f') and we apply the rule to the right branch, bringing us to point 5 ...

12   We climb to the left, bringing us to point 6 ...

13   Again, we climb to the left, bringing us to point 7 ...

14   There are no branches at point 7, so we just write down 'f' (so our notebook contains 'a', 'c', 'd', 'f', 'f') and return to point 6 ...

15   We write down 'l' (so our notebook contains 'a', 'c', 'd', 'f', 'f', 'l') and since there's no right branch we return to point 5 ...

16   We now write down 'x' (so our notebook contains 'a', 'c', 'd', 'f', 'f', 'l', 'x'). Again, there's no right branch so we return to the ground.

Our notebook now contains all the letters in alphabetical order - second objective achieved! Phew, again! That intricate sequence of steps was designed to convince you that by following a simple recursive rule, we can write the letters down in order. If you didn't follow it the first time round, it's worth pausing to try again. Then, try it for yourself, rule in one hand, tree in the other.

As humans, we're better than computers at tasks like this. We can actually predict our journey through the tree shown by the dotted line. This line starts to the left of the trunk and follows the 'outside' of the tree back to the ground. All you need to do is follow this path, writing down each letter when you pass it for the second time. You might like to try this as an experiment. The rule, however, is easy to follow, and as we'll see, it's also easy for Turbo Pascal to cope with.

Trees in Turbo Pascal

Knowing how to sort letters on paper using binary trees is all very well. But it's a little awkward if we have thousands of letters! We'd like to be able to express our rules in Turbo Pascal so that our PC can do all the hard work. That's the purpose of this section. There should be no big surprises here because all the code that we're going to see follows naturally from our discussions so far.

The Parts of a Tree

Now's the time to find out how the bits and pieces of a tree are represented in Turbo Pascal.

Trunks and Branches as Pointers

The simplest pieces of our tree are the branches themselves. The principal property of a branch is that it leads somewhere, or to put it another way, it *points* somewhere. Turbo Pascal's pointer types are ideal for this purpose. We can draw them as trunks or branches:

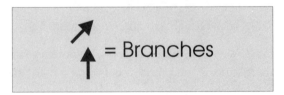

So what does a branch point at? Well, if you look at the figure again, you should be able to see that branches point at forks. If we assume for the moment that we have a convenient type lying around called **Fork**, we can say this:

```
Var
        A_branch1: ^Fork;
```

This tells Turbo Pascal that **A_branch1** is a pointer to a **Fork** type.

We can do even better by defining our own type:

```
Type
        Branch = ^Fork;
```

This says that anything declared as a **Branch** will be used to point to a **Fork**, and we can use this new type name in variable declarations:

```
Var
        A_branch, A_branch_too: Branch;
```

In fact, we can go right ahead and declare the trunk of our tree with the following:

```
Var
        trunk: Branch;
```

So, our variable names all indicate what they do.

The figure below shows a convenient way of drawing the trunk.

Forks as Records

Now that we've defined a type for **branches**, we have to decide how to define one for **Forks** (we side-stepped this issue earlier).

A **Fork** has some data in it - a string in this case (we'll use strings rather than individual characters, because this makes our forks more useful). It also has two branches emanating from it. Therefore it always has three components of different types and a Record is the ideal structure for this purpose. As a result we can define a **Fork** as follows:

```
Type
        Fork = Record
             Data: String;
             left_branch, right_branch: Branch
             End;
```

We can then declare **Fork** variables with:

```
Var
        A_fork, another_fork: Fork;
```

The fields of a **Fork** aren't in any particular order - we just declare them that way. However, we can do a better job when we draw them.

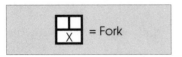

Here, we've split the **Fork** record into three smaller squares, one for the data ('x' in this case) and one each for the left and right branches. This allows us to add branches which point off in the appropriate direction:

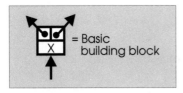

The next illustration shows a **Fork** containing the letter 'x' with a **branch** going up to the left and another going up to the right. There's also a **branch** coming in at the bottom so that we can climb up to the fork from below. This shows the basic building block for Turbo Pascal trees.

One more thing - we need to be able to represent a missing branch. In our picture, we can show this as a grayed-out square where a **branch** should start . We express this in Turbo Pascal by assigning the **nil** value, as in the following:

```
A_fork.right_branch := nil;
```

This marks the fact that **A_fork** hasn't got a right branch yet. We can also use the **nil** value to initialize the **trunk** variable that we declared above:

```
trunk := nil;
```

Putting the Parts Together

Using all these bits and pieces, we can translate the illustration of a tree (on the right) into our representation of it's Turbo Pascal equivalent (on the left).

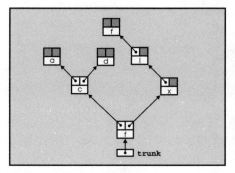
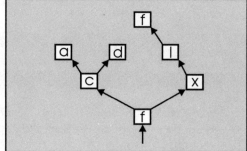

The rest is up to the recursive procedures described below.

Growing a Tree

Now we come back to the process of growing a tree. We've already seen how to do this on paper - now we'll do it in Turbo Pascal.

Growing Individual Branches

Before we can proceed, we need to know how to grow individual branches with forks at the end. This is where the really dynamic part comes in. We can't declare branches as ordinary variables, because we don't know how many we're going to need until run-time. That's the whole point - we don't *want* to know, because we don't want to fix how many strings we can handle before we run the program.

What we need is a way of plucking new branches out of thin air. The New procedure is provided for just such a purpose. If we write

```
New(trunk);
```

then Turbo Pascal will reserve a memory cell big enough for a **Fork** record and make **trunk** point to it.

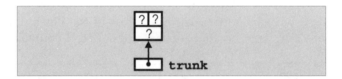

To place a string in a particular **fork**, we need to use the dereferencing mechanism. For example:

```
trunk^.data := 'f';
```

assigns '**f**' to the **data** field of the new **trunk** record - or to put it another way, it puts '**f**' in the fork at the top of the trunk. Notice how we can use the dereferenced variable as part of a file designator using the period. We can use the with statement to assign values to each of the fields in the dereferenced **trunk.**

```
New(trunk);
With trunk^ Do
        Begin
        left_branch := nil;
        data := 'f';
        right_branch := nil
End;
```

The effect of this initialization is illustrated below.

A Recursive Growing Procedure

We saw earlier, in great detail, how a recursive rule can be used to build the kind of tree we want. All we need to know now is how to translate such a recursive rule into Turbo Pascal. Here's the rule again:

If there's no branch, grow a new branch and put our letter in the new fork at the top
    OTHERWISE, climb to the fork at the top of this branch ...
        If the letter here is greater than ours, apply the rule to the left branch
            OTHERWISE, apply the rule to the right branch

Calling a procedure is very much like applying a rule When you finish applying a rule, you go back to the point at which you started to apply it. Similarly with a procedure, when the last statement of the procedure has been executed, the program returns to the point from where the procedure was called.

So, we should be able to define a procedure for adding letters to trees - **add** seems an appropriate name - which is equivalent to the written rule. If one of the statements in the **add** procedure calls **add** itself, then it will be recursive.

We need to tell the **add** procedure which branch (or trunk) to start at, so we need to give it an appropriate parameter. We also need another parameter for passing in the letter to be added. Therefore our procedure heading should look something like:

```
Procedure Add(this_branch: Branch; new_data: String);
```

This isn't quite right. At some point, **add** is going to have to assign to **this_branch** to make it point to a new record. So it must be a *variable* parameter and we change the heading to:

```
Procedure Add(var this_branch: Branch; new_data: String);
```

We can now use the rule as the design for the procedure, and without too much ado, we can convert it into Turbo Pascal:

```
Procedure Add(var this_branch: Branch; new_data: String);
   { Adds new_data to the tree starting at this_branch }
   Begin
   If this_branch = nil Then   { If there's no branch, }
      Begin
      New(this_branch);           { grow a new branch }
      With this_branch^ Do
         Begin
         left_branch := nil;
         Data := new_data;   { and put our letter in the new fork at the top }
         right_branch := nil
         End
      End
   Else                          { OTHERWISE }
      Begin
      With this_branch^ Do   { Climb to the fork at the top of this branch }
         Begin
         If data > new_data Then { If the letter here is greater than ours, }
            Begin
            Add(left_branch, new_data)  { apply the rule to the left branch }
            End
         Else
            Begin                        { OTHERWISE }
            Add(right_branch, new_data) { Apply the rule to the right branch }
            End
         End
      End
   End;
```

Don't worry too much if this procedure looks a little daunting. It's based on a couple of nested If statements which implement the **OTHERWISE** mechanism of the rule.

We won't bore you with a detailed attempt to execute this procedure on paper. We did quite enough of that with the written version earlier. But, remember that we've shown you that the rule works, and that Turbo Pascal has all the right bits and pieces to implement it. That's plenty good enough for now.

We've seen all the statements in this procedure at various points throughout the chapter. Take a stroll through the procedure body and notice that there is a direct correspondence between each part of the written rule and the piece of code which implements it as we have shown by adding the written rule as comments.

Climbing a Tree

Now that we can grow a Turbo Pascal tree, we need to work out how to climb it.

A Recursive Climbing Procedure

No prizes for guessing that we're going to translate the recursive climbing rule into another recursive procedure. However, instead of writing the strings down in a notebook, we'll get the procedure to print them on the screen — so, **print** is a good name for it. Here's the written version of the rule again:

If there is a branch, climb to the fork at the top of the branch ...
  Apply the rule to the left branch.
  Write down the letter at this fork.
  Apply the rule to the right branch.

We'll need a **Branch** parameter to direct **print** to a particular part of the tree. It won't be modified in the procedure body, so it can be a *value* parameter. The procedure heading looks like this:

```
Procedure print(this_branch: Branch);
```

This time, the body is easier to write because the rule is somewhat simpler:

```
Procedure print(this_branch: Branch);
   { Prints the tree starting at this_branch }
   Begin
   If this_branch <> nil Then { If there's a branch here, }
      Begin
      With this_branch^ Do     { climb to the fork at the top of the branch }
         Begin
         Print(left_branch);   { Apply the rule to the left branch }
         WriteLn(data);        { Write down the letter at this fork }
         Print(right_branch);  { Apply the rule to the right branch }
         End
      End
   End;
```

Again, we've formed the comments directly from the written version of the rule to indicate what's going on.

The Tree Sort Program

Having translated our two recursive rules, we're ready to proceed to a main program which uses the types, variables and procedures we've looked at to sort some strings. It looks like this:

```
Program Ex_10_2;
{ Sorts an arbitrary number of strings entered by the user }
Uses Crt;
Type
    Branch = ^Fork;
    Fork = Record
        data: String;
        left_branch, right_branch: Branch
        End;
Var
    trunk: Branch;
    str: String;
< Procedure definitions go here >
Begin
Clrscr;

trunk := nil;          { Initialize the tree }

{ Prompt for input }
WriteLn('Please type in some strings (blank line to finish)');

ReadLn(str);           { Read the first string }
While str <> '' Do     { While we have a string to add }
    Begin
    Add(trunk, str);   { Add it }
    Readln(str)        { And read another }
    End;
Print(trunk)           { Print the tree }
End.
```

This program simply reads a sequence of strings from the user and adds them to the tree. When the user has had enough, the program prints the contents of the tree before exiting.

Of course, a user typing at the keyboard isn't likely to enter all that many strings by hand, but these procedures could easily be hooked up to a text file, or a database of customer names, or some other large collection of strings.

Summary

In this chapter, we introduced Turbo Pascal's pointer type which is fundamental to dynamic data structures.

We described alternatives to the storage mechanisms we've seen in previous chapters, namely **dynamic data structures** (lists, trees and graphs). Dynamic data structures are more flexible and are, indeed, essential for some complex applications.

We saw how a binary tree could be used on paper to perform an insertion sort of an arbitrary collection of letters. Here, we described simple recursive rules which, when followed precisely, did the tricky parts for us.

Next, we saw the mechanisms that Turbo Pascal provides for representing branches and forks using pointers. Finally, we saw how to translate the written rules into an application that will quickly sort any number of strings entered by the user.

This chapter has been something of a walk-through. We don't expect you to rush off and use the techniques described here to writing your own airline booking system - that's beyond the scope of this book. But you have had a good look at important techniques for advanced programming. Also, with a little effort, you should be able to adapt the final program to similar tasks.

Quiz Questions

1   How do you initialize a pointer variable?

2   How do you allocate a new piece of memory for a pointer variable, and how do you release the memory when you don't need it any more?

3   What are the three main varieties of dynamic data structure?

4   What makes a tree structure recursive?

5   What makes a procedure or function recursive?

6   Why are the forks of a Turbo Pascal tree represented as records?

Exercises

1   In `EX_10_2`, we used procedure `add()` to grow a tree with a "left is less than, right is greater than or equal" rule. Because of this property, the following three statements in `Print()` are guaranteed to visit the strings in ascending order:

```
Print(Left_branch);   { Apply the rule to the left branch }
WriteLn(Data);        { Write down the letter at this fork }
Print(Right_branch)   { Apply the rule to the right branch }
```

Modify `Print()`, by rearranging these statements, so that it prints the strings in reverse order.

2   The types, such as Fork, and procedures such as `Add()` that we defined for `EX_10_2` could be used to sort any set of strings, not just a small set entered at the keyboard. We should include these definitions in their own Turbo Pascal unit.

Using the techniques described in Chapter 6, create a file called **SORT.PAS**, which is the same as `EX_10_2` except that the procedures and

type definitions have been moved into a unit file **SORTUNT.TPU**
Compile the unit and the program and check that everything still
works.

3   The techniques described in this chapter can be used to sort all manner
of types, not just strings. What you sort depends on three things:

   ▶ How you define the fork record.

   ▶ What parameters you pass to Add().

   ▶ What kind of data you read from the user.

Modify your tree sorting code to sort Real values instead of String
values. Does everything work as expected?

# CHAPTER 11

Interacting With the User

In this final chapter, we're going to finish off our study of Turbo Pascal by writing the most important part of any program, the part the user sees. Making your programs look good and easy to use is the packaging of your program. If your program looks dull, unattractive and difficult to use (see DOS), users won't be encouraged to use it (and this includes you!). On the other hand, if you make your programs attractive, people will be queuing up.

The techniques we'll teach you in this chapter include:

▶ Creating text windows and using color

▶ Designing a menu system

▶ Selecting background procedures

▶ Refining the system

Designing a User Interface

In Chapter 9, we designed a personal information system. At the moment, it's a collection of unrelated programs. To add new records or to change records, you'd have to load up a new program each time. In this chapter, we're going to build a menu system we can use to select the various available options.

In Chapter 9, we wrote the programs to perform the tasks we need in the system. The task in hand now is to display a list of choices on screen, and link this menu with the procedures. When the user selects an option we have to make sure the appropriate procedure runs.

No Pane, No Gain - Opening Windows

The first step is to be able to write text to the screen and to control where the text appears. To draw a text window we can use the Turbo Pascal procedure Window().

Window()

The procedure Window() has the following structure:

Window(*Left_Column*, *Top_Row*, *Right_ Column*, *Bottom_ Row*);

Where *Left_Column*, *Top_Row*, *Right_Column* and *Bottom_Row* are the integer numbers of the relevant column or row. The window is drawn from the corner of the *Left_Column* and the *Top_Row* to the corner of the *Right_Column* and the *Bottom_Row*. Having drawn the window, the cursor then appears in the top left corner.

The number of columns in the window is equal to

Right_Column - *Left_Column* + 1

and the number of rows is equal to

Bottom_Row - *Top_Row* + 1

The following short program draws a text window and then adds some text:

```
Program Ex_11_1;
Uses CRT;
Begin
 ClrScr;
 Window(10,10,21,21);
 Write('What happens to this string');
End.
```

This is the result of running the program:

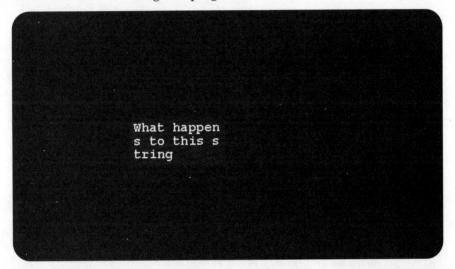

> Notice how the text wraps around on to the next line if it's too long. If text reaches the bottom of the window it scrolls the previous text up. This earlier text is then lost.

Coloring In

The window in the example is difficult to see because the background color is the same for the main screen as it is for the text window. To make your windows stand out, you need to do some coloring. Back in Chapter 4 we showed you the procedures TextBackground() and TextColor(). These allow you to select the background color and the color of the text.

To briefly recap, each procedure has the following format:

TextBackground(*Back_Color*);
TextColor(*Txt_Clr*);

where ***Back_Color*** can be any of **Black, Blue, Green, Cyan, Red, Magenta, Brown** or **LightGray** and ***Txt_Clr*** can be any of **Black, Blue, Green, Cyan, Red, Magenta, Brown, LightGray, DarkGray, LightBlue, LightGreen, LightCyan, LightRed, LightMagenta, Yellow** or **White**.

Clearing the Screen

We also need the procedure ClrScr. This clears the current window by writing a blank in each position, and changes the entire window to the background color. The cursor then appears in the top left-hand corner of the screen.

We have combined this all together in program **EX_11_2**.

```
Program Ex_11_2;
Uses CRT;
Begin
   ClrScr;
   TextBackground(Blue);
   TextColor(Black);
   Window(10,10,21,14);
   Clrscr;
   Writeln('This should appear on 2 lines');
   Write('Then this will appear on a new line');
End.
```

which gives the result below.

> Notice how the text scrolls up as it's written, so that you lose the top line of text.

> By counting the columns and rows you can see that the drawn window includes column 21 and row 14. So the numbers in the Windows() procedure are inclusive.

The System Requirements - Designing the Main Menu

Now that we know how to draw a text window, we need to examine what we need from the system. Below is a list of the basic requirements for our personal information system. You need to be able to do the following:

- Create a new file
- Open an existing file
- Add a new record to the file
- Find a specific record
- Amend a field in a record
- Exit the system

This should be our main menu.

Adding a Frame

We want to add a little pizzazz to our system, so we are going to add a frame to our menu using the following ASCII characters:

Chr(186) = ||
Chr(187) = ¬|
Chr(188) = ⌋|
Chr(200) = |L
Chr(201) = |⌐
Chr(205) = _

Framing a window is going to be a useful technique, so we'll write this as the procedure `Rectangle()`.

Writing Rectangle()

The procedure needs four parameters which are the same as the parameters of Window(). **Left_Col** and **Top_Row** are the coordinates of the upper left corner of the frame, and **Right_Col** and **Btm_Row** are the coordinates of the lower right corner of the frame. The procedure needs to draw the frame within the current window, but if you write a character in the final column of a text window, Turbo Pascal automatically moves the cursor to the next line. To avoid this, we'll leave the first and last columns empty to enhance the appearance.

First we need to draw the top line. Starting with a space then the appropriate corner piece, we need to write the double lines. We then finish off with a corner and move to the next line. The following statements:

```
Write(' ');
Write(Chr(201));
For I := (Left_Col + 2) to (Right_Col - 2) do
   Begin
   Write(Chr(205));
   End;
WriteLn(Chr(187));
```

draw the upper part of the frame (as in the figure below).

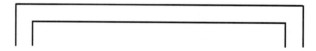

Next we need to draw the lines on either side. We do this by writing a space, then a double line on the left and a double line on the right and filling the gap in between with spaces using the following statements:

```
For I := Top_Row +1 to Btm_Row - 1 do
Begin
   Write(' ');
   Write(Chr(186));
   For J := Left_Col + 2 to Right_Col - 2 do
      Begin
      Write(' ');
      End;
   WriteLn(Chr(186));
End;
```

The picture now looks like the figure below:

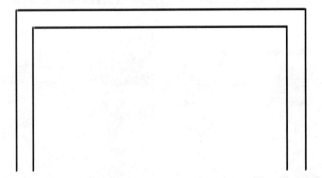

We draw the final line with the statements below. This completes the drawing:

```
Write(` `);
Write(Chr(200));
For I := Left_Col + 2 to Right_Col - 2 do
   Begin
   Write(Chr(205));
   End;
Write(Chr(188));
```

This is a list of the complete procedure:

```
Procedure Rectangle(Left_Col,Top_Row,Right_Col,Btm_Row : Integer);
Var
   I, J : Integer;
Begin
{Draw the space and the corner piece}
   Write(' ');
   Write(Chr(201));
{Draw the top line}
   For I := (Left_Col + 2) to (Right_Col - 2) do
      Begin
      Write(Chr(205));
      End;
{Draw corner piece and move to next line}
   WriteLn(Chr(187));
{From the top to the bottom}
   For I := (Top_Row +1) to (Btm_Row - 1) do
   Begin
{Draw the space and then the lines}
      Write(' ');
      Write(Chr(186));
{Draw the spaces in the middle}
      For J := (Left_Col + 2) to (Right_Col - 2) do
         Begin
         Write(' ');
         End;
      WriteLn(Chr(186));
   End;
{Draw the bottom line}
   Write(' ');
   Write(Chr(200));
   For I := (Left_Col + 2) to (Right_Col - 2) do
      Begin
      Write(Chr(205));
      End;
   Write(Chr(188));
End;
```

Talking to the User

So far our main menu consists of a different color window with a frame around it. We now need to decide what text to display. To make our system user-friendly, we need to ask the user to choose an option. To do this, we will need to open another text window inside the frame. We'll need to calculate how big this window will be. Inside the window, we'll want a message to appear, so we use the following statements:

```
Writeln(' Select an action and press Enter');
For I := 1 to 34 do
   Begin
   Write(Chr(205));
   End;
```

The For loop writes a double line under the message to separate it from the menu. We've added an extra space to the front of the message for clarity. Leaving room for a space at the end as well, the For loop prints 34 double-line characters. Printing the final character automatically moves the cursor down a line, but we can allow for that with the window size.

Displaying the Options

In our main window we need to write the list of options. If we declare an array of strings we can then assign the following values:

```
A[1] := '          Create          ';
A[2] := '          Open            ';
A[3] := '          Add             ';
A[4] := '          Find            ';
A[5] := '          Amend           ';
A[6] := '          Exit            ';
```

The user message is 34 characters long (including the space at either end). To center the text in the menu we have added 13 spaces before each word and then padded out the line to 33 characters (avoiding the final column). We can then use the following statements to write these values to the screen.

```
Writeln(A[1]);
Writeln(A[2]);
Writeln(A[3]);
Writeln(A[4]);
Writeln(A[5]);
Write  (A[6]);
```

We have used Write() for the last value to stop the lines scrolling up the screen.

Sizing the Windows

We now need to work out the size of the windows.

The message string is the longest part of the menu at 32 characters. With a space, lines either side from the rectangle and then another space at each end, we need to add on 6 more columns. So the window with the rectangle needs to be 38 columns wide. The screen has 80 columns. To center our window we need half the columns to the left of the 40th column. So we need to start the window in column 40 - 19 = 21.

The number of columns = 38 = Right_Col - Left_Col + 1, and we know Left_Col =21. So Right_Col =58.

Counting the number of rows, we have the top line, the message, the separating line, the 6 options and the final line. This equals 10 rows. It's easiest to read an article that's about a third of the way down the page, rather than one exactly in the middle. There are 25 rows in the screen so we shall start the window at row 6. Then, using the same formula as above, the bottom row will be row (10 + 6 - 1) = 15.

So, now we have the parameters for the main window and the rectangle:

Left_Col = 21, Top_Row = 6, Right_ Col = 58, and Btm_ Row = 15.

Now we need two more windows - one for the message, and one for the options. Both need to be inside the frame. So, in each case we need to allow 2 columns on each side for the space and the lines.

For the message, we need just 3 rows: one for the text, one for the line and one extra. We need to place this message one row down from the main window, so the parameters will be:

Left_Col = (23), Top_Row = (7), Right_ Col = (56), and Btm_ Row = (9)

For the options menu, we need 6 rows and we must start the window from where the message window finishes. So for the menu window the parameters are:

Left_Col = (23), Top_Row = (9), Right_ Col = (56), and Btm_ Row = (14).

The Main Menu

Now we have all the tools to build the program for the main menu below.

```
Program Ex_11_3;
Uses Crt;
Var
   A : Array[1..6] of String;
   I : Integer;
{_____}
```

```
{PROCEDURE RECTANGLE}
Procedure Rectangle(Left_Col,Top_Row,Right_Col,Btm_Row : Integer);
Var
   I, J : Integer;
Begin
{Draw the corner piece}
  Write(' ');
  Write(Chr(201));
{Draw the top line}
   For I := (Left_Col + 2) to (Right_Col - 2) do
      Begin
      Write(Chr(205));
      End;
{Draw corner piece and move to next line}
   WriteLn(Chr(187));
{From the top to the bottom}
   For I := (Top_Row + 1) to (Btm_Row - 1) do
   Begin
{Draw the space and the lines}
     Write(' ');
     Write(Chr(186));
{Draw the spaces in the middle}
     For J := (Left_Col + 2) to (Right_Col - 2) do
        Begin
        Write(' ');
        End;
{Draw the lines and move to next line}
     WriteLn(Chr(186));
   End;
{Draw the bottom line}
  Write(' ');
  Write(Chr(200));
   For I := (Left_Col + 2) to (Right_Col - 2) do
      Begin
      Write(Chr(205));
      End;
   Write(Chr(188));
End;
{_____}
{MAIN PROGRAM}
Begin
{Clear the Screen of any DOS messages}
   Clrscr;
{Assign the Strings}
   A[1] := '          Create          ';
   A[2] := '          Open            ';
   A[3] := '          Add             ';
   A[4] := '          Find            ';
   A[5] := '          Amend           ';
   A[6] := '          Exit            ';
{Draw background window in Blue}
   TextBackground(Blue);
   Window(21,6,58,15);
```

```
   Clrscr; {converts background to chosen color}
{Set the color for the frame and the message}
   TextColor(Red);
{Draw the frame}
   Rectangle(21,6,58,15);
{Write the User Message}
   Window(23,7,56,8);
   WriteLn(' Select an action and press Enter');
   For I := 1 to 34 do
      Begin
      Write(Chr(205));
      End;
{Dwrite the menu}
   TextBackground(Blue);
   TextColor(Yellow);
   Window(23,9,56,14);
   WriteLn(A[1]);
   WriteLn(A[2]);
   WriteLn(A[3]);
   WriteLn(A[4]);
   WriteLn(A[5]);
   Write  (A[6]);
End.
```

Highlighting an Option

Our next step is to highlight one of the options and to be able to move the highlight bar up or down, depending on which arrow key is pressed.

Blinking Create

To highlight one option, we'll use a window with a height of one row. This window will be a different color from the background. We will apply this first to highlight the word 'Create'.

The window which contains the text of the options had the following dimensions:

Left_Col = (23), Top_Row = (9), Right_ Col = (56), and Btm_ Row = (14).

and the option 'Create' is on the 9th row.

We can easily reset the background color and the foreground character color using these procedures:

```
TextBackground(Green);
TextColor(White + Blink);
```

We even set the characters blinking to attract the users attention.

We then need to create the one row window on row 9.

```
Window(23, 9, 56, 9);
```

Remember, the Window procedure includes the bottom row as well, so this must also be 9 to make the window one row. Now we write the text of the option in the window:

```
Write (A[1]);
```

So to add a blinking line over the Create option we need to add the following statements to **EX_11_3**.

```
TextBackground(Green);
TextColor(White + Blink);
Window(23, 9, 56, 9);
Write (A[1]);
Window(23, 9, 56, 9);
```

By opening the window the second time, we move the cursor to the left column of the window.

By adding these statements and running the program you will see the following screen. Unfortunately we can't show the color.

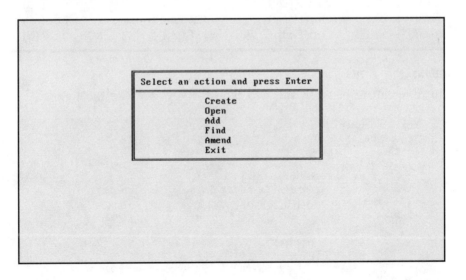

```
Select an action and press Enter
        Create
        Open
        Add
        Find
        Amend
        Exit
```

Function Keys and Readkey

Controlling the movement of the highlight bar isn't very complex, but we will need some additional knowledge about the function Readkey.

Both Read() and Readkey return the value of the last character pressed on the keyboard. Using ReadKey, however, the information doesn't appear on the screen. What's more, Readkey distinguishes between keys with an ASCII code, like 'A', '1' or even *Esc,* and **function** keys like the arrow keys or *F1* through *F12.*

If a function key is pressed, then the keyboard first sends the 'null' character. The null character is ASCII code number 0. Having sent the null character, the keyboard then sends the **extended key code** for the function key. This is a unique code for each function key.

As with ASCII codes, the extended key codes are numbered. This allows you to use the function Ord() to find the number of the key code.

Below is a short list of some of the numbers of the extended key codes. A more comprehensive list is in Appendix H.

Key	Code	Key	Code	Key	Code	Key	Code
Ord(←)	75	Ord(*PgUp*)	73	Ord(*F1*)	59	Ord(*F5*)	63
Ord(↑)	72	Ord(*PgDn*)	81	Ord(*F2*)	60	Ord(*F6*)	64
Ord(→)	77	Ord(*Home*)	71	Ord(*F3*)	61	Ord(*F7*)	65
Ord(↓)	80	Ord(*End*)	79	Ord(*F4*)	62	Ord(*F8*)	66

Separating the Keys

To differentiate between the two types of keys we use the following statements:

```
Ch_1:= Readkey;
 If Ord(Ch_1) <> 0
    Then
       Begin
          Write('You pressed ', Ch_1);
          WriteLn('which is ASCII value ', Ord(Ch_1));
       End
    Else
       Begin
          Ch_2 := Readkey;
          Write('You pressed a functional key ');
          WriteLn('whose extended key code number is ', Ord(Ch_2));
       End;
```

If the first character is the null character, then we switch to the Else statements and use ReadKey again. This time it assigns the extended key code to the variable **Ch_2**. The function **Ord(Ch_2)** then returns the number of the extended key code of the function key pressed.

Using the Arrow Keys

The number of the extended key code for the ↑ key is 72 and for the ↓ key is 80. Using ReadKey we know how to tell if the arrow keys have been pressed. With this information, we can continue with the problem of how to move the highlight bar up or down over the six options.

The skeleton of the program would be as follows:

```
Repeat
   ...
< draw main menu >
   ...
< draw highlighted window >
   ...
   Ch_1 := Readkey;
   If Ord(Ch_1) = 0
      Then
         Begin
            Ch_2 := Readkey;
            If Ord(Ch_2) = 80
               Then
                     < move highlighted window down >
               Else
                  If Ord(Ch_2) = 72
                     < move highlighted window up >
         End;
Until Ord(Ch_1) = 13;
```

The loop will continue until **Ord(Ch_1) = 13** which is the ASCII number for the *Enter* key.

Within the loop, we only react to the two arrow keys, and we only enter the If statements if a function key is pressed. Otherwise, control remains within the loop until the *Enter* key is pressed.

Moving the Window

Having established how to test which keys have been pressed, the next step is to consider how we'll move the highlight bar. In practical terms, this means redrawing the text of the options and the highlight bar. Because the computer does this so fast, it looks to the user as though we have just moved the bar.

Remember the statements to draw the highlighted window:

```
TextBackground(Green);
TextColor(White + Blink);
Window(23, 9, 56, 9);
Write  (A[1]);
Window(23, 9, 56, 9);
```

This only re-draws the first option so we will need to make these statements more flexible by altering them to be the following:

```
TextBackground(Green);
TextColor(White + Blink);
Window(23,8 + No_line, 56, 8 + No_line);
Write  (A[No_line]);
Window(23, 8 + No_line, 56, 8 + No_line);
```

The variable **No_line** now gives the position within the main menu which must be highlighted. If the value of **No_line** is one then the option Create will be highlighted, and so on. The value of **No_line** must be an integer between one and six.

To link the two parts we must reduce the value of **No_line** by one each time the ↑ key is pressed, and increase it by one each time the ↓ key is pressed. We can now write the following statements to control the movement of the highlighted window:

```
No_line := 1;
Repeat
   TextColor(Yellow);
   TextBackground(Blue);
   Window(23,9,56,14);
   WriteLn(A[1]);
   WriteLn(A[2]);
   WriteLn(A[3]);
   WriteLn(A[4]);
   WriteLn(A[5]);
   Write  (A[6]);
   TextBackground(Green);
   TextColor(White + Blink);
   Window(23, 8 + No_line, 56, 8 + No_line);
   Write  (A[No_line]);
   Window(23, 8 + No_line, 56, 8 + No_line);
   Ch_1 := Readkey;
   If Ord(Ch_1) = 0
      Then
         Begin
```

```
        Ch_2 := Readkey;
        If Ord(Ch_2) = 80
           Then
               Begin
                   No_line := No_line + 1;
               End
           Else
               If Ord(Ch_2) = 72
                  Then
                      Begin
                          No_line := No_line - 1;
                      End
      End;
Until Ord(Ch_1) = 13;
```

Each pass through the loop re-draws the menu and moves the highlight to another option.

Executing these statements, the value of **No_line** is initially set to one. After that, the value is only changed by pressing the ↑ or the ↓ keys. When the *Enter* key is pressed the loop ceases.

Preventing an Error

However, we still need further control over the movement of the highlight bar. At the moment, if a user pressed the ↑ key ten times then **No_line** would be equal to -10, but there are only six options in the main menu. To avoid this problem you control the movement of the highlight bar in the following ways:

1 If the value of **No_line** would become greater than six, reset the value to one.

2 If the value of **No_line** would become less than one, set the value to six.

Implementing these changes, we revise the If statements as follows:

```
Ch_1 := Readkey;
If Ord(Ch_1) = 0
   Then
      Begin
          Ch_2 := Readkey;
          If Ord(Ch_2) = 80
             Then
                 Begin
                     No_line := No_line + 1;
```

```
                    If No_line > 6
                        Then
                            Begin
                            No_line := 1;
                            End;
              End
          Else
              If Ord(Ch_2) = 72
                  Then
                      Begin
                      No_line := No_line - 1;
                      If No_line < 1
                          Then
                              Begin
                              No_line := 6;
                              End;
                  End;
      End;
```

This final feature provides us with a robust menu system which only reacts to the ↑ and the ↓ keys and restricts movement to the list of options.

Choosing Which Part to Execute

Now we have the menu system working the next part to consider is how we pass control to the programs for each option. For the time being, we will assume that we have written procedures for each of the options, and a Case statement can be used to issue a procedure call.

We already have a variable **No_line** that's used to indicate which option we have chosen. When the *Enter* key is pressed, the value of **No_line** is fixed at the number of the line corresponding to this option. So we can use the following Case statement to select the procedure:

```
Case No_line of
        1 : Begin
            Create;
            End;
        2 : Begin
            Open;
            End;
        3 : Begin
            Add;
            End;
        4 : Begin
            Find;
            End;
```

```
         5 : Begin
               Amend;
               End;
         6 : Begin
                 If External_name <> ''
                    Then
                       Begin
                       Close(My_file);
                       End;
                 End;
End; {Case}
```

You'll notice we haven't written a separate procedure for the Exit option, as this is a simple question of closing any opened files and ending the program. If you selected Exit immediately, then no files would be open, so we need a test to deal with this. In this instance, the value of the variable **External_name** would be an empty string and so we can use this to end the program.

Going Back to the Menu

Once you have executed a procedure you must return to the main menu, so we need another Repeat statement. This must enclose the earlier Repeat statement and the Case statement so the structure of the program needs to be as follows:

```
Repeat
   Repeat
      ...
   < draw main menu >
      ...
   < draw highlighted window >
      ...
   < manipulate highlight bar >
      ...
   Until Ord(Ch_1) = 13;
   Case No_line of
1 : Begin
               Create;
               End;
         2 : Begin
               Open;
               End;
         3 : Begin
               Add;
               End;
         4 : Begin
               Find;
               End;
```

```
        5 : Begin
            Amend;
            End;
        6 : Begin
            If External_name <> ''
               Then
                  Begin
                  Close(My_file);
                  End;
            End;
    End;{Case}
Until No_line = 6;
```

The loop repeats until the user chooses to exit.

The Main Menu - The Code

If we now assume that our procedures (including **rectangle**) are stored in the unit **MY_SYS**, the full program for running the menu is listed below:

```
Program Ex_11_4;
Uses Crt, My_Sys;
Var
    A : Array[1..6] of String;
    I, No_line : Integer;
    Ch_1, Ch_2 : Char;
Begin
{Clear the Screen of any DOS messages}
    Clrscr;
{Assign the Strings}
    A[1] := '        Create        ';
    A[2] := '        Open          ';
    A[3] := '        Add           ';
    A[4] := '        Find          ';
    A[5] := '        Amend         ';
    A[6] := '        Exit          ';
{Draw background window in Blue}
    TextBackground(Blue);
    Window(21,6,58,15);
    Clrscr; {converts background to chosen color}
{Set the color for the frame and the message}
    TextColor(Red);
{Draw the frame}
    Rectangle(21,6,58,15);
{Write the User Message}
    Window(23,7,56,9);
    WriteLn(' Select an action and press Enter');
    For I := 1 to 34 do
       Begin
```

```
      Write(Chr(205));
      End;
{Initialize the variable}
   No_line := 1;
   Repeat
     Repeat
{Write the menu}
     TextBackground(Blue);
     TextColor(Yellow);
     Window(23,9,56,14);
     Writeln(A[1]);
     Writeln(A[2]);
     Writeln(A[3]);
     Writeln(A[4]);
     Writeln(A[5]);
     Write(A[6]);
{Draw the Highlight bar}
     TextBackground(Green);
     TextColor(White + Blink);
     Window(23, 8 + No_line, 56, 8 + No_line);
     Write    (A[No_line]);
     Window(23, 8 + No_line, 56, 8 + No_line);
{Test which key pressed and move the bar accordingly}
     Ch_1 := Readkey;
     If Ord(Ch_1) = 0
        Then
           Begin
               Ch_2 := Readkey;
               If Ord(Ch_2) = 80
                   Then
                       Begin
                           No_line := No_line + 1;
                           If No_line > 6
                               Then
                               Begin
                               No_line := 1;
                               End;
                       End
                   Else
                       If Ord(Ch_2) = 72
                           Then
                               Begin
                                   No_line := No_line - 1;
                                   If No_line < 1
                                   Then
                                       Begin
                                       No_line := 6;
                                       End;
                               End;
           End;
     Until Ord(Ch_1) = 13;
```

```
     Case No_line of
          1 : Begin
              Create;
              End;
          2 : Begin
              Open;
              End;
          3 : Begin
              Add;
              End;
          4 : Begin
              Find;
              End;
          5 : Begin
              Amend;
              End;
          6 : Begin
                If External_name <> ''
                     Then
                        Begin
                        Close(My_file);
                        End;
              End;
     End;{Case}
Until No_line = 6;
End.
```

Adding the Procedures

The main menu is now ready and we need to write the five procedures: 'Create', 'Open', 'Add', 'Find', and 'Amend'. The body of the procedures were written in Chapter 9. We just need to make them more user-friendly, and to add a dialog window to let the user and the program exchange information.

Creating a File

The aim of this procedure is to create a file, so we need to elicit the name of the file to be created. We then need to check whether or not the file already exists. If it already exists, then the procedure must ask what action the user wishes to take. There are two possibilities:

- The user really wants to overwrite the file

- Or, the user has made a mistake.

Our procedure must be capable of dealing with both situations.

Talking to the User

Firstly, we need to ask the user for the name of the file to be created and then read that name.

```
WriteLn('Enter a file name : ');
ReadLn(External_name);
```

Now we must check whether or not the file exists. To do this we need to use the compiler directive **{$I-}** and the function IOResult.

The Compiler Directive {$I-}

By default, all calls by the standard input and output procedures such as Read(), Write() Reset() and Rewrite() are automatically checked for errors. When you write

```
Reset(My_file);
```

Turbo Pascal checks to see whether the file has already been created. If this is the case, everything will work fine. If the file hasn't been created, however, the automatic checking will report a run-time error and the program will crash.

Because there are occasions when you'll anticipate there being an error and you want to prevent the program crashing, Turbo Pascal allows you to turn this automatic checking off and on using the **{$I-}** and **{$I+}** compiler directives.

> Compiler directives are instructions directed at the compiler. They allow you to switch a wide variety of aspects on and off from within your program. The format of a directive is a $ sign signifying a directive, followed by the initial letter of the action, followed by a + or a - sign to signify turning the aspect on or off. All this is enclosed in {}.

To turn the Input/Output checking off whilst we call the Reset() procedure you add the directive **{$I-}** before the procedure call. It is a good habit to turn the checking back on again as soon as you can by adding **{$I+}** so the statements above now become as follows:

```
WriteLn('Enter a file name : ');
ReadLn(External_name);
Assign(My_file, External_name);
{$I-}
Reset(My_file);
{$I+}
```

Now, if the file doesn't exist, an error is still reported, but the program won't crash. The function IOResult reports whether or not an error has occurred.

IOResult Function

If there are no errors during the execution of Input/Output procedures, IOResult returns the value zero. If there *is* an error, the result is non-zero. So we can test the value of IOResult to make a decision about which actions to take. The procedure now becomes this:

```
WriteLn('Enter a file name : ');
ReadLn(External_name);
Assign(My_file, External_name);
{$I-}
Reset(My_file);
{$I+}
If IOResult = 0
   Then
      Begin
         TextColor(White+blink);
         WriteLn('File already exists!');
         TextColor(White);
         WriteLn('Overwrite? Reply y/n : ');
         Readln(Ch);
         If (Ch = 'y') or (Ch = 'Y')
            Then
               Begin
                  Rewrite(My_file);
                  Write('DONE! Press any key to continue:');
                  Readkey;
               End;
      End
   Else
      Begin
         Rewrite(My_file);
         Write('DONE! Press any key to continue:');
         Readkey;
      End;
```

If IOResult returns the value zero there was no error in the Input/Output procedure Reset so the file must already exist. As we are trying to create the file, we must inform the user of this fact and ask the user to make a decision about whether or not to continue. If the user goes ahead, the file is overwritten, otherwise the user is sent back to the main menu.

On the other hand, if IOResult returns a non-zero value, it means that Reset() was unable to find a file. This is actually what we wanted, so the procedure creates the file as requested.

Attracting Attention

If the file already exists, we want to alert the user that something is wrong. By changing the color of the text to white, and setting the blink option with the statement:

```
TextColor(White+blink);
```

we should be able to attract their attention.

Pausing the Procedure

So that we confirm to the user that the file has been created, we use the following statements:

```
Write('DONE! Press any key to continue:');
Readkey;
```

The Readkey procedure waits for a key to be pressed. In this instance, that is all we use it for and the particular key is ignored. When a key is pressed the program resumes.

A Dialog box for Create

Now we know what we want to say, we are in a position to design a dialog box for the procedure. We'll maintain the continuity with the central window within the frame, so we need to work out how big these new windows need to be.

Counting the Columns

The longest string is the line

```
Write('DONE! Press any key to continue:');
```

with 32 characters, so the inner window must be at least 32 columns wide. As the main menu window allows 34 characters, we are well advised to re-use the coordinates of this window. It also saves us time working out how to re-center the window.

Counting the Rows

If you step through the procedure as it stands, you can see the following statements affect the number of rows.

```
WriteLn('Enter a file name : ');
ReadLn(External_name);
    ...
         WriteLn('File already exists!');
    ...
         WriteLn('Overwrite? Reply y/n : ');
         Readln(Ch);
    ...
             Write('DONE! Press any key to continue:');
    ...
      Write('DONE! Press any key to continue:');
```

The first statement writes a message to the screen and moves to the next line. The ReadLn() reads the value entered onto the screen and then moves to the next line, so we need at least 2 rows in the window. Working through the program like this, and counting the number of lines output to the screen, you can see that you can count the number of rows to fit all the information on the screen. Choosing the branches of the If statements that lead to the most number of lines written to the screen we can count that we need at most 5 rows.

So the internal text window must be at least 5 rows deep. The text window for the main menu has 6 rows, has at least the right number of columns, and fits in the frame. Rather than do any more calculation, we'll just re-use the code for this window.

The Dialog Window

As a result, the window for our dialog box uses the following statements:

```
TextBackground(Blue);
TextColor(Yellow);
Window(23,9,56,14);
Clrscr;
```

Creating a File - the Code

The full procedure is shown below.

```
Procedure Create;
Var
   Ch : Char;
Begin
   TextBackground(Blue);
   TextColor(Yellow);
   Window(23,9,56,14);
   Clrscr;
```

```
WriteLn('Enter a file name : ');
ReadLn(External_name);
Assign(My_file, External_name);
{$I-}
Reset(My_file);
{$I+}
If IOResult = 0
    Then
        Begin
            TextColor(White+blink);
            WriteLn('File already exists!');
            TextColor(White);
            Writeln('Overwrite? Reply y/n : ');
            Readln(Ch);
            If (Ch = 'y') or (Ch = 'Y')
                Then
                    Begin
                        Rewrite(My_file);
                        Write('DONE! Press a key to continue.');
                        Readkey;
                    End;
        End
    Else
        Begin
            Rewrite(My_file);
            Write('DONE! Press a key to continue.');
            Readkey;
        End;
   TextBackground(Blue);
   TextColor(Yellow);
End;
```

The two statements at the end

```
TextBackground(Blue);
TextColor(Yellow);
```

reset the background and text colors, as the text will sometimes have become white.

This is a picture of the dialog box on screen.

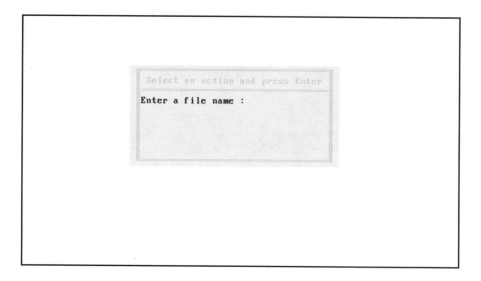

Opening a File

This procedure is very similar to the procedure for **create** as it must also check whether the file already exists.

Checking the File Exists

The corner-stone of the procedure **Open** is the following statements:

```
WriteLn('Enter a file name : ');
ReadLn(External_name);
Assign(My_file, External_name);
{$I-}
Reset(My_file);
{$I+}
If IOResult <> 0
   Then
      Begin
      TextColor(White+blink);
      WriteLn('Sorry' , External_name );
      WriteLn('doesn''t exist!');
      WriteLn('You must create it first.');
      WriteLn('Press any key to continue:');
      Readkey;
      End
```

```
Else
   Begin
   Write('DONE! Press any key to continue:');
   Readkey;
   End;
```

The procedure asks you for the name of the file to be opened, reads in the name, and then links the external name to the internal name. The next step, similar to the procedure for **create**, is to turn off the automatic check for Input/Output errors. Having done this, the procedure tries to open the file. Based on the value of IOResult, we either find that the file can't be opened because it hasn't yet been created, or the file is opened successfully.

In both cases we inform the user of the result and wait for them to press a key.

A Dialog Box for Open

All that is left is to add a dialog box and the procedure is complete.

As the procedure includes the line

```
WriteLn('DONE! Press any key to continue:');
```

you can see that we need the 34 columns of the main menu window. Working through the program, choosing the branches of the If statements that cause the most output, we can see that we need 6 rows. Once again, we save ourselves the trouble of doing any calculations and re-use the existing code.

Opening a File - the Code

Putting these two parts together we get the full listing below.

```
Procedure Open;
Begin
   TextBackground(Blue);
   TextColor(Yellow);
   Window(23,9,56,14);
   Clrscr;
   WriteLn('Enter a file name : ');
   ReadLn(External_name);
   Assign(My_file, External_name);
   {$I-}
   Reset(My_file);
   {$I+}
   If IOResult <> 0
```

```
   Then
      Begin
      TextColor(White+blink);
      WriteLn('Sorry ' , External_name );
      WriteLn('doesn''t exist!');
      WriteLn('You must create it first.');
      WriteLn('Press a key to continue.');
      Readkey;
      End
   Else
      Begin
         Write('DONE! Press a key to continue.');
         Readkey;
      End;
   TextBackground(Blue);
   TextColor(Yellow);
End;
```

Adding, Finding, and Amending a Record

Having opened the file, we then want to process the information in one of three ways. With the file open, the procedures written in Chapter 9 will apply the chosen option. To make these procedures compatible with our new system, we just need to add some user interaction to each procedure.

The Add Dialog Box

The body of the **Add** procedure is shown below:

```
Seek(My_file, FileSize(My_file));
WriteLn('Enter a name:');
ReadLn(Rec_var.Name);
WriteLn('Enter a date of birth:');
ReadLn(Rec_var.Date_of_birth);
WriteLn('Enter a telephone number:');
ReadLn(Rec_var.Telephone_number);
Write(My_file, Rec_var);
```

To accommodate this output we need a window at least 6 rows deep. As for the number of columns, to accommodate someone's name we can probably survive with the 34 columns available in our dialog box. Again we just need to repeat the statements we used before.

Adding a Record - the Code

The full procedure is listed on the following page.

```
Procedure Add;
Begin
   TextBackground(Blue);
   TextColor(Yellow);
   Window(23,9,56,14);
   Clrscr;
   Seek(My_file, FileSize(My_file));
   Writeln('Enter a name:');
   ReadLn(Rec_var.Name);
   Writeln('Enter a date of birth:');
   ReadLn(Rec_var.Date_of_birth);
   Writeln('Enter a telephone number:');
   ReadLn(Rec_var.Telephone_number);
   Write(My_file, Rec_var);
   TextBackground(Blue);
   TextColor(Yellow);
End;
```

Interacting with Find

We now repeat this process for the **Find** Procedure. The body of the procedure is as follows:

```
Counter := 0;
Writeln('Enter a name to be found : ');
ReadLn(Sought_Name);
Repeat
   Seek(My_file, Counter);
   Read(My_file, Rec_var);
   Found := (Rec_var.Name = Sought_Name);
   Counter := Counter + 1;
   If Found
      Then
          Begin
          Found_ind := Counter;
          End;
Until Found or Eof(My_file);
If Found
   Then
      Begin
          Seek(My_file, Found_ind - 1);
          Read(My_file, Rec_var);
          WriteLn(Rec_var.Name);
          WriteLn(Rec_var.Date_of_birth);
          WriteLn(Rec_var.Telephone_number);
      End
   Else
      Begin
          WriteLn(Sought_Name);
          WriteLn('is not in the file');
      End;
```

To make the procedure more user-friendly, we need to pause the program after either message is displayed, whether or not the record was found, so that the user can see what happened. To do this we add the statements:

```
Write('DONE! Press any key to continue:');
Readkey;
```

after each message.

We also need to alert the user if we don't find the name so we include the statement:

```
TextColor(White+blink);
```

before the warning message and afterwards:

```
TextColor(White);
```

Finally we need to add the text window, and again we re-use the code from before.

Finding a Record - the Code

The full procedure for finding a record is listed below:

```
Procedure Find;
Var
    Sought_Name         : String;
    Found               : Boolean;
    Counter, Found_ind  : Integer;
Begin
    TextBackground(Blue);
    TextColor(Yellow);
    Window(23,9,56,14);
    Clrscr;
    Counter := 0;
    Writeln('Enter a name to be found : ');
    ReadLn(Sought_Name);
    Repeat
        Seek(My_file, Counter);
        Read(My_file, Rec_var);
        Found := (Rec_var.Name = Sought_Name);
        Counter := Counter + 1;
        If Found
            Then
                Begin
```

```
                    Found_ind := Counter;
                End;
    Until Found or Eof(My_file);
    If Found
       Then
          Begin
             Seek(My_file, Found_ind - 1);
             Read(My_file, Rec_var);
             WriteLn(Rec_var.Name);
             WriteLn(Rec_var.Date_of_birth);
             WriteLn(Rec_var.Telephone_number);
             Write('Press a key to continue.');
             Readkey;
          End
       Else
          Begin
             TextColor(White+blink);
             WriteLn(Sought_Name);
             WriteLn('is not in the file');
             TextColor(White);
             Write('Press a key to continue.');
             Readkey;
          End;
    TextBackground(Blue);
    TextColor(Yellow);
End;
```

Amending a Record - the Code

Applying a similar analysis to the **amend** procedure we get the following statements:

```
Procedure Amend;
Var
   Sought_Name         : String;
   Found               : Boolean;
   Counter, Found_ind  : Integer;
Begin
   TextBackground(Blue);
   TextColor(Yellow);
   Window(23,9,56,14);
   Clrscr;
   Counter := 0;
   Writeln('Enter a name to be found : ');
   ReadLn(Sought_Name);
   Repeat
      Seek(My_file, Counter);
      Read(My_file, Rec_var);
      Found := (Rec_var.Name = Sought_Name);
      Counter := Counter + 1;
```

```
        If Found
            Then
                Begin
                Found_ind := Counter;
                End
    Until Found or Eof(My_file);
    If Found
        Then
            Begin
                Seek(My_file, Found_ind - 1);
                Read(My_file, Rec_var);
                WriteLn('Enter new telephone number : ');
                ReadLn(Rec_var.Telephone_number);
                Seek(My_file, Found_ind - 1);
                Write(My_file, Rec_var);
                Writeln('Press a key to continue.');
                Readkey;
            End
        Else
            Begin
                TextColor(White+blink);
                WriteLn(Sought_Name);
                WriteLn('is not in the file');
                TextColor(White);
                WriteLn('Press a key to continue.');
                Readkey;
            End;
    TextBackground(Blue);
    TextColor(Yellow);
End;
```

Writing the Unit - My_Sys

Now that we've written all the procedures, we need to gather them together and write our unit. When you write a unit, you'll sometimes need some types, variables or even procedures from another unit to be available globally to all of the procedures in your unit. To make this possible, you need to include the necessary declarations and definitions after the reserved word interface and before the list of sub-program headings. In this way, a unit has the same structure as a normal Turbo Pascal program.

In our unit we will need the following:

> A uses clause so that the **Crt** unit can be used by each of our procedures

> A definition of **rec_type**, and

> A declaration of the three variables **My_file**, **External_name** and **Rec_var** which are common to most of the procedures.

We now have all the information we need to write the interface.

> As we have already listed the complete procedures earlier, we will limit the statement list below to the procedure headings, including all declarations and definitions, and in the body of the unit we'll simply have an indication of where the individual procedures need to go.

```
Unit My_sys;

Interface

Uses Crt;

Type Rec_type = Record
                  Name             : String;
                  Date_of_birth    : String;
                  Telephone_number : String;
                End;
Var
   My_file       : File of Rec_type;
   External_name : String;
   Rec_var       : Rec_type;

Procedure Rectangle(Left_Col,Top_Row,Right_Col,Btm_Row : Integer);
Procedure Create;
Procedure Open;
Procedure Add;
Procedure Find;
Procedure Amend;

Implementation

Procedure Rectangle(Left_Col,Top_Row,Right_Col,Btm_Row : Integer);
<Body of Procedure Rectangle goes here>
End;

Procedure Create;
<Body of Procedure Create goes here>
End;

Procedure Open;
<Body of Procedure Open goes here>
End;

Procedure Add;
```

```
<Body of Procedure Add goes here>
End;

Procedure Find;
<Body of Procedure Find goes here>
End;

Procedure Amend;
<Body of Procedure Amend goes here>
End;
End.   {End this unit as you would a program}
```

Having written the unit, you need to compile it. So that the unit is available when you exit Turbo Pascal, change the Destination option in the Compile menu to Disk. Once compiled, the module **MY_SYS.TPU** will be available for all your programs.

The final step is to compile the main program. Again we must set the Destination option to Disk. This will produce an executable file **EX_11_4.EXE**. This file can now be run from DOS. If you quit Turbo Pascal and type **EX_11_4** at the DOS prompt, you should see the main menu in front of you as in the following screenshot:

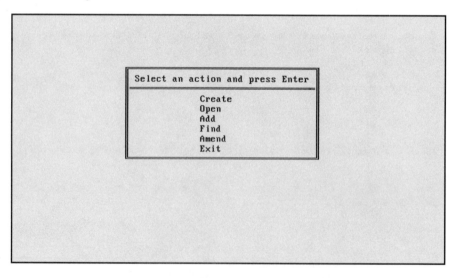

If you wanted to amend some records you would see the following screen:

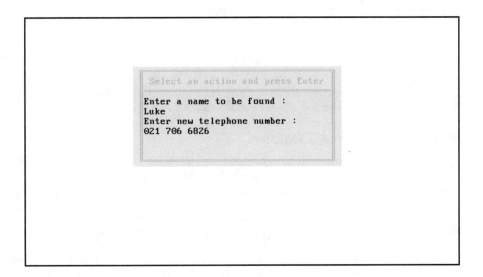

```
   Select an action and press Enter

Enter a name to be found :
Luke
Enter new telephone number :
021 706 6826
```

This is now a fully working system from which you can create files, amend records and so on. But this is only the first version of the system. We must now look at ways of improving the program.

Evaluating and Improving Your Program

In all our years of programming, we've never got a perfect result at the first stage of a program. Even with relatively small programs, it's easy to overlook things. It's often best to write a first version of the system, and then to test it and evaluate how well it performs the task you originally set yourself. Having done these tests, you can then rewrite fragments of the program to improve the system.

Testing the current version of the system we soon found an error. The user can try and add, find or amend a file, before opening the file. This causes a run-time error and the program fails. We need to change the system so that this can't happen.

Hiding Options

To prevent the user trying to select the activity options before the file is opened, we need to restrict the user so that they can only select the Create, Open, or Exit options. We can do this by 'hiding' the Add, Find or Amend options from view when the program starts. The user can then choose to create or open a file or even exit the system. We need to leave the user with only these options until they open a file. Once they have opened a file, we then need to remove the Create and Open options from the menu.

Restricting the Users Choice

We can limit the options available to the user by only allowing the highlight bar to highlight the specific options. As the variable to indicate the position of the bar is used to select the particular procedure, limiting the movement of the bar limits the choice for the user.

We want to restrict the user to the three options Create, Open or Exit, so the variable `No_line` must only take the values 1, 2, or 6. Also, the highlight bar should cycle through these options. So if the bar is on the option Open pressing the ↓ key must move the bar to the Exit option. Pressing it again must move the bar back to the Create option. The following program fragment restricts the movement of the highlight bar to cycling through the three options.

```
Ch_1:= Readkey;
If Ord(Ch_1) = 0
  Then
  Begin
    Ch_2 := Readkey;
    If Ord(Ch_2) = 80
      Then
        Begin
        {Down key pressed so increase No_line by 1}
        No_line := No_line + 1;
        {Check if now bar would move down past "Open"}
          If No_line > 2
            Then
            Begin
            {Check if now bar would move down past "Exit"}
              If No_line > 6
                Then
                Begin
                {If yes to both questions move bar to "Create"}
                No_line := 1;
                End
              Else
```

```
                    Begin
                    {If yes to first and no to second move bar to "Exit"}
                    No_line := 6;
                    End
            End
        End
    Else
      If Ord(Ch) = 72
        Then
        Begin
        {Up key pressed so decrease No_line by one}
        No_line := No_line - 1;
        {Check if bar would move up past "Create"}
        If No_line < 1
          Then
          Begin
          {If yes move bar to "Exit"}
          No_line := 6;
          End
        Else
          Begin
          {If no check if bar would move up above "Exit"}
          If (No_line < 6) and (No_line > 2)
            Then
            Begin
            {If yes move bar to "Open"}
            No_line := 2;
            End;
          End;
        End;
    End;
```

Telling the Program a File is Open

Once a file has been opened, we then need to offer the user the activity options. This requires some communication between the **open** procedure and the main program.

Changing the Open Procedure

Within the **open** procedure we need to declare a boolean variable **Opened**. Depending on what happens within the procedure, we can then assign **Opened** the value **true** or **false**. By making **Opened** a variable parameter of the procedure, we can then return its value to the main program. You'll need to change the procedure to include the new lines as below.

```
Procedure Open(Var Opened : Boolean);
Begin
   TextBackground(Blue);
```

```
   . . .
   If IOResult <> 0
      Then
         Begin
         Opened := False;
   . . .

         End
      Else
         Begin
            Opened := True;
            Write('DONE! Press a key to continue.');
            Readkey;
         End;
   TextBackground(Blue);
   TextColor(Yellow);
End;
```

Remember to also change the procedure heading in the unit.

Changing the Main Program

Within the main program, we also need to declare a boolean variable to indicate which menu items can be selected. This time we'll call it **File_Open**. We need to initially set the variable to **false** so we add a statement to the beginning of the program so that it now reads:

```
. . .
No_line  := 1;
File_Open := False;
Repeat
. . .
```

By calling the open procedure with **File_Open** as the actual parameter, the value of **File_Open** will be set equal to the value of **Opened** when the procedure has finished. So we also need to change the procedure call to the following:

```
Open(File_Open);
```

Once the file has been opened, we want the options in the menu to be restricted to the activity options only, so we also fix the variable **No_line** at 3. The next time through the Repeat loop the Add option will be highlighted. If the file hasn't been opened we need to take the user back to the Create, Open and Exit options only. This time we need to set **No_line** to 1.

To make these changes, the Case statement now becomes:

```
...
2 : Begin
    Open(File_Open);
    If File_Open
      Then
        Begin
        No_line := 3;
        End
      Else
        Begin
        No_line := 1;
        End
    End;
...
```

Finally, we can use our new variable to check whether we need to close a file when we exit by changing the If statement in the Exit option to the following:

```
If File_Open
```

Restricting the Menu When the File is Open

With the menu displayed, and an arrow key pressed, we must now check what the value of **File_Open** is set to. If it is **false** we need to execute the set of statements above, and restrict the menu to the Open, Create and Exit options. The other case is when **File_Open** is **true**. In this instance, we need to restrict the highlight bar to the options Add, Find, Amend, and Exit. To achieve this, **No_line** may only take the values 3, 4, 5, and 6. We implement these cases using the two extra If statements as below:

```
...
        {Down key pressed so increase No_line by 1}
        No_line := No_line + 1;
        If (File_Open = false)
        Then
          {if File_Open is false restrict bar to Open, Create and Exit}
          Begin
            {Check if now bar would move down past "Open"}
            If No_line > 2
          ...
          End
        Else
          {Otherwise If File_Open is true}
          Begin
            {When bar is to go beyond "Exit" put back to "Add"}
            If No_line > 6
            Then
              Begin
```

```
                No_line := 3;
                End;
            Else
            {When bar is to go above "Add" put back to "Exit"}
              If No_line < 3
                Then
                   Begin
                   No_line := 6;
                   End
        End;
      End;
  Else
    If Ord(Ch) = 72
    Then
      Begin
      {Up key pressed so decrease No_line by one}
      No_line := No_line - 1;
      If (File_Open = false)
      Then
        {if File_Open is false restrict bar to Open, Create and Exit}
        Begin
        {Check if bar would move up past "Create"}
        ...
        End;
      Else
        {Otherwise If File_Open is true}
        Begin
        {When bar is to go beyond "Exit" put back to "Add"}
        If No_line > 6
          Then
             Begin
             No_line := 3;
             End;
           Else
           {When bar is to go above "Add" put back to "Exit"}
             If No_line < 3
               Then
                  Begin
                  No_line := 6;
                  End
        End;
  End;
...
```

Making these changes our new improved version of the program looks like this:

```
Program Ex_11_5;
Uses Crt, My_Sys;
Var
```

```
   A : Array[1..6] of String;
   I, No_line : Integer;
   Ch_1, Ch_2 : Char;
   File_Open  : Boolean;
Begin
   {Clear the Screen of any DOS messages}
   Clrscr;
   {Assign the Strings}
   A[1] := '          Create              ';
   A[2] := '          Open                ';
   A[3] := '          Add                 ';
   A[4] := '          Find                ';
   A[5] := '          Amend               ';
   A[6] := '          Exit                ';
   {Draw background window in Blue}
   TextBackground(Blue);
   Window(21,6,58,15);
   Clrscr; {converts background to chosen color}
   {Set the color for the frame and the message}
   TextColor(Red);
   {Draw the frame}
   Rectangle(21,6,58,15);
   {Write the User Message}
   Window(23,7,56,9);
   WriteLn(' Select an action and press Enter');
   For I := 1 to 34 do
      Begin
      Write(Chr(205));
      End;
   {Initialize the variables}
   No_line  := 1;
   File_Open := False;
   Repeat
     Repeat
     {Write the menu}
     TextBackground(Blue);
     TextColor(Yellow);
     Window(23,9,56,14);
     ClrScr;
     Writeln(A[1]);
     Writeln(A[2]);
     Writeln(A[3]);
     Writeln(A[4]);
     Writeln(A[5]);
     Write(A[6]);
     {Draw the Highlight bar}
     TextBackground(Green);
     TextColor(White + Blink);
     Window(23, 8 + No_line, 56, 8 + No_line);
     Write    (A[No_line]);
     Window(23, 8 + No_line, 56, 8 + No_line);
```

```
{Test which key pressed and move the bar accordingly}
Ch_1:= Readkey;
If Ord(Ch_1) = 0
  Then
  Begin
    Ch_2 := Readkey;
    If Ord(Ch_2) = 80
      Then
        Begin
        {Down key pressed so increase No_line by 1}
        No_line := No_line + 1;
        If (File_Open = false)
        Then
          {if File_Open is false restrict bar to Open, Create and Exit}
          Begin
            {Check if now bar would move down past "Open"}
            If No_line > 2
            Then
            Begin
            {Check if now bar would move down past "Exit"}
              If No_line > 6
                Then
                Begin
                {If yes to both questions move bar to "Create"}
                No_line := 1;
                End
              Else
                Begin
                {If yes to first and no to second move bar to "Exit"}
                No_line := 6;
                End
            End
          End
        Else
          {Otherwise If File_Open is true}
          Begin
            {When bar is to go beyond "Exit" put back to "Add"}
            If No_line > 6
            Then
              Begin
              No_line := 3;
              End;
          End;
        End
    Else
      If Ord(Ch_2) = 72
      Then
        Begin
        {Up key pressed so decrease No_line by one}
        No_line := No_line - 1;
        If (File_Open = false)
        Then
          {if File_Open is false restrict bar to Open, Create and Exit}
          Begin
```

```
                    {Check if bar would move up past "Create"}
                      If (No_line < 1)
                        Then
                          Begin
                          {If yes move bar to "Exit"}
                          No_line := 6;
                          End
                        Else
                          Begin
                          {If no check if bar would move up above "Exit"}
                            If (No_line < 6) and (No_line > 2)
                              Then
                                Begin
                                {If yes move bar to "Open"}
                                No_line := 2;
                                End
                      End
                End
            Else
            {Otherwise If File_Open is true}
                Begin
                {When bar is to go beyond "Exit" put back to "Add"}
                  If No_line > 6
                    Then
                      Begin
                      No_line := 3;
                      End
                    Else
                      {When bar is to go above "Add" put back to "Exit"}
                      If No_line < 3
                        Then
                          Begin
                          No_line := 6;
                          End
                End
              End
          End
  Until (Ord(Ch_1) = 13);
  {From position of bar select action}
  Case No_line of
          1 : Begin
              Create;
              End;
          2 : Begin
              Open(File_Open);
              If File_Open
                Then
                  Begin
                  No_line := 3;
                  End
                Else
                  Begin
                  No_line := 1;
                  End
```

```
                 End;
          3 : Begin
                 Add;
                 End;
          4 : Begin
                 Find;
                 End;
          5 : Begin
                 Amend;
                 End;
          6 : Begin
                   If File_Open
                   Then
                       Begin
                       Close(My_file);
                       End;
                   End;
      End; {Case}
   Until No_line = 6;
   Window(1,1,80,25);
   Clrscr;
End.
```

There is always room for improvement, and this program is no exception. You now have all the tools you need to polish it up, so we will leave you to it. Good luck!

Summary

What your user sees of your program is very important. This is the 'bridge' connecting the user and the program. As a result, you need to consider it very carefully. In this chapter we showed you how to draw text windows on screen and use the color to make the menu system look interesting. We also showed you how to create a highlight bar and move it up and down through the system.

Having designed your menu system, you need to consider how you will pass control from the user's selection to the individual background programs. We showed you one method of writing the background programs as procedures and storing them in a unit. We then used a Case statement to call the procedures.

Finally, we looked at re-evaluating your system. Once you have the basic structure of a program together, it's often useful to write a working copy of the program. If you then test this as though you were an innocent user trying out different input data, you will soon find out how robust your system is and what you need to change to improve it.

Quiz Questions

1 Write a Turbo Pascal statement to create a window 10 characters wide and 11 rows high, in the middle of the screen.

2 How would you set the text to flashing red on a yellow background?

3 How would you put text into the window?

4 How do you tell if the special key *F1* has been pressed?

5 How do you go about implementing a highlight bar which can be moved up and down a menu?

6 How do you stop Turbo Pascal halting when it encounters an input/ output error?

Exercises

1 The following lines appear in **EX_11_5.PAS**:

```
TextBackground(Blue);
TextColor(Yellow);
Window(23,9,56,14);
ClrScr;
```

These statements redraw the dialog area of the main window ready for displaying the menu. The same four statements are also used in several places in **MY_SYS.PAS** to prepare the dialog area for user input. Write a procedure, in **MY_SYS.PAS**, called **Dialog_Box**, which performs the four statements above. Replace all occurrences of the statements in both files by calls to **Dialog_box**;

2 When a menu is displayed during a run of **EX_11_5.PAS**, you may only move the selection bar to valid menu items. However, the invalid items still appear. Modify **EX_11_5.PAS** so that it displays '————' for inactive items. For example, when there is no file open, the menu should be displayed as follows:

> Create
> Open
> ————
> ————
> ————
> Exit

3 When running **EX_11_5**, if a user selects a menu option they must provide valid input when the dialog box appears. There is no chance of escaping if, for example, they selected Open accidentally. Change the procedures of **MY_SYS.PAS** which prompt for input so that they perform no action if the user just types *Enter*, that is when they enter an empty string.

APPENDIX A

Editing Commands

Cursor Movement Commands

Command	Keys
Character left	*Ctrl+S*
Character right	*Ctrl+D*
Word left	*Ctrl+A*
Word right	*Ctrl+F*
Line up	*Ctrl+E*
Line down	*Ctrl+X*
Scroll up one line	*Ctrl+W*
Scroll down one line	*Ctrl+Z*
Page up	*Ctrl+R*
Page down	*Ctrl+C*

Quick Movement Commands

Command	Keys
Beginning of line	*Ctrl+Q, S*
End of line	*Ctrl+Q, D*
Top of window	*Ctrl+Q, E*
Bottom of window	*Ctrl+Q, X*
Top of file	*Ctrl+Q, R*
Bottom of file	*Ctrl+Q, C*
Beginning of block	*Ctrl+Q, B*
End of block	*Ctrl+Q, K*
Move to previous position	*Ctrl+Q, P*

Insert and Delete Commands

Command	Keys
Delete character	*Ctrl+G*
Delete character to left	*Ctrl+H*
Delete line	*Ctrl+Y*
Delete to end of line	*Ctrl+Q, Y*
Delete to end of word	*Ctrl+T*
Insert new line	*Ctrl+N*

Block Commands

Command	Keys
Mark block-begin	*Ctrl+K, B*
Mark block-end	*Ctrl+K, K*
Mark single word	*Ctrl+K, T*
Mark line	*Ctrl+K, L*
Copy block	*Ctrl+K, C*
Move block	*Ctrl+K, V*
Delete block	*Ctrl+Del*
Hide/Show block	*Ctrl+K, H*
Print selected block	*Ctrl+K, P*
Read block from disk	*Ctrl+K, R*
Write block to disk	*Ctrl+K, W*

Find and Replace Commands

Command	Keys
Find	*Ctrl+Q, F*
Find and replace	*Ctrl+Q, A*
Repeat last find	*Ctrl+L*

Miscellaneous Commands

Command	Keys
Invoke main menu	*F10*
Open file	*F3*
Save file	*F2*
Exit the IDE	*Alt+X*
Help	*F1*

APPENDIX B

Turbo Pascal Menus

- ▶ The File Menu
- ▶ The Edit Menu
- ▶ The Search Menu
- ▶ The Run Menu
- ▶ The Compile Menu
- ▶ The Debug Menu
- ▶ The Tools Menu
- ▶ The Options Menu
- ▶ The Window Menu
- ▶ The Help Menu

The File Menu

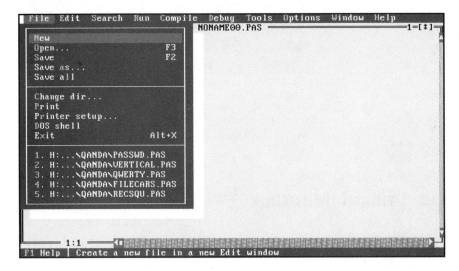

Option	What It Does
New	This opens a new file to edit and gives it the name **NONAME00.PAS**. After this, you can load the file to be edited or write new source text
Open	This opens an existing file. The prompt appears to help you select the file. Use the *Tab*, ←, ↑, → and ↓ keys to search through the list of files
Save	Saves the file in the current window to your hard disk with the name at the top of the window. It is a good idea, from time to time, to save the file being edited
Save as...	Also saves the file in the current window to disk, but offers you the chance to change the name
Save all	Saves all files being modified during your current session. The files are saved to disk under their current name. One of the features of the Borland IDE is its ability to edit multiple files at the same time
Print	Prints a copy of the program in the current window
Printer setup	This option allows you to change the settings on your printer

Continued

Option	What It Does
DOS shell	This option allows you to temporarily quit the Integrated Development Environment to execute DOS commands. To return to the IDE, you must type Exit. You will then return to the screen you were on before you went into DOS
Exit	This option takes you completely out of the Integrated Development Environment

The Edit Menu

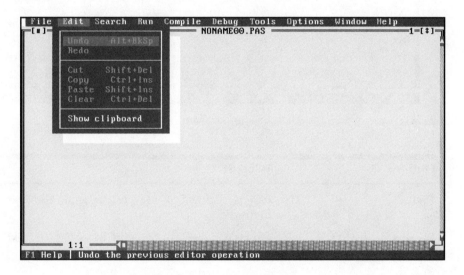

Option	What It Does
Undo	Undoes your most recent edit action
Redo	Redoes your most recent edit action
Cut	Removes the highlighted text and stores it on the clipboard
Copy	Copies the highlighted text and stores it on the clipboard
Paste	Pastes the text from the clipboard into the program
Clear	Removes the highlighted text permanently
Show clipboard	Shows what text is currently stored on the clipboard

The Search Menu

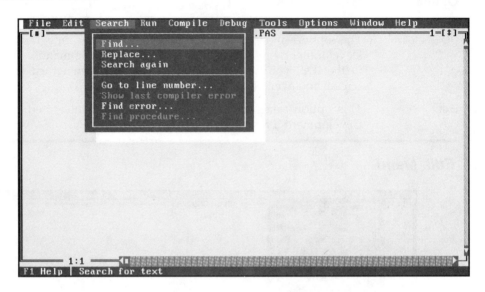

Option	What It Does
Find ...	Opens dialog box for you to enter the text you wish to find
Replace ...	Opens dialog box for you to enter the text you wish to search for and replace
Search again	Repeats the last search
Go to line number ...	Opens dialog box for you to enter a number. When you select *Enter* the cursor will jump to this line
Show last compiler error	Displays the last error message again
Find error ...	When a run-time error occurs Turbo Pascal tells you the memory address of the error. This option calls up a dialog box for you to enter the address and for Turbo Pascal to locate this error
Find procedure ...	Opens a dialog box to allow you to enter a name of a procedure or function when you are debugging a program. Turbo Pascal then searches for that procedure call and moves the cursor to it

The Run Menu

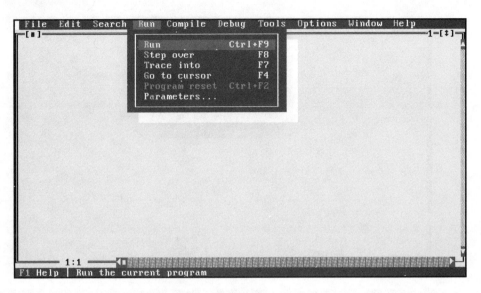

Option	What It Does
Run	This option lets you run the current program stored in the editor. If a program wasn't previously compiled, the Run option will cause it to compile before execution
Step over	Executes your program step by step
Trace into	Executes your program step by step and switches control into sub-programs and continues to show program executing
Go to cursor	When the debugger finds a fault, the position of the fault is marked by the cursor. By selecting this option you will move directly to the cursor
Program reset	Resets the program so that you can run it from the beginning again
Parameters ...	Opens a dialog box for you to enter the parameters for your program to use

The Compile Menu

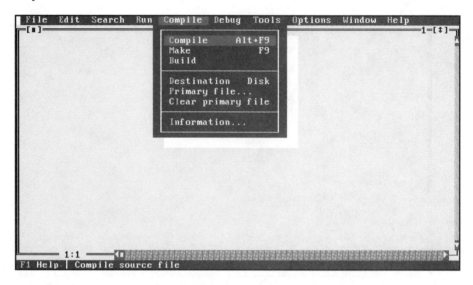

Option	What It Does
Compile	Causes the current source code file to be compiled. The destination of the code is decided by the option below
Make	Re-compiles the primary source file and any other associated files that have been modified
Build	Re-compiles the primary source file and any other associated files
Destination	This option allows you to select the destination of the compiled code. You have two choices. Either the code can go into the computer's memory or to your hard disk. You select the different options by pressing *Enter* at this option. The setting toggles between the two options.
Primary file ...	Opens a dialog box so that you can enter the **.PAS** file you wish to be the source file for the compile, make or build options
Clear primary file	Clears the file name
Information ...	Shows you information about the file such as the number of lines, the code size, how much memory you have free and so on

The Debug Menu

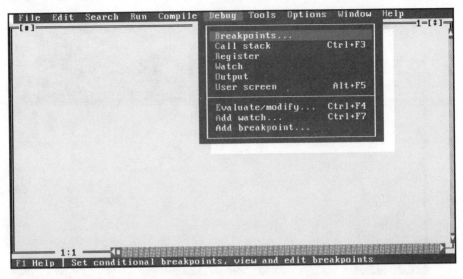

Option	What It Does
Breakpoints ...	Opens screen which gives you information about breakpoints you have set
Call stack	Shows you the procedures your program has called to reach this point
Register	Opens the register window. This displays memory addresses
Watch	Opens the Watch window
Output	Opens the Output window
User screen	Switches you to the DOS output screen to see the results of your program
Evaluate/modify	Opens a dialog box with the name of the expression the cursor is currently sitting at. You can use this option to evaluate an expression and then modify it
Add watch ...	Opens a dialog box to allow you to add a variable to the Watch window
Add breakpoint ...	Opens a dialog box to allow you to set a breakpoint. You can select the line number, the file and whether the breakpoint should wait for a loop to be executed a number of times before breaking

The Tools Menu

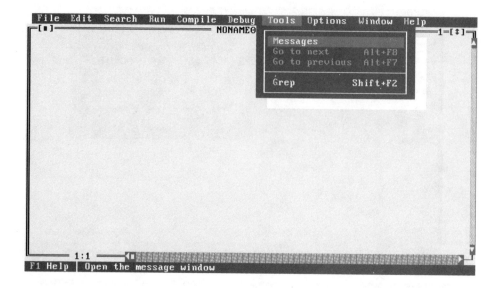

Option	What It Does
Messages	Opens the messages window. This displays information from programs that output through a DOS filter
Go to next	Takes you to the next message
Go to previous	Takes you to the previous message
Grep	Allows you to run Grep, a utility supplied with Turbo Pascal

The Options Menu

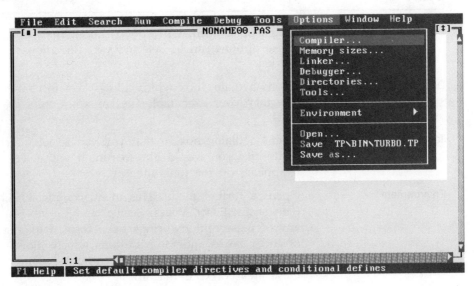

Option	What It Does
Compiler...	Shows you the current status of various directives to the compiler. This includes such items as whether range checking or I/O checking is on or off. You can use the mouse or the *tab* key to move around the form and the spacebar to toggle options on and off
Memory Sizes ...	Shows you a form detailing the current memory sizes of the 'stack' and the 'heap'
Linker ...	Brings up a form with options about the 'linker'. This is the tool for linking large programs to units

Continued

Option	What It Does
Debugger ...	Brings up a form with options about the Debugger. These options can be selected with the mouse or the tab key
Directories ...	Opens a dialog box which allows you to change which directory your executable files or your units are stored in
Tools ...	Opens a dialog box so that you can select which add-in utilities you would like to run. If you select a utility it appears on the tools menu
Environment	Opens a further menu. This menu contains the list - Preferences, Editor, Mouse, Startup and Colors. Selecting any of these options brings up a form with a selection of check boxes and radio buttons which allow you to choose various states for your computer which affect these areas of your machine
Open ...	Selects a file to open when you run Turbo Pascal
Save TP\BIN\TURBO.TP	Saves all the changes to settings you have made from the various choices in the options menu
Save as ...	Saves all the changes to settings, but allows you to choose a different file name

The Window Menu

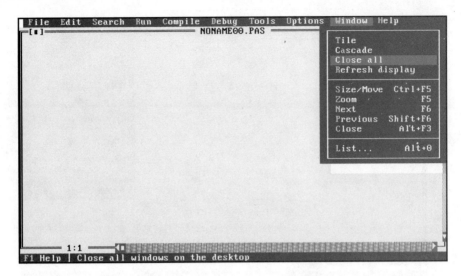

Option	What It Does
Tile	This arranges all the open windows like tiles.
Cascade	This arranges all the open windows in a cascade with the windows overlapping. The window at the front is the active window.
Close all	Closes all windows on the screen.
Size/Move	Changes the size or the location of the window currently being used. The Shift + ↑ and Shift + ↓ keys move the lower border of the window and the Shift+ ← and Shift+ → arrow keys move the window's right border. To move the whole window use the ←, ↑, → or ↓ keys. To fix the size or location press the *Enter* key.
Zoom	Zooms into and pulls out of the active window.
Next	Activates the next window.
Previous	Activates the previous window.
Close	Closes the current active window.
List ...	Shows a list of all the open windows from which you can select any window

The Help Menu

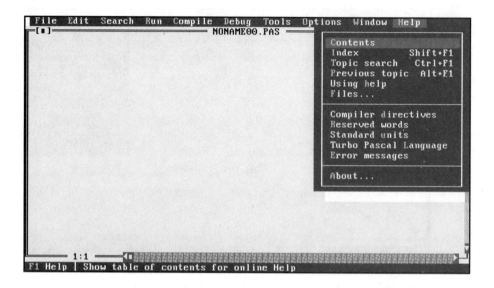

Option	What It Does
Contents	Shows you the contents menu screen for online help
Index	Shows you the index for online help. You can type in the word you are looking for and Turbo Pascal will take you to the topic
Topic search	Displays the help index highlighting the word the cursor is currently on
Previous topic	Allows you to look back through the topics you have selected
Using help	Opens a window with information about using the online help
Files ...	Opens a dialog box with a directory listing of help files so that you can add or delete them
Compiler directives	Displays a list of the compiler directives. Selecting the individual directive will take you to more information

Continued

Option	What It Does
Reserved words	Displays a list of the reserved words in Turbo Pascal. By selecting the individual word you will display more information on its application
Standard units	Displays a list of the standard units such as CRT. Selecting a unit will show you more information.
Turbo Pascal Language	Displays a list of important concepts in Turbo Pascal. You can select a concept and the help system will show you an explanation of how this concept is applied in programming
Error messages	Displays a list of the error messages in Turbo Pascal. By selecting a message you will see the single line comment displayed with the message
About ...	Opens a window with information about your version of Turbo Pascal

APPENDIX C

Reserved Words in Turbo Pascal

and	array	asm	begin	case
const	constructor	destructor	div	do
downto	else	end	file	for
function	goto	if	implementation	in
inherited	inline	interface	label	mod
nil	not	object	of	or
packed	procedure	program	record	repeat
set	shl	shr	string	then
to	type	unit	until	uses
var	while	with	xor	

Operations

Operations on Single Variables

Symbol	Operation	Type of Operands	Type of Result
+	identity	integer real	integer real
-	sign inversion	integer real	integer real

Operations on Two Variables

Symbol	Operation	Type of Operands	Type of Result
+	addition	integer real	integer real
-	subtraction	integer real	integer real
*	multiplication	integer real	integer real
/	division	integer real	real real
div	division with truncation	integer	integer
mod	modulo or remainder	integer	integer

Comparative Operations

Symbol	Operation	Type of Operands	Type of Result
=	Equals	Integer, real, string, char or pointer	boolean
<>	Not equal to		
>	Greater than	Integer, real, string or char	
>=	Greater than or equal to		
<	Less than		
<=	Less than or equal to		

Truth Table

Variables		Results	
A	B	A and B	A or B
True	True	True	True
True	False	False	True
False	True	False	True
False	False	False	False

Common Standard Functions and Procedures

Math Functions

Function	Value Returned
Abs(*x*)	Absolute value of x
ArcTan(*x*)	Arctangent of x
Cos(*x*)	Cosine of x
Exp(*x*)	Exponential part of x
Frac(*x*)	Fractional part of x
Int(*x*)	Integer part of x
Ln(*x*)	Natural logarithm of x
Pi	Value of Pi
Round(*x*)	Rounded value of (real) x
Sin(*x*)	Sine of x
Sqr(*x*)	Square of x
Sqrt(*x*)	Square root of x
Trunc(*x*)	Truncated value of (real) x

Miscellaneous Procedures and Functions

Function	Result
Assign(*External_name,File_name*)	Assigns the name of an external file to a file variable
Chr(*x*)	Returns a character with a specified ordinal number
Close(*File_name*)	Closes an open file
Eof(*File_name*)	Returns the end-of-file status of a file
Eoln(*File_name*)	Returns the end-of-line status of a text file
Exit	Exits from the current block
FileSize(*File_name*)	Returns the current size of a file
GotoXY(*x, y*)	Moves the cursor to the given coordinates
IOResult	Returns the status of the last I/O operation performed
New(*Pointer*)	Creates a new dynamic variable and sets a pointer variable to point to it
Odd(*x*)	Tests if the argument X is an odd number
Ord(*ch*)	Returns the ordinal value of a character
Random	Returns a random number
Randomize	Initializes the built-in random generator with a random value
Read(*A, B, C, ...*)	Reads values from the screen or from a file
ReadKey	Reads a character from the keyboard
ReadLn(*A, B, C, ...*)	As Read, but then skips to the next line
Reset(*File_name*)	Opens an existing file
Rewrite(*File_name*)	Creates and opens a new file

Continued

Function	Result
Seek(*File_name,Number*)	Moves the current position of a file to a specified component
TextBackground(*Color*)	Selects the background color
TextColor(*Color*)	Selects the foreground character color
WhereX	Returns the X-coordinate of the current cursor position
WhereY	Returns the Y-coordinate of the current cursor position
Window(*X1,Y1,X2,Y2*)	Defines a text window onscreen
Write(*A,B,C,...*)	Writes values to the screen or to a file
WriteLn(*A,B,C,...*)	As Write, but then outputs an end-of-line marker

String Procedures and Functions

Function	Result
Concat(*s1,s2,...*)	Joins a sequence of strings
Copy(*s,Start_char,Char_num*)	Returns a substring of a string
Delete(*s,Start_char,Char_num*)	Deletes a substring from a string
Insert(*s1,s2,Start_char*)	Inserts a substring into a string
Length(*s*)	Returns the dynamic length of a string
Pos(*s1,s2*)	Searches for a substring in a string
Str(*Number:Digits:Decimals,S*)	Converts a numeric value to its string representation
Val(*s,Value,Error_code*)	Converts the string value to its numeric representation

APPENDIX F

ASCII Table

	0	1	2	3	4	5	6	7	8	9	A	B	C	D	E	F
00	NUL 0	☺ 1	● 2	♥ 3	→ 4	⇓ 5	♠ 6	• 7	◙ 8	○ 9	◎ 10	♂ 11	♀ 12	♪ 13	♫ 14	☼ 15
10	▶ 16	◀ 17	↕ 18	‼ 19	¶ 20	§ 21	▬ 22	↨ 23	 24	¬ 25	Ø 26	♦ 27	└ 28	♦ 29	▲ 30	▼ 31
20	 32	! 33	" 34	# 35	$ 36	% 37	& 38	' 39	(40	) 41	* 42	+ 43	, 44	- 45	. 46	/ 47
30	0 48	1 49	2 50	3 51	4 52	5 53	6 54	7 55	8 56	9 57	: 58	; 59	< 60	= 61	> 62	? 63
40	@ 64	A 65	B 66	C 67	D 68	E 69	F 70	G 71	H 72	I 73	J 74	K 75	L 76	M 77	N 78	O 79
50	P 80	Q 81	R 82	S 83	T 84	U 85	V 86	W 87	X 88	Y 89	Z 90	[91	\ 92	] 93	^ 94	_ 95
60	` 96	a 97	b 98	c 99	d 100	e 101	f 102	g 103	h 104	i 105	j 106	k 107	l 108	m 109	n 110	o 111
70	p 112	q 113	r 114	s 115	t 116	u 117	v 118	w 119	x 120	y 121	z 122	{ 123	| 124	} 125	~ 126	△ 127

Continued

	0	1	2	3	4	5	6	7	8	9	A	B	C	D	E	F
80	Ç 128	ü 129	é 130	â 131	ä 132	à 133	å 134	ç 135	ê 136	ë 137	è 138	ï 139	î 140	ì 141	Ä 142	Å 143
90	É 144	æ 145	Æ 146	ô 147	ö 148	ò 149	û 150	ù 151	ÿ 152	Ö 153	Ü 154	¢ 155	£ 156	¥ 157	₧ 158	ƒ 159
A0	á 160	í 161	ó 162	ú 163	ñ 164	Ñ 165	ª 166	º 167	¿ 168	⌐ 169	¬ 170	½ 171	¼ 172	¡ 173	« 174	» 175
B0	░ 176	▒ 177	▓ 178	│ 179	┤ 180	╡ 181	╢ 182	╖ 183	╕ 184	╣ 185	║ 186	╗ 187	╝ 188	╜ 189	╛ 190	┐ 191
C0	└ 192	┴ 193	┬ 194	├ 195	─ 196	┼ 197	╞ 198	╟ 199	╚ 200	╔ 201	╩ 202	╦ 203	╠ 204	═ 205	╬ 206	╧ 207
D0	╨ 208	╤ 209	╥ 210	╙ 211	╘ 212	╒ 213	╓ 214	╫ 215	╪ 216	┘ 217	┌ 218	█ 219	▄ 220	▌ 221	▐ 222	▀ 223
E0	α 224	ß 225	Γ 226	π 227	Ý 228	σ 229	µ 230	τ 231	Φ 232	θ 233	Ω 234	δ 235	× 236	ø 237	238	↔ 239
F0	─ 240	± 241	≥ 242	≤ 243	⇔ 244	245	÷ 246	³ 247	° 248	· 249	· 250	│ 251	n 252	² 253	■ 254	255

Error Messages

Occasionally, you'll get error messages when you compile or run your program. Below, we've listed all the compile-time messages, and some of the more common run-time messages. You can also use the online help in Turbo Pascal.

Compile-Time Error Messages

These occur during compilation of the program. When an error is detected by the compiler, Turbo Pascal loads the program and moves the cursor to the error. The number and the message (below) will be displayed in a highlighted bar at the top of the screen. Where possible, the message will also include a filename or identifier. For example:

Error 15: File not found (MY_SYS.TPU)

We've included some hints to help you resolve the error for some of the more common, but obscure messages.

No.	Message	Hints
1	Out of memory	Try compiling to Disk or splitting your program into smaller units
2	Identifier expected	
3	Unknown identifier	Have you declared the Identifier?
4	Duplicate identifier	
5	Syntax error	An illegal character was found. Have you left the quotes off a string?
6	Error in real constant	Check you have declared the constant correctly
7	Error in integer constant	Check you have declared the constant correctly
8	String constant exceeds line	Have you forgotten the end quote on the string?
10	Unexpected end of file	Did you close all your comments? Do your Begins and Ends match?
11	Line too long	A line can only have 127 characters
12	Type identifier expected	
13	Too many open files	Check your **CONFIG.SYS** and look for a line Files=*nn* and increase the value
14	Invalid file name	
15	File not found	
16	Disk full	
17	Invalid compiler directive	
18	Too many files	Try to use fewer files
19	Undefined type in pointer definition	
20	Variable identifier expected	
21	Error in type	Have you used an illegal character in defining your type?
22	Structure too large	A structured type can be a maximum of 65,535 bytes
23	Set base type out of range	
24	File components may not be files or objects	You can't declare a **file of file**
25	Invalid string length	The maximum length of a string is 255 characters

Continued

No.	Message	Hints
26	Type mismatch	Are the variable and the result of the expression of different type?
27	Invalid subrange base type	
28	Lower bound > than upper bound	
29	Ordinal type expected	
30	Integer constant expected	
31	Constant expected	
32	Integer or real constant expected	
33	Pointer Type identifier expected	
34	Invalid function result type	
35	Label identifier expected	
36	BEGIN expected	
37	END expected	
38	Integer expression expected	
39	Ordinal expression expected	
40	Boolean expression expected	
41	Operand types do not match	
42	Error in expression	Have you used a symbol incorrectly?
43	Illegal assignment	Files can't be assigned values and function identifiers can only be assigned a value within the function
44	Field identifier expected	
45	Object file too large	
46	Undefined external	
47	Invalid object file record	
48	Code segment too large	The maximum size of the code of a program is 65,520 bytes. Try creating smaller units
49	Data segment too large	The maximum size of a program's data segment is 65,520 bytes. Try declaring large structures as pointers
50	DO expected	
51	Invalid PUBLIC definition	
52	Invalid EXTRN definition	
53	Too many EXTRN definitions	
54	OF expected	

Continued

No.	Message	Hints
55	INTERFACE expected	
56	Invalid relocatable reference	
57	THEN expected	
58	TO or DOWNTO expected	
59	Undefined forward	
61	Invalid typecast	
62	Division by zero	
63	Invalid file type	
64	Cannot read or write variables of this type	
65	Pointer variable expected	
66	String variable expected	
67	String expression expected	
68	Circular unit reference	Two units are not allowed to use each other in the **Interface** part
69	Unit name mismatch	The name of the unit must be the same in the **.TPU** file and the uses clause
70	Unit version mismatch	A unit has changed since this unit was compiled
71	Internal stack overflow	Have you nested too deeply? Try moving internal nesting to a procedure
72	Unit file format error	Try re-compiling the **.TPU** file
73	IMPLEMENTATION expected	
74	Constant and case types don't match	Check the type of the result of the expression to select the case
75	Record or object variable expected	
76	Constant out of range	
77	File variable expected	
78	Pointer expression expected	
79	Integer or real expression expected	
80	Label not within current block	Have you been using **GOTO**? (*see Chapter 5*)
81	Label already defined	
82	Undefined label in preceding stmt part	
83	Invalid @ argument	
84	UNIT expected	

Continued

No.	Message	Hints
85	";" expected	
86	":" expected	
87	"," expected	
88	"(" expected	
89	")" expected	
90	"=" expected	
91	":=" expected	
92	"[" or "(." expected	
93	"]" or ".)" expected	
94	"." expected	
95	".." expected	
96	Too many variables	You can only have 64K worth of variables in a program or sub-program
97	Invalid FOR control variable	Have you declared the variable in the current sub-program?
98	Integer variable expected	
99	Files types are not allowed here	
100	String length mismatch	
101	Invalid ordering of fields	The fields of a record must be in the order they were declared
102	String constant expected	
103	Integer or real variable expected	
104	Ordinal variable expected	
105	INLINE error	
106	Character expression expected	
107	Too many relocation items	
108	Overflow in arithmetic operation	The math you've just done is outside the **longint** range
109	No enclosing For, While or Repeat statement	
112	CASE constant out of range	Integer case statements must be within -32,768 through 32,767
113	Error in statement	Have you used an illegal symbol in a statement?
114	Cannot call an interrupt procedure	
116	Must be in 8087 mode to compile	You need to issue the compiler directive {$N+}

Continued

No.	Message	Hints
117	Target address not found	
118	Include files are not allowed here	
119	No inherited methods are accessible here	
121	Invalid qualifier	
122	Invalid variable reference	
123	Too many symbols	You can only declare 64K of symbols in a unit or program
124	Statement part too large	You can only have about 24K in the statement part
126	Files must be var parameters	
127	Too many conditional symbols	
128	Misplaced conditional directive	
129	ENDIF directive missing	
130	Error in initial conditional defines	
131	Header does not match previous definition	
133	Cannot evaluate this expression	
134	Expression incorrectly terminated	
135	Invalid format specifier	
136	Invalid indirect reference	
137	Structured variables are not allowed here	
138	Cannot evaluate without System unit	
139	Cannot access this symbol	
140	Invalid floating-point operation	
141	Cannot compile overlays to memory	
142	Pointer or procedural variable expected	
143	Invalid procedure or function reference	
144	Cannot overlay this unit	
145	Too many nested scopes	
146	File access denied	
147	Object type expected	
148	Local object types are not allowed	
149	Virtual expected	
150	Method identifier expected	
151	Virtual constructors are not allowed	
152	Constructor identifier expected	
153	Destructor identifier expected	
154	Fail only allowed within constructors	

Continued

No.	Message	Hints
155	Invalid combination of opcode and operands	
156	Memory reference expected	
157	Cannot add or subtract relocatable symbols	
158	Invalid register combination	
159	286/287 instructions are not enabled	
160	Invalid symbol reference	
161	Code generation error	
162	ASM expected	
163	Duplicate dynamic method index	
164	Duplicate resource identifier	
165	Duplicate or invalid export clause	
166	Procedure or function identifier expected	
167	Cannot export this symbol	
168	Duplicate export name	
169	Executable file header too large	

Run-Time Error Messages

Some errors that occur whilst you are running the program will cause the program to halt. On some occasions, you'll see an error message which will look like the following:

Run_time error *nnn* at *xxxx:yyyy*

nnn is the number of the error message.

Run-time errors can also be split into:

- DOS errors   1 through 99
- Input/Output errors   100 through 149
- Critical errors   150 through 199
- Fatal errors   200 through 255.

Below we've listed some of the more common errors

DOS Errors

No.	Message	Hints
2	File not found	Check you have spelt the file name correctly
3	Path not found	Check you have spelt the path correctly
4	Too many open files	DOS allows a maximum of 15 files to be open
5	File access denied	
...		
15	Invalid drive number	Check you have specified a valid drive
16	Cannot remove current directory	
17	Cannot rename across drives	
18	No more files	DOS can't find any files matching the file name

Input/Output Errors

Reported if in {$I+} state

No.	Message	Hints
100	Disk read error	Check to see if you tried to read past the end of the file
101	Disk write error	Check if the disk is full
102	File not assigned	Check you've used the assign procedure properly
103	File not open	Check you've opened the file
104	File not open for input	Check you've opened the file correctly
105	File not open for output	Check you've opened the file correctly
106	Invalid numeric format	Check the number just read from a text file

Critical Errors

If you see any of these errors, DOS has reported a sharing violation or a network error. To resolve the error, you'll need to consult your DOS guru or even the manual

No.	Message	Hints
150	Disk is write protected	
151	Unknown unit	
152	Drive not ready	
153	Unknown command	
154	CRC error in data	
155	Bad drive request structure length	
156	Disk seek error	
157	Unknown media type	
158	Sector not found	
159	Printer out of paper	
160	Device write fault	
161	Device read fault	
162	Hardware failure	

Fatal Errors

These errors will immediately terminate a program

No.	Message	Hints
200	Division by zero	Try testing the denominator before doing the division. (See Chapter 7)
201	Range check error	Reported if in {$R+} state. Check whether you are trying to assign a value outside the range of the variable's type
...		
205	Floating point overflow	Check your math. The operation resulted in a number too large for Turbo Pascal
...		
207	Invalid floating point operation	Check your math as you tried to do something outside the rules (like getting the square root of a negative number)

APPENDIX H

The Extended Key Codes

Num	Char	Num	Char	Num	Char	Num	Char
...		59	*F1*	92	*Shift+F9*	124	*Alt+5*
3	NUL	60	*F2*	93	*Shift+F10*	125	*Alt+6*
...		61	*F3*	94	*Ctrl+F1*	126	*Alt+7*
15	*Shift Tab*	62	*F4*	95	*Ctrl+F2*	127	*Alt+8*
16	*Alt+Q*	63	*F5*	96	*Ctrl+F3*	128	*Alt+9*
17	*Alt+W*	64	*F6*	97	*Ctrl+F4*	129	*Alt+0*
18	*Alt+E*	65	*F7*	98	*Ctrl+F5*	130	*Alt+-*
19	*Alt+R*	66	*F8*	99	*Ctrl+F6*	131	*Alt+=*
20	*Alt+T*	67	*F9*	100	*Ctrl+F7*	132	*Ctrl+PgUp*
21	*Alt+Y*	68	*F10*	101	*Ctrl+F8*	133	*F11*
22	*Alt+U*	...		102	*Ctrl+F9*	134	*F12*
23	*Alt+I*	71	*Home*	103	*Ctrl+F10*	135	*Shift+F11*
24	*Alt+O*	72	↑	104	*Alt+F1*	136	*Shift+F12*
25	*Alt+P*	73	*PgUp*	105	*Alt+F2*	137	*Ctrl+F11*
...		...		106	*Alt+F3*	138	*Ctrl+F12*
30	*Alt+A*	75	←	107	*Alt+F4*	139	*Alt+F11*
31	*Alt+S*	...		108	*Alt+F5*	140	*Alt+F12*
32	*Alt+D*	77	→	109	*Alt+F6*		
33	*Alt+F*	...		110	*Alt+F7*		
34	*Alt+G*	79	*End*	111	*Alt+F8*		
35	*Alt+H*	80	↓	112	*Alt+F9*		
36	*Alt+J*	81	*PgDn*	113	*Alt+F10*		
37	*Alt+K*	82	*Ins*	114	*Ctrl+PrtScr*		
38	*Alt+L*	83	*Del*	115	*Ctrl+ ←*		
...		84	*Shift+F1*	116	*Ctrl+ →*		
44	*Alt+Z*	85	*Shift+F2*	117	*Ctrl+End*		
45	*Alt+X*	86	*Shift+F3*	118	*Ctrl+PgDn*		
46	*Alt+C*	87	*Shift+F4*	119	*Ctrl+Home*		
47	*Alt+V*	88	*Shift+F5*	120	*Alt+1*		
48	*Alt+B*	89	*Shift+F6*	121	*Alt+2*		
49	*Alt+N*	90	*Shift+F7*	122	*Alt+3*		
50	*Alt+M*	91	*Shift+F8*	123	*Alt+4*		

APPENDIX

I

Model Answers to the Exercises

Chapter 1

1

1. Select bread.
2. Select spread.
3. Select cheese.
4. Select pickle.
5. Take two slices of bread.
6. Coat one side of each slice with spread.
7. Cover spread side of one slice with cheese.
8. Cover the cheese with pickle.
9. Cover the pickle with other slice of bread, spread side down.

Input data:
        Bread (rye, pumpernickel, etc.)
        Spread (butter, margarine, etc.)
        Cheese (Limburger, Emmenthal, etc.)
        Pickle (Farmhouse, Cucumber, etc.)

Transformed into (output data):
        The sandwich.

2

```
Program Myprog2;
Begin
WriteLn('This is an odd line of output.');
WriteLn('This is an even line of output.');
WriteLn('This is an odd line of output.');
WriteLn('This is an even line of output.');
WriteLn('This is an odd line of output.');
WriteLn('This is an even line of output.');
WriteLn('This is an odd line of output.');
WriteLn('This is an even line of output.');
WriteLn('This is an odd line of output.');
WriteLn('This is an even line of output.');
End.
```

Chapter 2

1

```
Program Address_Label;
{ Print my address label }
Uses Crt;
Begin
{ Clear any existing text from the screen }
ClrScr;
{ Print the label }
WriteLn('-------------------------------------');
WriteLn('|                                   |');
WriteLn('|   Seth Squirrel      ____||__     |');
WriteLn('|   1 Forest lane     /_____\    |');
WriteLn('|   Nuttley           ||_| _  |     |');
WriteLn('|   Connecticut    |..\|__|_|_|..|.. |');
WriteLn('|   02150           \.\/..\..../\/.//.\. |');
WriteLn('|                                   |');
WriteLn('-------------------------------------');

End.
```

2

```
Program Limerick;
{ Personalizes a limerick with the user's name }
Uses Crt;
Var
   Users_name: String; { For storing the user's name }
Begin
{ Clear any existing text from the screen }
ClrScr;

{ Ask the user what their name is }
Write('Please type in your name and press <Return> ');
ReadLn(Users_name);
```

```
{ Clear the screen again for presentation of the result }
ClrScr;

{ Print out the limerick, line by line }
WriteLn('"Hey! These computers are great!"');
WriteLn('Said ', Users_name, ', a coder of late.'); { Personalized bit }
WriteLn('   "They can calculate stuff');
WriteLn('   "And, if that''s not enough,');
WriteLn('They can even arrange you a date!"');

End.
```

3

```
Program Days_to_hours;
{ Converts a number of days entered by the user }
{ into the equivalent number of hours }
Uses Crt;
Var
    Days, Hours: Integer; { Days entered and the corresponding hours }
Begin
{ Clear any existing text from the screen }
ClrScr;

{ Ask the user how many days they want to convert}
Write('Please enter the number of days: ');
ReadLn(Days);

{ Calculate the equivalent number of hours }
Hours := Days * 24;

{ Print the result }
WriteLn(Days, ' days is the same as ', Hours, ' hours.');

End.
```

Chapter 3

1

```
Program Chicks_and_rabbits;
{ A program to calculate the number of chickens and rabbits in }
{ a pen from the total number of heads and legs }
Uses Crt;
Var
    Heads, Legs: LongInt;          { For user responses }
    Rabbits, Chickens: LongInt; { For calculations }
Begin
ClrScr;

{ Find out how many legs there are }
Write('What''s the total number of legs in the pen? ');
ReadLn(Legs);
```

```
{ Find out how many heads there are }
Write('What''s the total number of heads in the pen? ');
ReadLn(Heads);

{ Do the calculations }
Rabbits := ( Legs - 2 * Heads ) div 2;
Chickens := Heads - Rabbits;

{ Print the results }

{ (messages are different for single animals and multiple animals, }
{ so use If statements to choose between them) }

If Rabbits = 1 Then
   Begin
   Write('There is 1 rabbit ')
   End
Else
   Begin
   Write('There are ', Rabbits, ' rabbits ')
   End;

If Chickens = 1 Then
   Begin
   WriteLn('and 1 chicken in the pen.')
   End
Else
   Begin
   WriteLn('and ', Chickens, ' chickens in the pen.')
   End;
End.
```

2

```
Program Sales_tax;
{ A program to calculate the sales tax and total price of an }
{ article being bought from a shop }
Uses Crt;
Const
   Sales_tax_rate = 7.5;
Var
   Net_price: Real;          { Net price from user }
   Tax, Total_price: Real; { Calculation results }
Begin
ClrScr;

{ Ask the user for the net price }
Write('Please type in the net price (dollars.cents): ');
ReadLn(Net_price);

{ Do the calculations }
Tax := Net_price * Sales_tax_rate / 100;
Total_price := Net_price + Tax;
```

```
{ Print the results }
WriteLn;
WriteLn('Tax (', Sales_tax_rate:3:1, '%):  $', Tax:4:2);
WriteLn('Total price: $', Total_price:4:2);

End.
```

3

```
Program Give_change;
{ Works out how many nickels, dimes, quarters and pennies to give }
{ in change (up to 99 cents) }
Uses Crt;
Const
   { Declare value of each coin, for clarity }
   Quarter_value = 25;
   Dime_value = 10;
   Nickel_value = 5;
   Penny_value = 1;
Var
   Change: Integer; { Amount of change requested by user }
   Quarters, Dimes, Nickels, Pennies: Integer; { Count of each coin type }
Begin
ClrScr;

{ Ask the user for the change amount }
Write('How much is the change (up to 99 cents) ? ');
ReadLn(Change);

{ Quarters is the whole part when dividing Change by Quarter_value... }
Quarters := Change div Quarter_value;

{ ...change still to give is the remainder... }
Change := Change mod Quarter_value;

{ ...similarly for dimes... }
Dimes := Change div Dime_value;
Change := Change mod Dime_value;

{ ...similarly for nickels... }
Nickels := Change div Nickel_value;
Change := Change mod Nickel_value;

{ ...what's left are the Pennies. }
Pennies := Change;

{ Print the results (only report used coins) }
If Quarters > 0 Then
   Begin
   WriteLn('Quarters: ', Quarters);
   End;
```

```
If Dimes > 0 Then
   Begin
   WriteLn('Dimes:     ', Dimes);
   End;

If Nickels > 0 Then
   Begin
   WriteLn('Nickels: ', Nickels);
   End;

If Pennies > 0 Then
   Begin
   WriteLn('Pennies:  ', Pennies);
   End

End.
```

Chapter 4

1

```
Program Vertical;
{ Prints a user's string down the middle of the screen }
Uses Crt;
Const
   Offset = 40; { 'Distance' to the middle of the screen }
Var
   In_string: String; { String read and reversed version }
   Spaces: String[Offset]; { A string for the indent }
   I: Integer; { For loop index }
Begin
ClrScr;

{ Fill in the indent string }
For I := 1 To Offset Do
   Begin
   Spaces := Spaces + ' '
   End;

{ Get the user's string }
WriteLn('Please type in a String:');
ReadLn(In_String);

{ Write each character on a new line, preceded by the indent }
For I := 1 to Length(In_string) Do
   Begin
   WriteLn(Spaces, In_string[I])
   End;

End.
```

2

```
Program Reverse;
{ Reverses a string using the '+' operator }
Uses Crt;
Var
  In_string, Out_string: String; { String read and reversed version }
  I: Integer; { For loop index }
Begin
ClrScr;

{ Get the user's string }
WriteLn('Please type in a String:');
ReadLn(In_String);

{ Reverse it into the other string}
Out_string := ''; { Initialize the receiver }
For I := 1 to Length(In_string) Do
   Begin
   Out_string :=  In_string[I] + Out_string { This does the reversing! }
   End;

{ Print the result }
WriteLn('And the result is:');
WriteLn(Out_string);

End.
```

3

```
Program Get_password;
{ Reads a fixed length password from the user without }
{ displaying the characters as they are typed }
Uses Crt;
Const
   Len = 10; { The length of the password }
Var
   Password: String[Len]; { The password entered }
   I: Integer;            { For loop index }
Begin
ClrScr;

{ Get the password }
Write('Please enter your password: ');
For I := 1 To Len Do
   Begin
   Password := Password + ReadKey { Store each character }
   End;
WriteLn;

{ Print the password quietly! }
Write('Make sure noone''s looking, then press <Return>...');
```

```
ReadLn;
WriteLn('Your password is: ', Password);
Write('Press <Return> to continue...');
ReadLn;

End.
```

Chapter 5

1

```
Program Black_Jack;
{ Calculate the number of points for a card in Black Jack }
Uses Crt;
Var
    Card: String; { Card code read from the user }
Begin
ClrScr;

{ Ask the user to name the card }
Write('What card do you have ( a, 2-10, j, q or k) ? ');
ReadLn(Card);

{ Print the score}
Write('That scores ');
Case Card[1] of { We only need to examine the first character }
    'a', 'A':                        { It's an ace }
       Begin
       Write('1 or 11')
       End;
    '2'..'9':                        { It's a 2, 3, 4, 5, 6, 7, 8 or 9 }
       Begin
       Write(Card)
       End;
    '1':                             { Make 10 a separate case, for clarity }
       Begin
       Write(10)
       End;
    'j', 'J', 'q', 'Q', 'k', 'K': { It's a court card }
       Begin
       Write(10)
       End;
    End;

    Write(' points.');
End.
```

2

```
Program Freda;
{ Calculate how many hops Freda will need to get back to the pond }
Uses Crt;
Var
   Distance: Real; { Distance from the pond (in feet) }
   Hops: LongInt;  { Number of hops required }
Begin
ClrScr;

{ Read current distance }
Write('How far is Freda from the pond (in feet)? ');
ReadLn(Distance);

{ Get Freda to hop while she's too far to crawl }
Hops := 0;                       { No hops yet }
While Distance > 0.5 Do          { Hop while more than six inches away }
   Begin
   Distance := Distance * 0.5; { Hop half the distance }
   Hops := Hops + 1            { Increment the count }
   End;

{ Print results }
Write('Freda needs ', hops:4, ' hop(s) to get near enough to crawl.')

End.
```

3

```
Program Validate_time;
{ Asks the user to enter a formatted time until they get it right }
Uses Crt;
Var
   Time: String;                    { Time entered by user }
   Hours, Minutes: Integer;         { Hour and minute values}
   Valid_punctuation, Valid_hours, { For test results }
      Valid_minutes, Valid_length,
      Valid_chars, Hours_is_number,
      Minutes_is_number: Boolean;
   Val_error: Integer;              { For Val error code }

Begin
ClrScr;

{ Read a time repeatedly until it's valid }
Repeat

   { Ask for a time }
   Write('Please enter a time (HH:MM) ');
   ReadLn(Time);
```

```pascal
        { Check it's the right length }
        Valid_length := Length(Time) = 5;

        { Only continue if we have the correct length }
        If Valid_length Then
           Begin

           { Read the hours part }
           Val(Copy(Time, 1, 2), Hours, Val_error);
           Hours_is_number := (Val_error = 0); { and check it's a number }

           { Check that there's a colon in the middle }
           Valid_punctuation := Time[3] = ':';

           { Read the minutes part }
           Val(Copy(Time, 4, 2), Minutes, Val_error);
           Minutes_is_number := (Val_error = 0); { and check it's a number }

           Valid_chars := Hours_is_number and
                          Valid_punctuation and
                          Minutes_is_number;

           { Only continue if the characters are correct }
           If Valid_chars Then
              Begin

              { Hours must be in the range 0 to 23 }
              Valid_hours := ( Hours >= 0 ) and ( Hours <= 23 );

              { Minutes must be in the range 0 to 59 }
              Valid_minutes := ( Minutes >= 0 ) and ( Minutes <= 59 );

              End
           End

     Until Valid_length and Valid_chars and Valid_hours and Valid_minutes;

  WriteLn('Thank you.')

End.
```

Chapter 6

1

```
Program Test_on_screen;
{ Tests the operation of On_screen() }
Uses Crt;
Function On_screen(X, Y: Integer): Boolean;
   { Returns True if the given coordinates are on-screen, }
   { returns False otherwise }
   Const
      { Mark screen dimensions as constants }
      Screen_height = 25;
      Screen_width = 80;
   Var
      X_ok, Y_ok: Boolean; { Test results }
   Begin
      X_ok := (X >= 1) And (X <= Screen_width);    { Is X on-screen? }
      Y_ok := (Y >= 1) And (Y <= Screen_height);   { Is Y on-screen? }
      On_screen := X_ok And Y_ok    { Are the coordinates on-screen? }
   End;
Begin
ClrScr;

{ Test On_screen() for various coordinates by writing }
{ the expected result followed by the actual result }

{ Typical coordinates }
WriteLn('This result should be true: ', On_screen(9,9));
WriteLn('This result should be false: ', On_screen(-10,10));
WriteLn('This result should be false: ', On_screen(11,-11));
WriteLn('This result should be false: ', On_screen(-12,-12));

{ Extreme coordinates }
WriteLn('This result should be true: ', On_screen(1,1));
WriteLn('This result should be true: ', On_screen(1,25));
WriteLn('This result should be true: ', On_screen(80,1));
WriteLn('This result should be true: ', On_screen(80,25));

{ Nearest coordinates off-screen }
WriteLn('This result should be false: ', On_screen(0,0));
WriteLn('This result should be false: ', On_screen(0,26));
WriteLn('This result should be false: ', On_screen(81,0));
WriteLn('This result should be false: ', On_screen(81,26));

End.
```

2

```
Program Stick;
{ Draws a stick person in the middle of the screen }
Uses Crt;
Const
   { Characters for the head, arms and legs }
   Head_char = 'h';
   Arm_char = 'a';
   Leg_char = 'l';
Var
   X: Integer;    { For loop index for drawing the arms }
Function On_screen(X, Y: Integer): Boolean;
   { Returns True if the given coordinates are on-screen, }
   { returns False otherwise }
   Const
      { Mark screen dimensions as constants }
      Screen_height = 25;
      Screen_width = 80;
   Var
      X_ok, Y_ok: Boolean; { Test results }
   Begin
      X_ok := (X >= 1) And (X <= Screen_width);    { Is X on-screen? }
      Y_ok := (Y >= 1) And (Y <= Screen_height);   { Is Y on-screen? }
      On_screen := X_ok And Y_ok    { Are the coordinates on-screen? }
   End;
Procedure Draw_char(X, Y: Integer; A_char: Char);
   { Draws the character A_char at the coordinates (X, Y) }
   { Does nothing if the coordinates are off-screen }
   Begin
   If On_screen(X, Y) Then    { Only draw if on-screen }
      Begin
      GotoXY(X, Y);
      Write(A_char)
      End
   End;
Begin
ClrScr;

{ Draw the head }
Draw_char(40, 9, Head_char);
Draw_char(39, 10, Head_char);
Draw_char(41, 10, Head_char);
Draw_char(40, 11, Head_char);

{ Draw the arms }
For X := 37 To 43 Do
   Begin
   Draw_char(X, 12, Arm_char)
   End;
```

```
{ Draw the legs }
Draw_char(40, 13, Leg_char);
Draw_char(39, 14, Leg_char);
Draw_char(41, 14, Leg_char);
Draw_char(38, 15, Leg_char);
Draw_char(42, 15, Leg_char);

End.
```

3

```
Program A_square;
{ Draws a single square on the screen }
Uses Crt;
Function On_screen(X, Y: Integer): Boolean;
   { Returns True if the given coordinates are on-screen, }
   { returns False otherwise }
   Const
      { Mark screen dimensions as constants }
      Screen_height = 25;
      Screen_width = 80;
   Var
      X_ok, Y_ok: Boolean; { Test results }
   Begin
      X_ok := (X >= 1) And (X <= Screen_width);    { Is X on-screen? }
      Y_ok := (Y >= 1) And (Y <= Screen_height);   { Is Y on-screen? }
      On_screen := X_ok And Y_ok    { Are the coordinates on-screen? }
   End;
Procedure Draw_char(X, Y: Integer; A_char: Char);
   { Draws the character A_char at the coordinates (X, Y) }
   { Does nothing if the coordinates are off-screen }
   Begin
   If On_screen(X, Y) Then    { Only draw if on-screen }
      Begin
      GotoXY(X, Y);  { Goto the coordinates }
      Write(A_char)  { Draw the character }
      End
   End;
Procedure Draw_square(Origin_x, Origin_y, Side: Integer; Border: Char);
   { Draws a square whose top left corner is at }
   { (Origin_x, Origin_y), whose side is of length }
   { Side, and whose border is comprised of Border }
   { characers. Parts of the square which are off-screen }
   { are clipped. }
   Var
      Index: Integer; { For loop index }
   Begin
   { Draw the edges of the square clockwise }
   For Index := Origin_x To Origin_x + Side - 1 Do
      Begin
      Draw_char(Index, Origin_y, Border);
      End;
   For Index := Origin_y + 1 To Origin_y + Side - 1 Do
```

```
     Begin
     Draw_char(Origin_x + Side - 1, Index, Border);
     End;
   For Index := Origin_x + Side - 2 Downto Origin_x Do
     Begin
     Draw_char(Index, Origin_y + Side - 1, Border);
     End;
   For Index := Origin_y + Side - 2 Downto Origin_y + 1 Do
     Begin
     Draw_char(Origin_x, Index, Border);
     End
   End;
Begin
ClrScr;
{ Draw the square }
Draw_square(35, 8, 10, '#')
End.
```

4

```
Program Pattern1;
{ Draws a pattern of squares on the screen }
Uses Crt, Square;
Var
   Index: Integer;
Begin
ClrScr;
{ Draw a nested pattern on the screen }
For Index := 1 To 5 Do
   Begin
   Draw_square(25 + 2 * Index, 2 + 2 * Index, 21 - 4 * Index, 'Z')
   End
End.


Program Pattern2;
{ Draws a pattern of squares on the screen }
Uses Square, Crt;
Var
   Index: Integer;
Begin
ClrScr;
{ Draw a zooming pattern on the screen }
For Index := 1 To 11 Do
   Begin
   Draw_square(6 * Index, Index + 2, Index, '@')
   End
End.
```

5

```
Program Move;
{ Draws a moving, zooming square on the screen }
Uses Square, Crt;
Var
   Zoom, Index: Integer;
Begin
ClrScr;
{ Draw a moving, zooming pattern on the screen, six times }
For Zoom := 1 To 6 Do
   Begin
   For Index := 1 To 15 Do
      Begin
      Draw_square(6 * (Index - 1), (Index - 1), (Index - 1), ' ');
      Draw_square(6 * Index, Index, Index, ':');
      GotoXY(1, 25); { Move the cursor out of the way }
      Delay(140)
      End
   End
End.
```

Chapter 8

1

```
Program Enum_8_2;
{ Program to find the hottest month, using an enumerated type }
Uses Crt;
Type
   { Enumerated type to represent the months }
   Month = (Jan, Feb, Mar, Apr, May, Jun, Jul, Aug, Sep, Oct, Nov, Dec);
   { An array of Real numbers corresponding to each month }
   Weather = Array[Month] of Real;
Const
   { A constant array for converting the enumeration }
   { into a readable string }
   Month_strings: Array[Month] Of String = (
      'January',
      'February',
      'March',
      'April',
      'May',
      'June',
      'July',
      'August',
      'September',
      'October',
      'November',
      'December'
      );
```

```
Var
   Temp    : Weather; { An array of temperatures for each month }
   Cmpnent : Month;   { An index into the array }
   Hottest : Real;    { The hottest temperature in the search }
Begin
ClrScr;

{ Read all the temperatures from the user }
For Cmpnent := Jan to Dec do
   Begin
   { Use Month_strings to make the question prettier }
   Write('Enter temperature for ', Month_strings[Cmpnent], ': ');
   ReadLn(Temp[Cmpnent])
   End;

{ Search for the highest temperature }
Hottest := Temp[Jan]; { Initialise Hottest }
For Cmpnent := Feb To Dec Do
   Begin
   If Temp[Cmpnent] > Hottest Then { Replace Hottest if we've found higher }
      Begin
      Hottest := Temp[Cmpnent]
      End
   End;

{ Print result }
WriteLn('Hottest temperature is ', Hottest:5:2);

End.
```

2

```
Program Car_search;
{ Reads a list of car descriptions and prints the extra }
{ details of the most expensive one }
Uses Crt;
Const
   No_of_cars = 5; { Number of car descriptions }
Type
   Car = Record              { The information for a car }
      Make_model: String;    { The make and model }
      Price, Mpg: Real       { The price and fuel consumption }
      End;
   Car_range = 1..No_of_cars; { A useful integer subrange }
Var
   Cars: Array[Car_range] Of Car; { All the car descriptions }
   Index, High_index: Car_range;  { Working index and index of priciest }
Begin
ClrScr;

{ For every car, fill in the details from the user }
For Index := 1 To No_of_cars Do
   Begin
```

```
   WriteLn('Please enter details for car ', Index);
   With Cars[Index] Do  { Avoid some tedious typing }
      Begin
      Write('Make and model: ');
      ReadLn(Make_model);
      Write('Price: ');
      ReadLn(Price);
      Write('Fuel consumption: ');
      ReadLn(Mpg)
      End
   End;

{ Look for the priciest car }
High_index := 1;        { Assume it's the first one }
For Index := 2 To No_of_cars Do
   Begin
   If Cars[Index].Price > Cars[High_index].Price Then { If this one's pricier }
      Begin
      High_index := Index { record its index }
      End
   End;

{ Print the other details of the priciest one }
WriteLn;
With Cars[High_index] Do { Save some more tedious typing }
   Begin
   WriteLn('The most expensive car is the ', Make_model);
   WriteLn('Which has an average fuel consumption of ', Mpg:1:2)
   End
End.
```

3

```
Unit RecSqu;
{ Square drawing facilities using a record type for coordinates }

Interface
{-----------------------------------------------}

Uses Crt; { For drawing on the screen }

Type
   Coord = Record      { Regular 2D coordinates }
      X, Y: Integer
      End;

Function On_screen(Position: Coord): Boolean;
   { Returns True if Position is on-screen, }
   { returns False otherwise }
```

```
Procedure Draw_char(Position: Coord; A_char: Char);
   { Draws the character A_char at Position }
   { Does nothing if Position is off-screen }

Procedure Draw_square(Origin: Coord; Side: Integer; Border: Char);
   { Draws a square whose top left corner is at }
   { Origin, whose side is of length }
   { Side, and whose border is comprised of Border }
   { characers. Parts of the square which are off-screen }
   { are clipped. }

Implementation
{---------------------------------------------------}
Function On_screen(Position: Coord): Boolean;
   { Returns True if Position is on-screen, }
   { returns False otherwise }
   Const
      { Mark screen dimensions as constants }
      Screen_height = 25;
      Screen_width = 80;
   Var
      X_ok, Y_ok, Will_scroll: Boolean; { Test results }
   Begin
     With Position Do
       Begin
       X_ok := (X >= 1) And (X <= Screen_width);  { Is X on screen? }
       Y_ok := (Y >= 1) And (Y <= Screen_height); { Is Y on screen? }
       Will_scroll := (X = Screen_width)       { Would they cause scrolling? }
                      And
                      (Y = Screen_height);
         End;
       On_screen := X_ok And Y_ok And Not Will_Scroll
   End;
Procedure Draw_char(Position: Coord; A_char: Char);
   { Draws the character A_char at Position }
   { Does nothing if Position is off-screen }
   Begin
   If On_screen(Position) Then            { Only draw if on-screen }
      Begin
      GotoXY(Position.X, Position.Y);  { Goto the coordinates }
      Write(A_char)                    { Draw the character }
      End
   End;
Procedure Draw_square(Origin: Coord; Side: Integer; Border: Char);
   { Draws a square whose top left corner is at }
   { Origin, whose side is of length }
   { Side, and whose border is comprised of Border }
   { characers. Parts of the square which are off-screen }
   { are clipped. }
```

```
    Var
        Index: Integer; { For loop index }
        Pos: Coord;      { For building a coordinate }
    Begin
    With Origin Do
        Begin

        { Draw the edges of the square clockwise }

        Pos.Y := Y;
        For Index := X To X + Side - 1 Do
            Begin
            Pos.X := Index;
            Draw_char(Pos, Border);
            End;

        Pos.X := X + Side - 1;
        For Index := Y + 1 To Y + Side - 1 Do
            Begin
            Pos.Y := Index;
            Draw_char(Pos, Border);
            End;

        Pos.Y := Y + Side - 1;
        For Index := X + Side - 2 Downto X Do
            Begin
            Pos.X := Index;
            Draw_char(Pos, Border);
            End;

        Pos.X := X;
        For Index := Y + Side - 2 Downto Y + 1 Do
            Begin
            Pos.Y := Index;
            Draw_char(Pos, Border);
            End

        End
    End;

{-----------------------------------------------------}
End.

Program Record_move;
{ Draws a moving, zooming square on the screen }
{ but uses a record type to represent coordinates }
Uses Crt, RecSqu;
Var
    Zoom, Index: Integer;
    Pos: Coord; { For building a coordinate }
```

```
Begin
ClrScr;
{ Draw a moving, zooming pattern on the screen, six times }
For Zoom := 1 To 6 Do
   Begin
   For Index := 1 To 15 Do
      Begin
      { Overwrite the old position }
      Pos.X := 6 * (Index - 1);
      Pos.Y := Index - 1;
      Draw_square(Pos, Index - 1, ' ');
      { Draw the new positon }
      Pos.X := 6 * Index;
      Pos.Y := Index;
      Draw_square(Pos, Index, ':');
      GotoXY(1, 25); { Move the cursor out of the way }
      Delay(140)
      End
   End
End.
```

Chapter 9

1

```
Program Reverse;
{ Reads a text file and prints it out with each line reversed }
Uses Crt;
Var
   The_file: Text;
   C: Char;
   The_file_name: String;
   Back_line: String; { For building the reversed line }
Begin
ClrScr;

{ Ask for the file name and get the file }
Write('File name? ');
ReadLn(The_file_name);
Assign(The_file, The_file_name);
Reset(The_file);

{ Standard nested While loop for processing a text file }
While Not Eof(The_file) Do
   Begin
   { The backwards line is empty so far }
   Back_line := '';
   While Not Eoln(The_file) Do
      Begin
      Read(The_file, C);
      { Put the character at the front of the backwards line }
```

```
         { (this does the reversing for us) }
         Back_line := C + Back_line
         End;
      WriteLn(Back_line);
      Readln(The_file)
      End;
Close(The_file)
End.
```

2

```
Program Qwerty;
{ Measures letter frequency in a text file }

Uses Crt;

Type
  Letters = 'a'..'z';
  Letter_array = Array[Letters] Of LongInt; { An array for storing }
                                            { the totals for each character }

Var
   Counts: Letter_array;
   The_file_name: String;
   The_file: Text;
   C: Char; { A character from the file }
   L: Letters; { The lower case version of a letter }

{ Break the problem down into sub-programs... }

Procedure Init_letter_array(La: Letter_array);
   { Fill a letter array with zeroes }
   Var
      L: Letters;
   Begin
   For L := 'a' To 'z' Do
      Begin
      La[L] := 0
      End
   End;

Function To_lower(C: Char): Letters;
   { Returns the lower case version of C, which must be a letter }
   Begin
   If C < 'a' Then { If it's upper case, use Ord() to adjust it }
      Begin
      To_lower := Chr(Ord(C) + Ord('a') - Ord('A'))
      End
   Else              { Otherwise, it needs no adjusting }
      Begin
      To_lower := C
```

```
      End
   End;

Function Is_letter(C: Char): Boolean;
   { True if C is a letter, False otherwise }
   Begin
   Is_letter := ((C >= 'a') And (C <= 'z')) Or ((C >= 'A') And (C <= 'Z'))
   End;

Procedure Print_frequencies(La: Letter_array);
   { Prints the frequency of each member of La }
   Var
      L: Letters;
      Total: LongInt;
      Frequency: Real;
   Begin

   { Work out the total number of letters }
   Total := 0;
   For L := 'a' To 'z' Do
      Begin
      Total := Total + La[L]
      End;

   { Print the frequencies as percentages }
   For L := 'a' To 'z' Do
      Begin
      Frequency := (La[L] / Total * 100);
      WriteLn('Frequency of ''', L, ''' is ', Frequency:1:1, '%')
      End
   End;

Begin
ClrScr;
{ Get a file from the user }
Write('File name? ');
ReadLn(The_file_name);
Assign(The_file, The_file_name);
Reset(The_file);

Init_letter_array(Counts);

{ Process each character }
While Not Eof(The_file) Do
   Begin
   While Not Eoln(The_file) Do
      Begin
      Read(The_file, C);
      If Is_letter(C) Then { If it's a letter then increment its count }
         Begin
```

```
            L := To_lower(C);
            Counts[L] := Counts[L] + 1
            End
        End;
        Readln(The_file)
   End;

Print_frequencies(Counts);

{ Release the file }
Close(The_file)

End.
```

3

```
Program File_cars;
{ Reads a list of car descriptions and prints the extra }
{ details of the most expensive one. Uses a File so as not }
{ to restrict the number of cars }
Uses Crt;
Type
   Car = Record                { The information for a car }
      Make_model: String;       { The make and model }
      Price, Mpg: Real          { The price and fuel consumption }
      End;
Var
   File_name: String; { Name of the file to be read from the user }
   A_car: Car;          { Temporary car record for processing }
   Cars: File Of Car; { All the car descriptions }
   Index, High_index: Integer;  { Working index and index of priciest }
   High_price: Real;  { Highest price so far }
   Response: Char;
Begin
ClrScr;

{ Get a file for storing the cars }
Write('File name for storing the descriptions? ');
ReadLn(File_name);
Assign(Cars, File_name);
Rewrite(Cars);

{ Read and store car details from the user }
WriteLn('Please enter some car details');
Repeat
   With A_car Do  { Avoid some tedious typing }
      Begin
      Write('Make and model: ');
      ReadLn(Make_model);
      Write('Price: ');
```

```
      ReadLn(Price);
      Write('Fuel consumption: ');
      ReadLn(Mpg)
      End;
   Write(Cars, A_car); { Write the temporary car to the file }
   { Check for continue }
   Write('Continue (y or n)? ');
   Response := Readkey;
   WriteLn;
   Until (Response = 'n') Or (Response = 'N');

{ Flush the details to disk }
Close(Cars);


{ Re-open the file for reading }
Reset(Cars);

{ Look for the priciest car (choose random access for illustration) }
High_index := 0;  { Assume it's the first car }
High_price := -1; { its price must be higher than this! }
For Index := 0 To FileSize(Cars) - 1 Do
   Begin
   Seek(Cars, Index); { Find the car }
   Read(Cars, A_car); { Read it to temporary }
   If A_car.Price > High_price Then { If this one's pricier }
      Begin
      High_index := Index;        { Record its index }
      High_price := A_car.price { Overwrite the highest price }
      End
   End;

{ Print the other details of the priciest one }
WriteLn;
Seek(Cars, High_index); { Find it }
Read(Cars, A_car);        { Read it }
With A_car Do { Save some more tedious typing }
   Begin
   WriteLn('The most expensive car is the ', Make_model);
   WriteLn('Which has an average fuel consumption of ', Mpg:1:2)
   End
End.
```

Chapter 10

1

```
Program Reverse_sort;
{ Sorts an arbitrary number of strings entered by the user }
{ into reverse order }
Uses Crt;
Type
    Branch = ^Fork;
    Fork = Record
        Data: String;
        Left_branch, Right_branch: Branch
        End;
Var
    Trunk: Branch;
    User_data: String;

Procedure Add(Var This_branch: Branch; New_data: String);
    { Adds new_data to the tree starting at this_branch }
    Begin
    If This_branch = nil Then   { If there's no branch }
        Begin
        New(This_branch);        { Grow a new branch }
        With This_branch^ Do
            Begin
            Left_branch := Nil;
            Data := New_data;     { Put our letter in the new fork at the top }
            Right_branch := Nil
            End
        End
    Else                          { OTHERWISE }
        Begin
        With This_branch^ Do      { Climb to the fork at the top of this branch }
            Begin
            If Data > New_data Then { If the letter here is greater than ours }
                Begin
                Add(Left_branch, New_data) { apply the rule to the left branch }
                End
            Else
                Begin                           { OTHERWISE }
                Add(Right_branch, New_data) { Apply the rule to the right branch }
                End
            End
        End
    End;
```

```
Procedure Print(This_branch: Branch);
   { Prints the tree starting at this_branch }
   { in reverse order }
   Begin
   If This_branch <> Nil Then { If there's a branch here, }
      Begin
      With This_branch^ Do      { climb to the fork at the top of the branch }
         Begin
         Print(Right_branch);  { Apply the rule to the right branch }
         WriteLn(Data);        { Write down the letter at this fork }
         Print(Left_branch)    { Apply the rule to the left branch }
         End
      End
   End;

Begin
ClrScr;

Trunk := Nil;        { Initialise the tree }

{ Prompt for input }
WriteLn('Please type in some strings (blank line to finish)');

ReadLn(User_data);           { Read the first string }
While User_data <> '' Do { While we have a string to add }
   Begin
   Add(Trunk, User_data); { Add it }
   ReadLn(User_data)       { And read another }
   End;
Print(Trunk)            { Print the tree }
End.
```

2

```
Unit SortUnit;
{ A module which provides a tree sort and print facility }
{----------------------------------------------------------------}

Interface
{----------------------------------------------------------------}

Type
   Branch = ^Fork;
   Fork = Record
      Data: String;
      Left_branch, Right_branch: Branch
      End;

Procedure Add(Var This_branch: Branch; New_data: String);
   { Adds new_data to the tree starting at this_branch }

Procedure Print(This_branch: Branch);
   { Prints the tree starting at this_branch }
   { in reverse order }
```

```
Implementation
{---------------------------------------------------------------}

Procedure Add(Var This_branch: Branch; New_data: String);
   { Adds new_data to the tree starting at this_branch }
   Begin
   If This_branch = nil Then   { If there's no branch }
      Begin
      New(This_branch);            { Grow a new branch }
      With This_branch^ Do
         Begin
         Left_branch := Nil;
         Data := New_data;        { Put our letter in the new fork at the top }
         Right_branch := Nil
         End
      End
   Else                           { OTHERWISE }
      Begin
      With This_branch^ Do         { Climb to the fork at the top of this
branch }
         Begin
         If Data > New_data Then { If the letter here is greater than ours }
            Begin
            Add(Left_branch, New_data) { apply the rule to the left branch }
            End
         Else
            Begin                       { OTHERWISE }
            Add(Right_branch, New_data) { Apply the rule to the right branch }
            End
         End
      End
   End;

Procedure Print(This_branch: Branch);
   { Prints the tree starting at this_branch }
   { in reverse order }
   Begin
   If This_branch <> Nil Then { If there's a branch here, }
      Begin
      With This_branch^ Do       { climb to the fork at the top of the branch }
         Begin
         Print(Left_branch);  { Apply the rule to the left branch }
         WriteLn(Data);       { Write down the letter at this fork }
         Print(Right_branch); { Apply the rule to the right branch }
         End
      End
   End;

End.
```

3

```pascal
Program Real_sort;
{ Sorts an arbitrary number of numbers entered by the user }
Uses winCrt;
Type
    Branch = ^Fork;
    Fork = Record
       Data: Real;
       Left_branch, Right_branch: Branch
       End;
Var
   Trunk: Branch;
   User_data: Real;

Procedure Add(Var This_branch: Branch; New_data: Real);
   { Adds new_data to the tree starting at this_branch }
   Begin
   If This_branch = nil Then    { If there's no branch }
      Begin
      New(This_branch);           { Grow a new branch }
      With This_branch^ Do
         Begin
         Left_branch := Nil;
         Data := New_data;        { Put our number in the new fork at the top }
         Right_branch := Nil
         End
      End
   Else                           { OTHERWISE }
      Begin
      With This_branch^ Do        { Climb to the fork at the top of this branch }
         Begin
         If Data > New_data Then { If the number here is greater than ours }
           Begin
           Add(Left_branch, New_data) { apply the rule to the left branch }
           End
         Else
           Begin                     { OTHERWISE }
           Add(Right_branch, New_data) { Apply the rule to the right branch }
           End
         End
      End
   End;

Procedure Print(This_branch: Branch);
   { Prints the tree starting at this_branch }
   { in reverse order }
   Begin
   If This_branch <> Nil Then { If there's a branch here, }
      Begin
      With This_branch^ Do     { climb to the fork at the top of the branch }
         Begin
```

```
            Print(Left_branch);    { Apply the rule to the left branch }
            WriteLn(Data:1:3);     { Write down the number at this fork }
            Print(Right_branch)    { Apply the rule to the right branch }
          End
        End
    End;

Begin
ClrScr;

Trunk := Nil;         { Initialise the tree }

{ Prompt for input }
WriteLn('Please type in some positive numbers (-1 to finish)');

ReadLn(User_data);            { Read the first number }
While User_data <> -1 Do   { While we have a number to add }
    Begin
    Add(Trunk, User_data); { Add it }
    ReadLn(User_data)         { And read another }
    End;
Print(Trunk)            { Print the tree }
End.
```

Chapter 11

1

```
Program Dialog;
{ As Ex_11_6 but uses a dialog box procedure }
Uses Crt, Dial_sys;
Var
   A : Array[1..6] of String;
   I, No_line : Integer;
   Ch_1, Ch_2 : Char;
   File_Open  : Boolean;
Begin
   {Clear the Screen of any DOS messages}
   Clrscr;
   {Assign the Strings}
   A[1] := '        Create           ';
   A[2] := '        Open             ';
   A[3] := '        Add              ';
   A[4] := '        Find             ';
   A[5] := '        Amend            ';
   A[6] := '        Exit             ';
   {Draw background window in Blue}
   TextBackground(Blue);
   Window(21,6,58,15);
   Clrscr; {converts background to chosen color}
```

```
{Set the color for the frame and the message}
TextColor(Red);
{Draw the frame}
Rectangle(21,6,58,15);
{Write the User Message}
Window(23,7,56,9);
WriteLn(' Select an action and press Enter');
For I := 1 to 34 do
   Begin
   Write(Chr(205));
   End;
{Initialise the variables}
No_line  := 1;
File_Open := False;
Repeat
  Repeat
  {Write the menu}
  Dialog_box;
  Writeln(A[1]);
  Writeln(A[2]);
  Writeln(A[3]);
  Writeln(A[4]);
  Writeln(A[5]);
  Write(A[6]);
  {Draw the Highlight bar}
  TextBackground(Green);
  TextColor(White + Blink);
  Window(23, 8 + No_Line, 56, 8 + No_line);
  Write    (A[No_line]);
  Window(23, 8 + No_Line, 56, 8 + No_line);
  {Test which key pressed and move the bar accordingly}
  Ch_1:= Readkey;
  If Ord(Ch_1) = 0
     Then
     Begin
       Ch_2 := Readkey;
       If Ord(Ch_2) = 80
         Then
           Begin
           {Down key pressed so increase No_line by 1}
           No_line := No_line + 1;
           If (File_Open = false)
           Then
             {if File_Open is false restrict bar to Open, Create and Exit}
             Begin
               {Check if now bar would move down past "Open"}
               If No_line > 2
               Then
               Begin
               {Check if now bar would move down past "Exit"}
```

```
                If No_line > 6
                  Then
                  Begin
                  {If yes to both questions move bar to "Create"}
                  No_line := 1;
                  End
                Else
                  Begin
                  {If yes to first and no to second move bar to "Exit"}
                  No_line := 6;
                  End
            End
          End
       Else
         {Otherwise If File_Open is true}
         Begin
           {When bar is to go beyond "Exit" put back to "Add"}
           If No_line > 6
           Then
             Begin
             No_line := 3;
             End;
         End;
       End
  Else
    If Ord(Ch_2) = 72
    Then
      Begin
      {Up key pressed so decrease No_Line by one}
      No_line := No_line - 1;
      If (File_Open = false)
      Then
        {if File_Open is false restrict bar to Open, Create and Exit}
        Begin
        {Check if bar would move up past "Create"}
          If (No_line < 1)
            Then
            Begin
            {If yes move bar to "Exit"}
            No_line := 6;
            End
          Else
            Begin
            {If no check if bar would move up above "Exit"}
              If (No_line < 6) and (No_line > 2)
                Then
                  Begin
                  {If yes move bar to "Open"}
                  No_line := 2;
                  End
```

```
                          End
                    End
              Else
              {Otherwise If File_Open is true}
                    Begin
                    {When bar is to go beyond "Exit" put back to "Add"}
                      If No_line > 6
                        Then
                          Begin
                          No_line := 3;
                          End
                        Else
                          {When bar is to go above "Add" put back to "Exit"}
                          If No_line < 3
                            Then
                              Begin
                              No_line := 6;
                              End
                    End
              End
        End
  Until (Ord(Ch_1) = 13);
  {From position of bar select action}
  Case No_line of
          1 : Begin
              Create;
              End;
          2 : Begin
              Open(File_Open);
              If File_Open
                Then
                  Begin
                  No_line := 3;
                  End
                Else
                  Begin
                  No_line := 1;
                  End
              End;
          3 : Begin
              Add;
              End;
          4 : Begin
              Find;
              End;
          5 : Begin
              Amend;
              End;
          6 : Begin
                If File_Open
```

```
                    Then
                       Begin
                       Close(My_file);
                       End;
                 End;
        End;{Case}
   Until No_line = 6;
   Window(1,1,80,25);
   Clrscr;
End.


Unit Dial_Sys;
{ As My_Sysx but with a dialog procedure }
Interface

Uses Crt;

Type Rec_type = Record
                     Name              : String;
                     Date_of_birth     : String;
                     Telephone_number  : String;
                 End;
Var
   My_file       : File of Rec_type;
   External_name : String;
   Rec_var       : Rec_type;

Procedure Dialog_box;
Procedure Rectangle(Left_Col,Top_Row,Right_Col,Btm_Row : Integer);
Procedure Create;
Procedure Open(Var Opened : Boolean);
Procedure Add;
Procedure Find;
Procedure Amend;

Implementation

Procedure Dialog_box;
Begin
   TextBackground(Blue);
   TextColor(Yellow);
   Window(23,9,56,14);
   ClrScr;
End;

Procedure Rectangle(Left_Col,Top_Row,Right_Col,Btm_Row : Integer);
Var
   I, J : Integer;
Begin
{Draw the corner piece}
```

```
   Write(' ');
   Write(Chr(201));
{Draw the top line}
   For I := (Left_Col + 2) to (Right_Col - 2) do
      Begin
      Write(Chr(205));
      End;
{Draw corner piece and move to next line}
   WriteLn(Chr(187));
{From the top to the bottom}
   For I := (Top_Row + 1) to (Btm_Row - 1) do
   Begin
{Draw the space and the lines}
      Write(' ');
      Write(Chr(186));
{Draw the spaces in the middle}
      For J := (Left_Col + 2) to (Right_Col - 2) do
         Begin
         Write(' ');
         End;
{Draw the lines and move to next line}
      WriteLn(Chr(186));
   End;
{Draw the bottom line}
  Write(' ');
  Write(Chr(200));
   For I := (Left_Col + 2) to (Right_Col - 2) do
      Begin
      Write(Chr(205));
      End;
   Write(Chr(188));
End;

Procedure Create;
Var
   Ch : Char;
Begin
   Dialog_box;
   WriteLn('Enter a file name : ');
   ReadLn(External_name);
   Assign(My_file, External_name);
   {$I-}
   Reset(My_file);
   {$I+}
   If IOResult = 0
      Then
         Begin
            TextColor(White+blink);
            WriteLn('File already exists!');
            TextColor(White);
```

```
                Writeln('Overwrite? Reply y/n : ');
                Readln(Ch);
                If (Ch = 'y') or (Ch = 'Y')
                    Then
                        Begin
                            Rewrite(My_file);
                            Write('DONE! Press a key to continue.');
                            Readkey;
                        End;
          End
      Else
          Begin
              Rewrite(My_file);
              Write('DONE! Press a key to continue.');
              Readkey;
          End;
   TextBackground(Blue);
   TextColor(Yellow);
End;

Procedure Open(Var Opened : Boolean);
Begin
   Dialog_box;
   WriteLn('Enter a file name : ');
   ReadLn(External_name);
   Assign(My_file, External_name);
   {$I-}
   Reset(My_file);
   {$I+}
   If IOResult <> 0
      Then
          Begin
          Opened := False;
          TextColor(White+blink);
          WriteLn('Sorry ' , External_name );
          WriteLn('doesn''t exist!');
          WriteLn('You must create it first.');
          WriteLn('Press a key to continue.');
          Readkey;
          End
      Else
          Begin
              Opened := True;
              Write('DONE! Press a key to continue.');
              Readkey;
          End;
   TextBackground(Blue);
   TextColor(Yellow);
End;
```

```
Procedure Add;
Begin
   Dialog_box;
   Seek(My_file, FileSize(My_file));
   Writeln('Enter a name:');
   ReadLn(Rec_var.Name);
   Writeln('Enter a date of birth:');
   ReadLn(Rec_var.Date_of_birth);
   Writeln('Enter a telephone number:');
   ReadLn(Rec_var.Telephone_number);
   Write(My_file, Rec_var);
   TextBackground(Blue);
   TextColor(Yellow);
End;

Procedure Find;
Var
   Sought_Name        : String;
   Found              : Boolean;
   Counter, Found_ind : Integer;
Begin
   Dialog_box;
   Counter := 0;
   Writeln('Enter a name to be found : ');
   ReadLn(Sought_Name);
   Repeat
      Seek(My_file, Counter);
      Read(My_file, Rec_var);
      Found := (Rec_var.Name = Sought_Name);
      Counter := Counter + 1;
      If Found
         Then
            Begin
            Found_ind := Counter;
            End;
   Until Found or Eof(My_file);
   If Found
      Then
         Begin
            Seek(My_file, Found_ind - 1);
            Read(My_file, Rec_var);
            WriteLn(Rec_var.Name);
            WriteLn(Rec_var.Date_of_birth);
            WriteLn(Rec_var.Telephone_number);
            Write('Press a key to continue.');
            Readkey;
         End
      Else
         Begin
            TextColor(White+blink);
            WriteLn(Sought_Name);
            WriteLn('is not in the file');
            TextColor(White);
            Write('Press a key to continue.');
```

```
            Readkey;
        End;
   TextBackground(Blue);
   TextColor(Yellow);
End;


Procedure Amend;
Var
   Sought_Name          : String;
   Found                : Boolean;
   Counter, Found_ind : Integer;
Begin
   Dialog_box;
   Counter := 0;
   Writeln('Enter a name to be found : ');
   ReadLn(Sought_Name);
   Repeat
      Seek(My_file, Counter);
      Read(My_file, Rec_var);
      Found := (Rec_var.Name = Sought_Name);
      Counter := Counter + 1;
      If Found
         Then
            Begin
            Found_ind := Counter;
            End
   Until Found or Eof(My_file);
   If Found
      Then
         Begin
            Seek(My_file, Found_ind - 1);
            Read(My_file, Rec_var);
            WriteLn('Enter new telephone number : ');
            ReadLn(Rec_var.Telephone_number);
            Seek(My_file, Found_ind - 1);
            Write(My_file, Rec_var);
            Writeln('Press a key to continue.');
            Readkey;
         End
      Else
         Begin
            TextColor(White+blink);
            WriteLn(Sought_Name);
            WriteLn('is not in the file');
            TextColor(White);
            WriteLn('Press a key to continue.');
            Readkey;
         End;
   TextBackground(Blue);
   TextColor(Yellow);
End;
End.
```

2

```
Program Omit;
{ As Dialog but omits options that aren't available }
Uses Crt, Dial_sys;
Const
   Omit_string = '                ------                      '; { Text of unused items }
Var
   A : Array[1..6] of String;
   I, No_line : Integer;
   Ch_1, Ch_2 : Char;
   File_Open  : Boolean;
Begin
   {Clear the Screen of any DOS messages}
   Clrscr;
   {Assign the Strings}
   A[1] := '           Create              ';
   A[2] := '           Open                ';
   A[3] := '           Add                 ';
   A[4] := '           Find                ';
   A[5] := '           Amend               ';
   A[6] := '           Exit                ';
   {Draw background window in Blue}
   TextBackground(Blue);
   Window(21,6,58,15);
   Clrscr; {converts background to chosen color}
   {Set the color for the frame and the message}
   TextColor(Red);
   {Draw the frame}
   Rectangle(21,6,58,15);
   {Write the User Message}
   Window(23,7,56,9);
   WriteLn(' Select an action and press Enter');
   For I := 1 to 34 do
      Begin
      Write(Chr(205));
      End;
   {Initialise the variables}
   No_line  := 1;
   File_Open := False;
   Repeat
     Repeat
     {Write the menu}
     Dialog_box;
     If Not File_open Then
        Begin
        Writeln(A[1]);
        Writeln(A[2]);
        Writeln(Omit_string);
        Writeln(Omit_string);
        Writeln(Omit_string);
```

```
      Write(A[6])
      End
Else
   Begin
   Writeln(Omit_string);
   Writeln(Omit_string);
   Writeln(A[3]);
   Writeln(A[4]);
   Writeln(A[5]);
   Write(A[6])
   End;
{Draw the Highlight bar}
TextBackground(Green);
TextColor(White + Blink);
Window(23, 8 + No_Line, 56, 8 + No_line);
Write    (A[No_line]);
Window(23, 8 + No_Line, 56, 8 + No_line);
{Test which key pressed and move the bar accordingly}
Ch_1:= Readkey;
If Ord(Ch_1) = 0
   Then
   Begin
     Ch_2 := Readkey;
     If Ord(Ch_2) = 80
       Then
         Begin
         {Down key pressed so increase No_line by 1}
         No_line := No_line + 1;
         If (File_Open = false)
         Then
           {if File_Open is false restrict bar to Open, Create and Exit}
           Begin
             {Check if now bar would move down past "Open"}
             If No_line > 2
             Then
             Begin
             {Check if now bar would move down past "Exit"}
               If No_line > 6
                 Then
                 Begin
                 {If yes to both questions move bar to "Create"}
                 No_line := 1;
                 End
               Else
                 Begin
                 {If yes to first and no to second move bar to "Exit"}
                 No_line := 6;
                 End
             End
         End
```

```
        Else
          {Otherwise If File_Open is true}
          Begin
            {When bar is to go beyond "Exit" put back to "Add"}
            If No_line > 6
            Then
              Begin
              No_line := 3;
              End;
          End;
      End
  Else
    If Ord(Ch_2) = 72
    Then
      Begin
      {Up key pressed so decrease No_Line by one}
      No_line := No_line - 1;
      If (File_Open = false)
      Then
        {if File_Open is false restrict bar to Open, Create and Exit}
        Begin
        {Check if bar would move up past "Create"}
          If (No_line < 1)
            Then
              Begin
              {If yes move bar to "Exit"}
              No_line := 6;
              End
            Else
              Begin
              {If no check if bar would move up above "Exit"}
                If (No_line < 6) and (No_line > 2)
                  Then
                    Begin
                    {If yes move bar to "Open"}
                    No_line := 2;
                    End
          End
      End
    Else
    {Otherwise If File_Open is true}
        Begin
        {When bar is to go beyond "Exit" put back to "Add"}
          If No_line > 6
            Then
              Begin
              No_line := 3;
              End
```

```
                        Else
                          {When bar is to go above "Add" put back to "Exit"}
                          If No_line < 3
                            Then
                                Begin
                                No_line := 6;
                                End
                End
              End
          End
     Until (Ord(Ch_1) = 13);
     {From position of bar select action}
     Case No_line of
            1 : Begin
                Create;
                End;
            2 : Begin
                Open(File_Open);
                If File_Open
                  Then
                      Begin
                      No_line := 3;
                      End
                    Else
                      Begin
                      No_line := 1;
                      End
                End;
            3 : Begin
                Add;
                End;
            4 : Begin
                Find;
                End;
            5 : Begin
                Amend;
                End;
            6 : Begin
                    If File_Open
                    Then
                       Begin
                       Close(My_file);
                       End;
                End;
       End;{Case}
  Until No_line = 6;
  Window(1,1,80,25);
  Clrscr;
End.
```

3

```
Program Quit;
{ As Omit but allows the user to quit an action }
{ by hitting <Return> when asked for input }
Uses Crt, Quit_sys;
Const
   Omit_string = '              ------                    '; { Text of unused items }
Var
   A : Array[1..6] of String;
   I, No_line : Integer;
   Ch_1, Ch_2 : Char;
   File_Open  : Boolean;
Begin
   {Clear the Screen of any DOS messages}
   Clrscr;
   {Assign the Strings}
   A[1] := '          Create           ';
   A[2] := '          Open             ';
   A[3] := '          Add              ';
   A[4] := '          Find             ';
   A[5] := '          Amend            ';
   A[6] := '          Exit             ';
   {Draw background window in Blue}
   TextBackground(Blue);
   Window(21,6,58,15);
   Clrscr; {converts background to chosen color}
   {Set the color for the frame and the message}
   TextColor(Red);
   {Draw the frame}
   Rectangle(21,6,58,15);
   {Write the User Message}
   Window(23,7,56,9);
   WriteLn(' Select an action and press Enter');
   For I := 1 to 34 do
      Begin
      Write(Chr(205));
      End;
   {Initialise the variables}
   No_line  := 1;
   File_Open := False;
   Repeat
     Repeat
     {Write the menu}
     Dialog_box;
     If Not File_open Then
        Begin
        Writeln(A[1]);
        Writeln(A[2]);
        Writeln(Omit_string);
        Writeln(Omit_string);
```

```
      Writeln(Omit_string);
      Write(A[6])
      End
Else
      Begin
      Writeln(Omit_string);
      Writeln(Omit_string);
      Writeln(A[3]);
      Writeln(A[4]);
      Writeln(A[5]);
      Write(A[6])
      End;
{Draw the Highlight bar}
TextBackground(Green);
TextColor(White + Blink);
Window(23, 8 + No_Line, 56, 8 + No_line);
Write    (A[No_line]);
Window(23, 8 + No_Line, 56, 8 + No_line);
{Test which key pressed and move the bar accordingly}
Ch_1:= Readkey;
If Ord(Ch_1) = 0
  Then
  Begin
    Ch_2 := Readkey;
    If Ord(Ch_2) = 80
      Then
        Begin
        {Down key pressed so increase No_line by 1}
        No_line := No_line + 1;
        If (File_Open = false)
        Then
          {if File_Open is false restrict bar to Open, Create and Exit}
          Begin
            {Check if now bar would move down past "Open"}
            If No_line > 2
            Then
            Begin
            {Check if now bar would move down past "Exit"}
              If No_line > 6
                Then
                Begin
                {If yes to both questions move bar to "Create"}
                No_line := 1;
                End
              Else
                Begin
                {If yes to first and no to second move bar to "Exit"}
                No_line := 6;
                End
            End
```

```
            End
         Else
           {Otherwise If File_Open is true}
           Begin
             {When bar is to go beyond "Exit" put back to "Add"}
             If No_line > 6
             Then
               Begin
               No_line := 3;
               End;
           End;
       End
   Else
     If Ord(Ch_2) = 72
     Then
       Begin
       {Up key pressed so decrease No_Line by one}
       No_line := No_line - 1;
       If (File_Open = false)
       Then
         {if File_Open is false restrict bar to Open, Create and Exit}
         Begin
         {Check if bar would move up past "Create"}
           If (No_line < 1)
             Then
               Begin
               {If yes move bar to "Exit"}
               No_line := 6;
               End
             Else
               Begin
               {If no check if bar would move up above "Exit"}
                 If (No_line < 6) and (No_line > 2)
                   Then
                     Begin
                     {If yes move bar to "Open"}
                     No_line := 2;
                     End
               End
         End
       Else
       {Otherwise If File_Open is true}
         Begin
         {When bar is to go beyond "Exit" put back to "Add"}
           If No_line > 6
             Then
               Begin
               No_line := 3;
               End
```

```
                       Else
                          {When bar is to go above "Add" put back to "Exit"}
                          If No_line < 3
                             Then
                                Begin
                                No_line := 6;
                                End
                 End
              End
        End
    Until (Ord(Ch_1) = 13);
    {From position of bar select action}
    Case No_line of
            1 : Begin
                Create;
                End;
            2 : Begin
                Open(File_Open);
                If File_Open
                   Then
                      Begin
                      No_line := 3;
                      End
                    Else
                      Begin
                      No_line := 1;
                      End
                End;
            3 : Begin
                Add;
                End;
            4 : Begin
                Find;
                End;
            5 : Begin
                Amend;
                End;
            6 : Begin
                   If File_Open
                   Then
                      Begin
                      Close(My_file);
                      End;
                End;
      End;{Case}
   Until No_line = 6;
   Window(1,1,80,25);
   Clrscr;
End.
```

```
Unit Quit_Sys;
{ As Dial_sys but allows users to quit rather than entering items }
Interface

Uses Crt;

Type Rec_type = Record
                    Name               : String;
                    Date_of_birth      : String;
                    Telephone_number   : String;
               End;
Var
   My_file       : File of Rec_type;
   External_name : String;
   Rec_var       : Rec_type;

Procedure Dialog_box;
Procedure Rectangle(Left_Col,Top_Row,Right_Col,Btm_Row : Integer);
Procedure Create;
Procedure Open(Var Opened : Boolean);
Procedure Add;
Procedure Find;
Procedure Amend;

Implementation

Procedure Dialog_box;
Begin
   TextBackground(Blue);
   TextColor(Yellow);
   Window(23,9,56,14);
   ClrScr;
End;

Procedure Rectangle(Left_Col,Top_Row,Right_Col,Btm_Row : Integer);
Var
   I, J : Integer;
Begin
{Draw the corner piece}
  Write(' ');
  Write(Chr(201));
{Draw the top line}
   For I := (Left_Col + 2) to (Right_Col - 2) do
      Begin
      Write(Chr(205));
      End;
{Draw corner piece and move to next line}
   WriteLn(Chr(187));
{From the top to the bottom}
   For I := (Top_Row + 1) to (Btm_Row - 1) do
   Begin
```

```
{Draw the space and the lines}
    Write(' ');
    Write(Chr(186));
{Draw the spaces in the middle}
    For J := (Left_Col + 2) to (Right_Col - 2) do
        Begin
        Write(' ');
        End;
{Draw the lines and move to next line}
    WriteLn(Chr(186));
  End;
{Draw the bottom line}
  Write(' ');
  Write(Chr(200));
   For I := (Left_Col + 2) to (Right_Col - 2) do
      Begin
      Write(Chr(205));
      End;
   Write(Chr(188));
End;

Procedure Create;
Var
   Ch : Char;
Begin
   Dialog_box;
   WriteLn('Enter a file name : ');
   ReadLn(External_name);
   If External_name <> '' Then
      Begin
      Assign(My_file, External_name);
      {$I-}
      Reset(My_file);
      {$I+}
      If IOResult = 0
         Then
            Begin
               TextColor(White+blink);
               WriteLn('File already exists!');
               TextColor(White);
               Writeln('Overwrite? Reply y/n : ');
               Readln(Ch);
               If (Ch = 'y') or (Ch = 'Y')
                  Then
                     Begin
                        Rewrite(My_file);
                        Write('DONE! Press a key to continue.');
                        Readkey;
                     End;
            End
         Else
```

```
            Begin
                Rewrite(My_file);
                Write('DONE! Press a key to continue.');
                Readkey;
            End;
       End;
   TextBackground(Blue);
   TextColor(Yellow);
End;

Procedure Open(Var Opened : Boolean);
Begin
   Dialog_box;
   WriteLn('Enter a file name : ');
   ReadLn(External_name);
   If External_name <> '' Then
      Begin
      Assign(My_file, External_name);
      {$I-}
      Reset(My_file);
      {$I+}
      If IOResult <> 0
         Then
            Begin
            Opened := False;
            TextColor(White+blink);
            WriteLn('Sorry ' , External_name );
            WriteLn('doesn''t exist!');
            WriteLn('You must create it first.');
            WriteLn('Press a key to continue.');
            Readkey;
            End
         Else
            Begin
                Opened := True;
                Write('DONE! Press a key to continue.');
                Readkey;
            End;
      End;
   TextBackground(Blue);
   TextColor(Yellow);
End;

Procedure Add;
Begin
   Dialog_box;
   Seek(My_file, FileSize(My_file));
   Writeln('Enter a name:');
   ReadLn(Rec_var.Name);
   If Rec_var.Name <> '' Then
      Begin
      Writeln('Enter a date of birth:');
```

```
      ReadLn(Rec_var.Date_of_birth);
      Writeln('Enter a telephone number:');
      ReadLn(Rec_var.Telephone_number);
      Write(My_file, Rec_var);
      End;
   TextBackground(Blue);
   TextColor(Yellow);
End;

Procedure Find;
Var
   Sought_Name         : String;
   Found               : Boolean;
   Counter, Found_ind : Integer;
Begin
   Dialog_box;
   Counter := 0;
   Writeln('Enter a name to be found : ');
   ReadLn(Sought_Name);
   If Sought_name <> '' Then
      Begin
      Repeat
         Seek(My_file, Counter);
         Read(My_file, Rec_var);
         Found := (Rec_var.Name = Sought_Name);
         Counter := Counter + 1;
         If Found
            Then
               Begin
               Found_ind := Counter;
               End;
      Until Found or Eof(My_file);
      If Found
         Then
            Begin
               Seek(My_file, Found_ind - 1);
               Read(My_file, Rec_var);
               WriteLn(Rec_var.Name);
               WriteLn(Rec_var.Date_of_birth);
               WriteLn(Rec_var.Telephone_number);
               Write('Press a key to continue.');
               Readkey;
            End
         Else
            Begin
               TextColor(White+blink);
               WriteLn(Sought_Name);
               WriteLn('is not in the file');
               TextColor(White);
               Write('Press a key to continue.');
               Readkey;
            End;
```

```
      End;
   TextBackground(Blue);
   TextColor(Yellow);
End;

Procedure Amend;
Var
   Sought_Name         : String;
   Found               : Boolean;
   Counter, Found_ind : Integer;
Begin
   Dialog_box;
   Counter := 0;
   Writeln('Enter a name to be found : ');
   ReadLn(Sought_Name);
   If Sought_name <> '' Then
      Begin
      Repeat
         Seek(My_file, Counter);
         Read(My_file, Rec_var);
         Found := (Rec_var.Name = Sought_Name);
         Counter := Counter + 1;
         If Found
            Then
                Begin
                Found_ind := Counter;
                End
      Until Found or Eof(My_file);
      If Found
         Then
            Begin
               Seek(My_file, Found_ind - 1);
               Read(My_file, Rec_var);
               WriteLn('Enter new telephone number : ');
               ReadLn(Rec_var.Telephone_number);
               Seek(My_file, Found_ind - 1);
               Write(My_file, Rec_var);
               Writeln('Press a key to continue.');
               Readkey;
            End
         Else
            Begin
               TextColor(White+blink);
               WriteLn(Sought_Name);
               WriteLn('is not in the file');
               TextColor(White);
               WriteLn('Press a key to continue.');
               Readkey;
            End;
      End;
   TextBackground(Blue);
   TextColor(Yellow);
End;
End.
```

Index

C++ is widely taught as a first programming

language because of its power and simplicity.

This book provides wide coverage of the

language and is aimed squarely at the

beginner to C++.

Author: Ian Wilks   Price $19.95   ISBN 1-874416-29-X

INSTANT....................

Designed as a rapid introduction to the programming

language, these books deliver fundamental, essential

knowledge in an entertaining, painless way. These

books are ideal for students looking for a swift

grounding, or indeed for anyone wanting to make a

quick breakthrough into programming proficiency

The Book

Author: I. Horton   Price $24.95   ISBN 1-874416-15X

The Beginner's Guide to C

is the perfect introduction to programming in the most popular language of today. The book assumes

no prior knowledge and its approach is friendly and active. You learn best by doing, so the book

focuses on hands-on applications and examples, and gets you programming in the first chapter. Each

chapter ends with a useful and entertaining program which links together what you have learnt .

The Series

BEGINNER'S GUIDE TO ....

These guides are designed for beginners to the particular language or to

programming in general. The style is friendly and the emphasis is on

learning by doing. The chapters focus on useful examples that illustrate

important areas of the language. The wealth of examples and figures

help make the transition from beginner to programmer

both easy and successful

The Book

Author: Ben Ezzell (Includes disk)
Price $39.95 ISBN 1-874416-22-2

The Revolutionary Guide to Visual C ++ provides the reader with a comprehensive understanding of objects, thus making Windows programming with the MFC an easier task to accomplish. Section One allows the C programmer to quickly get to terms with the difference between C and C++, including the concepts involved in object oriented design and programming. In Sections Two and Three, you are guided through the various steps required to produce complete Windows applications.

The Series

REVOLUTIONARY GUIDE TO ....

Learn the programming techniques of the industry experts with the Revolutionary Guides. This series guides you through the latest technology to bring your skills right up to date. Example applications are used to illustrate new concepts and to give you practical experience in the language.

Authors: Various Price: $44.99 ISBN 1-874416-34-6

Assembly Language Master Class covers the 386,

486 and Pentium processors. This guide gives

aspiring experts a tutorial covering subjects such as

direct SVGA access, serial communications, device

drivers, protected mode and Windows, and virus

protection secrets.

............*MASTER CLASS*

The aim of this series is to bring together the ideas of a

number of the leading edge experts in one indispensable

book. Each chapter has a defined objective built around

the key application areas of the language.

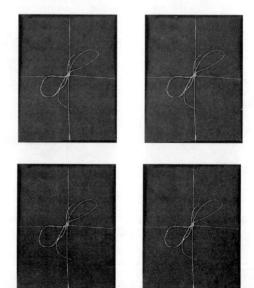

WIN FREE BOOKS!

TELL US WHAT YOU THINK!

Complete and return the bounce back card and you will:

- Help us create the books you want
- Receive an update on all Wrox titles.
- Enter the draw for 5 Wrox titles of your choice

FILL THIS OUT to enter the draw for free Wrox titles

Name _____

Address _____

_____

_____ Post code/Zip _____

Occupation _____

How did you hear about this book ?

- ☐ Book review (name) _____
- ☐ Advertisement (name) _____
- ☐ Recommendation
- ☐ Catalog
- ☐ Other _____

Where did you buy this book?

- ☐ Bookstore (name) _____
- ☐ Computer Store (name) _____
- ☐ Mail Order
- ☐ Other _____

What influenced you in the purchase of this book?

- ☐ Cover Design
- ☐ Contents
- ☐ Use of Color
- ☐ Other (please specify)

How did you rate the overall contents of this book?

- ☐ Excellent
- ☐ Good
- ☐ Average
- ☐ Poor

What did you find most useful about this book? _____

What did you find least useful about this book? _____

Please add any additional comments? _____

What other subjects will you buy a computer book on soon?

What is the best computer book you have used this year?

Please do not put me on your mailing list ☐

WROX

WROX PRESS INC.

Wrox writes books for you. Any
suggestions, or ideas about how you
want information given in your ideal
book will be studied by our team. Your
comments are always valued at WROX.

Free phone from USA 1 800 814 3461
Fax (312) 465 4063

Compuserve 100063,2152.
UK Tel. (4421) 706 6826 Fax (4421) 706 2967

———— *Computer Book Publishers* ————

NB. If you post the bounce back card below in the UK, please send it to:
Wrox Press Ltd. 1334 Warwick Road, Birmingham, B27 6PR

NO POSTAGE
NECESSARY
IF MAILED
IN THE
UNITED STATES

BUSINESS REPLY MAIL
FIRST CLASS MAIL   PERMIT#64   CHICAGO,IL.

POSTAGE WILL BE PAID BY ADDRESSEE

WROX PRESS
2710 WEST TOUHY AVE
CHICAGO IL 60645-3008
USA